ULTIMATE PS2 CHEATS

VOLUME 2

CODES & SECRETS

NEW AND FULLY UPDATED EDITION

COMPLETE A-Z GUIDE FEATURING OVER 260 PLAYSTATION2 GAMES!

Published independently in the UK

ISBN 0 9543643 1 7

Printed and bound in the United Kingdom by
Mackays of Chatham Limited, Chatham, Kent

Distributed by
Computer Bookshops Limited, Sparkhill, Birmingham

CONTENTS

Featuring Complete Solutions/Player Guides to the following great PS2 games:

Over 260 PS2 Games Inside!

CONTENTS ■ ✖ ● ▲

18 WHEELER: AMERICAN PRO TRUCKER

Unlock Bonus trailers:
Finish arcade mode with all four characters to unlock two bonus trailers in score attack mode, versus mode, and arcade mode.

Unlock Bonus parking levels:
Finish each of the four parking levels to unlock an additional parking level, then finish the bonus parking level to unlock the sixth parking level.

Unlock The Nippon Maru:
Hold ✖ and hit START at the main title screen, keeping ✖ held down until the mode selection screen appears. Choose any mode to drive the Nippon Maru truck.

2002 FIFA WORLD CUP

Unlock All-Asian team:
Win the World Cup with an Asian team.

Unlock All-African team:
Win the World Cup with an African team.

Unlock All-World team:
Unlock the All-Americas, All-European, All-Asian, and All-African teams to unlock the All-World team in a friendly match.

Unlock All-Americas team:
Win the World Cup with a North American or South American team.

Unlock All-European team:
Win the World Cup with a European or Oceania team.

4x4 EVOLUTION

Get a $25,000 Bonus:
Pause the game, and then hit L2, ■, R1, ■, R1, L1, Circle, L2, ■, R2, ■, R1 to get $25,000 in career mode.

Get a $1 million Bonus:
Pause the game, and then hit L2, ■, R1, ●, R1, L1, ●, L2, ■, R2, ■, and R1 to get $1 million in career mode.

Unlock All trucks:
Pause the game, then hit L1, L2, R1, R2, L1 and R1 to unlock all 18 trucks and custom colours.

Enable Slower game speed:
Pause the game, then hit L1, L2, R1, R2, ■, ●.

Enable Faster game speed:
Pause the game, then hit L1, L2, R1, R2, ■ x2.

Enable Normal game speed:
Pause the game, then hit L1, L2, R1, R2, ● x2.

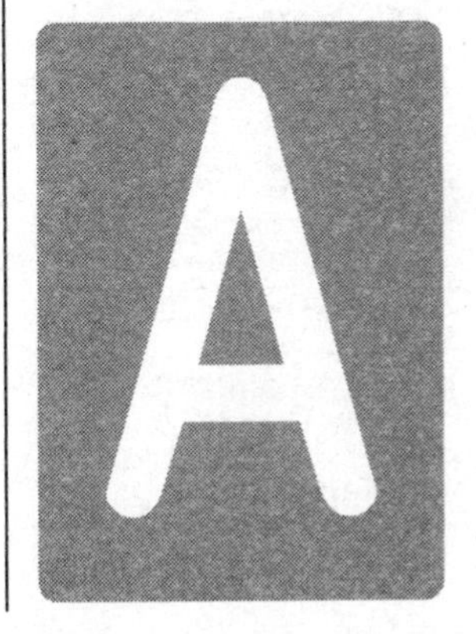

ACE COMBAT 4: SHATTERED SKIES

Unlock Expert mode:
Finish the game on the hard difficulty setting.

Unlock Ace mode:
Finish the game on the expert difficulty setting.

Unlock Alternate colours:
Finish the game in Ace mode.

Unlock Bonus options:
Finish all 18 missions and save the game, quit out and then reload the saved game to unlock the following new options at the main menu screen. The "Special Continue" option allows you to be able to replay the entire game with all the new fighters and weapons, plus the money earned during your first play. The "Free Mission" option allows you to be able to play any mission. The "Trial Mission" option opens up the "score attack" or "time attack" modes. The "Scene Viewer" allow you to be able to play all the game's numerous FMV sequences. Finally, the "Music Player" option allows you to play all of the in game music.

Safe Return: Easy completion:
You will notice that there are eleven balloons ahead of you, shoot them all down and then take a right across the mountain. From this point shoot down six more balloons and then take a right again and blasting more balloons until the timer runs out.

Easier X-02s:
The easy way to get win the three X-02s is to play the

"Free Mission" option you have unlocked. Then choose a difficulty setting to unlock the desired plane (normal for the grey X-02, hard for the black X-02, or expert for the silver X-02). Play and complete any mission with an "S" rank and the X-02 becomes available. Repeat this process to unlock all three

AGE OF EMPIRES 2: THE AGE OF KINGS

Build faster:
Continuously select the icon next to the percentage.

Barbarians:
Play in death match mode and choose the Vikings.

Explore enemy territory without being attacked:
Skip forward to the Feudal age and build a Market, and then a Trade Cart. You can now use this Trade Cart to safely explore your opponent's territory, without fear of attack.

AGGRESSIVE INLINE

Unlock Never Die Cheat
Enter K, H, U, F, and U as the code at the cheat selection screen.

Unlock Low gravity wall ride:
Enter ⇧, ⇩, ⇧, ⇩, ⇦, ⇨, ⇦, ⇨, A, B, A, B, S as the code at the cheat selection screen.

Unlock Super Spin:
Enter ⇦, ⇦, ⇦, ⇦, ⇨, ⇨, ⇨, ⇨, ⇦, ⇨, ⇦, ⇨, ⇧ as the code at the cheat selection screen.

Unlock Perfect manuals:
Enter Q, U, E, Z, D, O, N, T, S, L, E, E, and P as the code at the cheat selection screen.

Unlock Perfect hand plants:
Enter J, U, S, T, I, N, [Space], B, A, I, L, E, Y as the code at the cheat selection screen.

Unlock Level select, all park editor objects, full stats:
Enter ⇧, ⇧, ⇩, ⇩, ⇦, ⇨, ⇦, ⇨, B, A, B, A as the code at the cheat selection screen.

Unlock All bonus characters:
Enter ⇩, ⇨, ⇨, ⇩, ⇦, ⇩, ⇦, ⇩, ⇨, ⇨, ⇨ as the code at the cheat selection screen.

Unlock All keys:
Enter S, K, E, L, E, T, O, and N as the code at the cheat selection screen.

Unlock FMV sequences:
Finish the normal challenges in a level to unlock its FMV sequence.

Unlock Bonus characters:
Finish the normal and hidden challenges in a level to unlock a bonus character. The characters are as follows:

Movie Lot: The Bride
Civic Center: Goddess
Industrial: Junkie
Boardwalk: Captain
Cannery: Diver
Airfield: Bombshell
Museum: Mummy

Unlock Perfect grinds:
Enter B, I, G, U, P, Y, A, S, E, L, F as the code at the cheat selection screen.

Unlock Juice regeneration:
Enter ⇦, ⇦, ⇨, ⇨, ⇦, ⇨, ⇩, ⇧, ⇧, ⇩, A, I as the code at the cheat selection screen.

Unlock Juice bar is always full:
Enter B, A, K, A, B, A, K, A as the code at the cheat selection screen.

Unlock CHEAT:
Collect all juice boxes in a level to reveal a cheat code.

Unlock Power Skates:
Complete all challenges (normal and hidden) hidden on every the level.

Unlock Ultra Skates:
Complete all the levels with 100%.

AIRBLADE

Unlock Stunt attack mode:
Finish the game in story mode.

Unlock Hidden Future:
Finish with a "Master" rank in all four stages to unlock the Hidden Future in story puzzle mode.

Unlock J. J. Sawyer:
Finish the game with an "S" rank in all levels.

Unlock Naomi:
Finish the Downtown level with a "B" rank.

Unlock Oscar:
Finish the game with an "A" rank in all levels.

Unlock The Insider:
Finish the Storage level with a "B" rank.

ALONE IN THE DARK: THE NEW NIGHTMARE

Skip events:
Repeatedly hit Action to skip past events during in game .

APE ESCAPE 2

Play as Spike:
Successfully complete the game after finding all 297 monkeys. Highlight "New Game" at the main menu, then press L1 + START.

ARCTIC THUNDER

Unlock All Random mode:
Hit R1, R2, ■, ●, R1, R2, and START at the screen after the start-up.

Unlock All Atomic Snowballs mode:
Hit ■ x3, L1, ●, START at the screen after the start-up.

Unlock All Grappling Hooks and Random mode:
Hit ● x2, L2, ● x2, L1, START at the screen after start-up.

Unlock All Rooster Tails mode:
Hit R1, R2, L2, L1, ■, and START at the screen after start-up.

Unlock No drones mode:
Hit ■ x2, ● x2, L1, R1, START at the screen after the start-up.

Unlock Expert mode:
Hit ●, ■, and ● x2, ■, START at the screen after the start-up.

Unlock Clone mode:
Hit L1, L2 x2, ●, L1, ●, START at the screen after start-up.

Unlock Everyone invisible mode:
Hit ■, ●, ■, R2, ● x2, START at the screen after start-up.

Unlock No power-ups mode:
Hit ■ x2, ●, ■, R2, ■, and START at the screen after start-up.

Unlock All Snow Bombs and Random mode:
Hit ● x2, R1, R2, START at the screen after start-up.

Unlock All Boost modes:
Hit ●, R1 x2, ●, R2, START at the screen after start-up.

Unlock Super boost wheelie mode:
Hit ●, L1, ■, R2, ■, L2, and START at the screen after start-up.

Unlock Mooing:
Enter MOO as your initials after a race.

Unlock Snowman:
Win gold medals on all twelve tracks in race.

ARMORED CORE 2

Add defeated AC emblems:
Hit SELECT + START when the victory message appears in the arena.

Unlock Unlimited energy, weight, and arm weight:
Finish the game and allow the credits to complete.

Unlock Temporary invincibility:
Hit L2 + R2 + R3. A "Limiter Released" system error message will appear, and you will have unlimited energy during this time.

ARMY MEN: AIR ATTACK 2

Level:	Password:
2	⇧, ✖, ▲, ⇨, ⇦, ■, ●, ✖
3	▲, ●, ⇩, ⇦, ■, ■, ⇧, ⇧
4	✖, ⇨, ⇦, ✖, ●, ■, ■, ▲
5	⇩, ⇩, ●, ■, ●, ■, ⇨, ✖
6	▲, ✖, ⇧, ⇦, ⇨, ⇦, ●, ▲
7	⇨, ■, ⇨, ⇩, ●, ✖, ✖, ⇨
8	▲, ⇨, ■, ■, ●, ⇩, ⇩, ✖
9	⇧, ✖, ■, ⇦, ⇨, ●, ⇦, ⇦
10	▲, ⇧, ●, ✖, ■, ⇩, ⇩, ⇩
11	●, ●, ⇧, ⇦, ⇨, ✖, ▲, ■
12	⇨, ⇧, ✖, ⇨, ●, ■, ▲, ●
13	⇦, ⇦, ▲, ●, ✖, ✖, ⇩, ⇨
14	■, ⇨, ●, ⇧, ⇩, ■, ⇩, ✖
15	⇦, ⇨, ●, ✖, ■, ⇩, ⇩, ●
16	▲, ●, ✖, ⇨, ⇨, ●, ■, ⇩
17	■, ⇧, ⇧, ⇨, ⇦, ■, ⇩, ✖
18	●, ✖, ⇨, ▲, ■, ⇧, ✖, ✖
19	⇩, ⇨, ✖, ■, ⇨, ⇧, ●, ●
20	⇧, ✖, ●, ⇧, ⇦, ■, ●, ✖

ARMY MEN: GREEN ROGUE

Sink the Shark Submarine:
To sink the Shark Submarine at the end of level 2, kill all the tan soldiers that appear and then Hold L1 and hit the Right Analog-stick to aim for the gun turrets on top of the submarine. You must destroy all the turrets to sink the sub.

ARMY MEN: RTS

Unlock 5000 Plastic:
Hold R2 and hit ▲, ●, ■, ✖, ▲, ■ during in game.

Unlock Paratroopers:
Hold R2 and hit ●, ■, ●, ■, ▲, ▲ during in game.

Unlock Extra dump truck resources:
Hold R2 and hit ■, ■, ■, ▲, ●, and ✖ during in game.

Unlock Super soldiers:
Hold R2 and hit ■, ■, ✖, ▲, ✖, ■ during in game.

Unlock Super enemy soldiers:
Hold R2 and hit ▲, ▲, ✖, ■, ▲, and ▲ during in game.

Unlock 2000 Electricity:
Hold R2 and hit ▲, ■, ●, ✖, ▲, ✖ during in game.

Unlock Green army is blue:
Hold R2 and hit ■, ▲, ■, ■, ✖, ● during in game.

Unlock Tan army is green:
Hold R2 and hit ▲ x2, ✖, ■, ▲ x2 during in game.

Kill your soldiers:
Hold R2 and hit ■, ▲, ⇦ x2, ▲, ■ during in game.

ARMY MEN: SARGE'S HEROES 2

Unlock Level select:
Enter FREEPLAY as a password.

Unlock All weapons:
Enter GIMME as a password

Unlock Invincibility:
Enter NODIE as a password.

Unlock Invisible:
Enter NOSEEUM as a password.

Unlock Tiny mode:
Enter SHORTY as a password.

Unlock Big mode:
Enter IMHUGE as a password.

Unlock Debug info:
Enter THDOTEST as a password.

ATV OFF ROAD FURY

Unlock All ATVs:
Select pro-career mode, then enter CHACHING as a name.

Unlock All tracks:
Select pro-career mode, then enter WHATEXIT as a name.

Unlock Expert mode:
Select pro-career mode, then enter ALLOUTAI as a name.

Unlock Fast racers:
Select pro-career mode, then enter ALLQUIKI as a name.

Unlock Ravage 1000cc Quad ATV:
Finish the game in pro-career mode.

Preload:
To preload, hit ⇩ at bottom of a jump then hit ⇧.

Tricks:
To do tricks, hold ▲ or ● and move the Left Analog Stick or D-pad in any direction.

Quick resume:
Hit L1 + R1 if you go off-track or crash.

Win New Quads wheelers:
Go to any race and win the championship. Return to the same championship and go to the pro races to see that two new quads have been unlocked.

Split-X:
Hit ⇨ + ▲ to do the Split-X trick.

BALDUR'S GATE: DARK ALLIANCE

Unlock Cheat mode:
Hold R2 + L1 + ⇦ + ▲ then hit START during in game.

Unlock Super character:
Hold R2 + L1 + ⇦ + ▲ then hit R3 during in game.

Play as Drizzt:
Hold L1 + R1 then hit ✖ + ▲ at the main menu screen.

Control loading screen:
Move the Right Analog-stick and the flames surrounding "Loading" will move.

Unlock The Gauntlet level:
Finish the game under any difficulty setting.

Unlock Extreme mode:
Finish The Gauntlet level to unlock the extreme difficulty setting.

Unlock Play as Drizzt:
Finish the game under the extreme difficulty setting.

Alternate costume:
Highlight a character, and then hit R1 at the selection screen.

BARBARIAN

Alternate costume:
Highlight a character, then press R1 at the selection screen.

BATMAN VENGEANCE

Unlock Master code:
Hit L2, R2, L2, R2, ■ x2, ● x2 at the main menu screen.

Unlock all power moves and 120 Beatment points:
Hit L1 x2, R2 x2, L2, R2, L1, R2 at the main menu screen.

Unlock Unlimited Handcuffs:
Hit Square, Circle, Square, Circle, L2, R2 x2, L2 at the main menu screen.

Unlock Unlimited Batlauncher:
Hit Circle, Square, Circle, Square, L1, R1, L2, R2 at the main menu screen.

Unlock unlimited electric Batarangs:
Hit L1, R1, L2, and R2 at the main menu screen.

BIG MUTHA TRUCKERS

Master cheat code:
Enter CHEATINGMUTHATRUCKER as a cheat code in the options screen. All cheats and the Evil Truck will be unlocked.

Unlock $10 million:
Enter LOTSAMONEY as a cheat code in the options screen.

Unlock Level select:
Enter LAZYPLAYER as a cheat code in the options screen.

Unlock Evil Truck:
Play Trial By Trukin' 60 day mode, then win the race back to Big Mutha Trucking HQ.

BLADE 2

Level select:
Press and hold L1 and press ⇩, ⇧, ⇦ x2 , ●, ⇨, ⇩, ■ at the main menu.

Unlimited health:
Pause game play, then press and hold L1 and press ▲, ■, ▲, ■, ▲, ●, ▲, ●.

Unlimited rage:
Pause game play, then press and hold L1 and press ⇦, ⇩, ⇦, ⇩, ⇨, ⇧, ⇨, ⇧.

All weapons:
Press and hold L1 and press ■, ●, ⇩, ⇦, ●x2 , ▲ at the main menu.

Unlimited ammunition:
Pause game play, then press and hold L1 and press ⇦, ●, ⇨, ■, ⇧, ▲, ⇩, ✖.

Daywalker difficulty setting:
Press and hold L1 and press ⇦, ●, ⇧, ⇩, ■, ●, ✖ at the main menu.

BLOODYRAYNE

God Mode:
Enter TRIASSASSINDONTDIE as a cheat code to unlock the "God Mode" option at the main cheat menu. A message will confirm correct cheat code entry.

Restore Health:
Enter LAMEYANKEEDONTFEED as a cheat code to unlock the "Restore Health" option at the main cheat menu. A message will confirm correct cheat code entry.

Fill Bloodlust:
Enter ANGRYXXXINSANEHOOKER as a cheat code to unlock the "Fill Bloodlust" option at the main cheat menu. A message will confirm correct cheat code entry.

BLOODY ROAR 3

Unlock Kohryu:
Play through arcade mode until you face Kohryu and beat him.

Unlock Uranus:
Play through arcade mode and defeat Xion without using any continues up to that point and beat him.

Unlock Gallery pictures:
Finish the game with any character to unlock their images in the picture gallery.

Unlock Sudden death survival mode:
Survive nine fights in survival mode to unlock this option.

Unlock Survival ranking:
Win 100 matches in survival mode as all characters wins put together.

Unlock Super difficulty:
Finish Arcade mode once without continuing to unlock this option.

Unlock No blocking mode:
Get first place in arcade mode to unlock this option.

Unlock Low speed mode:
Gain a ranking with each character in arcade mode to unlock this option.

Unlock High-speed mode:
Win 100 battles in survival mode with a single character then enter your player namein the high scores screen to unlock this option.

Unlock One hit knockdowns:
Get first place in sudden death mode to unlock this option.

Unlock Hyper beast mode:
Win 10 fights with a single character in arcade mode and record your player nameto unlock this option.

Unlock Sumo wrestling battle mode:
Defeat twenty opponents in survival mode and earn a ranking.

Unlock One fall mode:
Win twenty rounds with a single character in survival mode to unlock this option.

Looping replay:
Hit ▲ during a replay to play it repeatedly.

BMX XXX

Unlock Level select:
Enter XXX RATED CHEAT as a code at the cheat menu.

Unlock Stage select:
Enter MASS HYSTERIA as a code at the cheat menu.

Unlock Play as Amish Boy:
Enter ELECTRICITYBAD as a code at the cheat menu.

Unlock All bikes:
Enter 65 SWEET RIDES as a code at the cheat menu.

Unlock Amish Boy's bikes:
Enter AMISHBOY1699 as a code at the cheat menu.

Unlock Hellkitty's bikes:
Enter HELLKITTY487 as a code at the cheat menu.

Unlock Itchi's bikes:
Enter ITCHI594 as a code at the cheat menu.

Unlock Joyride's bikes:
Enter JOYRIDE18 as a code at the cheat menu.

Unlock Karma's bikes:
Enter KARMA311 as a code at the cheat menu.

Unlock La'tey's bikes:
Enter LATEY411 as a code at the cheat menu.

Unlock Manuel's bikes:
Enter MANUEL415 as a code at the cheat menu.

Unlock Mika's bikes:
Enter MIKA362436 as a code at the cheat menu.

Unlock Nutter's bikes:
Enter NUTTER290 as a code at the cheat menu.

Unlock Rave's bikes:
Enter RAVE10 as a code at the cheat menu.

Unlock Skeeter's bikes:
Enter SKEETER666 as a code at the cheat menu.

Unlock Tripledub's bikes:
Enter TRIPLEDUB922 as a code at the cheat menu.

Unlock Twan's bikes:
Enter TWAN18 as a code at the cheat menu.

Unlock Launch Pad 69 level:
Enter SHOWMETHEMONKEY as a code at the cheat menu.

Unlock Rampage Skatepark level:
Enter IOWARULES as a code at the cheat menu.

Unlock The Dam level:
Enter THATDAMLEVEL as a code at the cheat menu.

Unlock Las Vegas level:
Enter SHOWMETHEMONEY as a code at the cheat menu.

Unlock Roots level:
Enter UNDERGROUND as a code at the cheat menu.

Unlock Sheep Hills level:
Enter BAABAA as a code at the cheat menu.

Unlock Syracuse level:
Enter BOYBANDSSUCK as a code at the cheat menu.

Unlock Night vision mode:
Enter 3RD SOG as a code at the cheat menu.

Unlock Happy bunny mode:
Enter FLUFFYBUNNY as a code at the cheat menu.

Unlock Ghost control mode:
Enter GHOSTCONTROL as a code at the cheat menu.

Unlock Super crash mode:
Enter HEAVYPETTING as a code at the cheat menu.

Unlock Green skin mode:
Enter MAKEMEANGRY as a code at the cheat menu.

Unlock Visible gap mode:
Enter PARABOLIC as a code at the cheat menu.

Unlock All FMV sequences:
Enter CHAMPAGNE ROOM as a code at the cheat menu.

Unlock Bonus Movie 1 FMV sequence:
Enter THISISBMXX as a code at the cheat menu.

Unlock Bonus Movie 2 FMV sequence:
Enter KEEPITDIRTY as a code at the cheat menu.

Unlock Dam 1 FMV sequence:
Enter BOING as a code at the cheat menu.

Unlock Final Movie FMV sequence:
Enter DDUULRRLDRSQUARE as a code at the cheat menu.

Unlock Las Vegas 1 FMV sequence:
Enter HIGHBEAMS as a code at the cheat menu.

Unlock Las Vegas 2 FMV sequence:
Enter TASSLE as a code at the cheat menu.

Unlock Launch Pad 69 1 FMV sequence:
Enter IFLINGPOO as a code at the cheat menu.

Unlock Launch Pad 69 2 FMV sequence:
Enter PEACH as a code at the cheat menu.

Unlock Rampage Skatepark 2 FMV sequence:
Enter BURLESQUE as a code at the cheat menu.

Unlock Sheep FMV sequence:
Enter ONEDOLLAR as a code at the cheat menu.

Unlock Sheep Hills 2 FMV sequence:
Enter 69 as a code at the cheat menu.

Unlock Syracuse 1 FMV sequence:
Enter FUZZYKITTY as a code at the cheat menu.

Unlock Syracuse 2 FMV sequence:
Enter MICHAELHUNT as a code at the cheat menu.

Unlock The Bronx, NYC 1 FMV sequence:
Enter LAPDANCE as a code at the cheat menu.

Unlock The Bronx, NYC 2 FMV sequence:
Enter STRIPTEASE as a code at the cheat menu.

Unlock UGP Roots Jam 2 FMV sequence:
Enter BOOTYCALL as a code at the cheat menu.

Unlock Park editor:
Enter BULLETPOINT as a code at the cheat menu.

THE BOUNCER

Unlock Alternate costumes:
Hold L1, L2, R1, or R2 and hit ✖ choose a person at the main character selection screen.

Unlock Hidden FMV sequence:
Finish the game as Sion.

Unlock Bonus characters:
Finish the game in story mode to unlock more characters each time that it is finished.

Increased character rank:
Every time the game is completed in story mode, the rank of the extra characters in versus and survival modes will increase. This does not include Volt, Sion, and Kou.

Unlock Echidna:
Finish the MSD Cargo Train level to unlock Echidna in versus and survival modes.

Unlock Dauragon shirtless:
Complete the game for a third time using any character.

Unlock Dauragon fighting with one arm:
Play the game in story mode and defeat Dauragon at his first encounter.

Unlock Dominique:
Play the game in story mode until Dominique destroys the group of PD-4s to unlock her.

Unlock Kaldea:
Defeat Kaldea before the final encounter with Dauragon in story mode to unlock her.

Team attack:
Immediately hit R2 whenever you hear one of your teammates uses their taunt.

BRITNEY'S DANCE BEAT

Unlock Baby One More Time video:
Get at least 9999 points in audition mode.

Unlock Britney:
Finish audition mode then go to practice mode. Britney Spears will now be unlocked as your dancing partner.

BURNOUT

Unlock All racers:
Hit R2 x3, L1, ▲, L2 x3, R1, ■ at the main title screen.

Ending bonuses:
Finish the game to unlock the Free Run mode, Free Run Twin mode and Credits options.

Unlock Face Off option:
Finish championship mode once to unlock Face off one against the Roadster.

Unlock Roadster:
Defeat the Roadster in Face off one to unlock it and Face off two against another car.

Unlock Tow truck:
Play in championship mode until you unlock Face off two in the special options screen, now you must defeat the Tow truck to unlock it.

Unlock Saloon GT:
Defeat the Saloon GT in Face off three.

Unlock Bus:
Defeat the bus in Face off four.

Increase boost:
Drive on the wrong side of the road to keep increasing your boost.

Full bonus:
Drive a perfect lap and your bonus will be automatically filled.

Crash horn:
Hold Circle to use the horn while driving and then when you crash, the horn will stay on.

Quick start:
Accelerate immediately before the "1" fades during the pre-race countdown.

Rush Hour: Boost:
On Rush Hour, you can drive on the wrong side of the road to keep your boost up.

Supermini: Flip:
Select the Supermini as your car and while at high speeds ram a car while going around a corner.

Worst Driver List:
To get on the Worst Driver List, crash up your car and then go through all the checkpoints at the very last second.

BURNOUT 2: POINT OF IMPACT

Cheat mode:
Unlock any cheat and the "Cheat Mode" selection will appear at the options screen. Note: Races will not be counted as wins with any cheat activated.

Invulnerability:
Complete all Grand Prix Championships with gold medals to unlock the "Invulnerability" option at the "Cheat Mode" menu.

Runaway:
Complete Crash mode with all gold medals on all fifteen tracks to unlock the "Runaway" option at the "Cheat Mode" menu.

Face Off:
Win all the face offs in the first championship.

Custom Championship:
Get all gold medals in every race and win everything in the first championship to unlock the Custom Championship.

1997 Eclipse and 2001 Focus SVT:
Complete the Custom championship two times and get best score possible in the races.

Classic 1970 car:
Win Pursuit 2 by destroying the classic 1970 car with the police car.

Drivers Ed car:
Complete Driving 101 with all gold medals.

Oval Racer:
Race Face-Off 2 against the Oval Racer. The race is five laps around Airport Terminal 3.

Police car:
Win Pursuit 1 by destroying the criminal's car before it gets away.

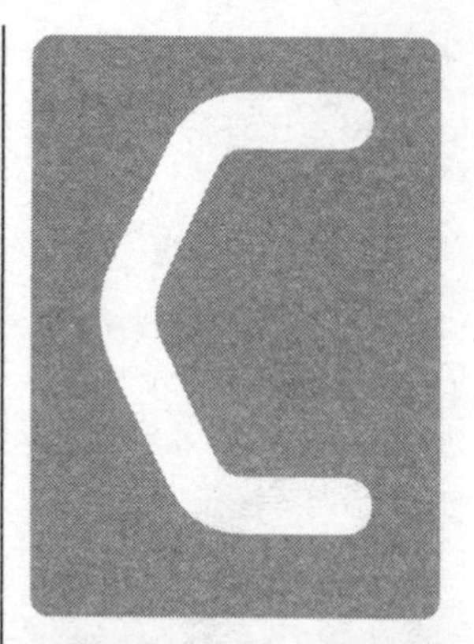

CART FURY: CHAMPIONSHIP RACING

Unlock All cars:
Hit ▲, ✖, ▲, ■, L2, ▲ at the cheat menu.

Unlock All tracks:
Hit R1, ▲, ✖ x2, R2, L1 at the cheat menu.

Unlock Unlimited turbo:
Hit ✖ x2, ■ x2, and L2 x2 at the cheat menu.

Unlock Infinite continues:
Hit L1, L2, L1, ■, ▲, ● at the cheat menu.

Unlock Big head mode option:
Hit ▲, ■ x2, L2, L1, and R2 at the cheat menu.

Unlock Low gravity:
Hit R2, R1, ■ x2, L1 x2 at the cheat menu.

Unlock Jump option:
Hit L1, L2, L1, R2, ✖ x2 at the cheat menu.

Unlock Thick fog:
Hit R2, R1, ✖, ■ x2, ● at the cheat menu. Thick Fog and New York track options at the cheat menu.

Unlock Night drive:
Hit ✖, ●, ▲, L2, R2, L1 at the cheat menu.

Unlock Rocket wheels:
Hit L1, R2, ▲, ■ x2, ▲ at the cheat menu.

Unlock Death car:
Hit L1, ■, R1, R2, L2, L1 at the cheat menu.

Unlock Opponent Death cars:

COLIN McRAE RALLY 3

Cheat code notes:
The game's cheat codes are matched to the bonus cheat code of each game.

Unlock Jet:
Enter GOBUUR as a cheat code
Enter LOWWOH as a cheat code
Enter YJBATU as a cheat code
Enter RUGSSH as a cheat code
Enter YJBUUZ as a cheat code

Unlock Baja Buggy:
Enter NQFIPE as a cheat code
Enter PHOUOT as a cheat code
Enter VURCNU as a cheat code
Enter VURKFA as a cheat code

Unlock Hovercraft:
Enter IURUOT as a cheat code
Enter MHXIPE as a cheat code
Enter NXDLLB as a cheat code
Enter BKQBAU as a cheat code
Enter NXDZPS as a cheat code

Unlock Battle Tank:
Enter LHZWOH as a cheat code
Enter ZIIUUR as a cheat code
Enter ZSSDBU as a cheat code
Enter LWXEIF as a cheat code

Unlock R/C cars:
Enter WWBDBU as a

cheat code
Enter AQVATU as a cheat code
Enter GBPWOH as a cheat code
Enter PFKCXQ as a cheat code
Enter GBPNXU as a cheat code

Unlock Ford Super Focus:
Enter OQJZZY as a cheat code
Enter UYNFVA as a cheat code
Enter LPGXUE as a cheat code
Enter WSNBSB as a cheat code

Unlock All cars:
Enter MKCLLB as a cheat code
Enter WWACNU as a cheat code
Enter FMGUOT as a cheat code
Enter OQJHOK as a cheat code
Enter FMGGPL as a cheat code
Enter OHCIIZ as a cheat code

Unlock All tracks:
Enter ODIATU as a cheat code
Enter XWUDBU as a cheat code
Enter RVNUUR as a cheat code

Enter ODIFCS as a cheat code
Enter RVNBLQ as a cheat code
Enter BKQOHP as a cheat code

Unlock All parts:
Enter FHPCNU as a cheat code
Enter UZVLLB as a cheat code
Enter HZUWOH as a cheat code
Enter KEZIPE as a cheat code
Enter FHPIWQ as a cheat code
Enter KEZMGO as a cheat code
Enter RUGWOL as a cheat code

All difficulties:
Enter WSNXZU as a cheat code
Enter AUNAMA as a cheat code
Enter UXNKFB as a cheat code
Enter UXNPBG as a cheat code

Hit L2, ■, L1, R2, R2, and ✖ at the cheat menu.
Unlock Death wall:
Hit ✖, ■, R2, ▲, R1, R2 at the cheat menu.
Unlock All FMV sequences:
Hit L1, ●, and R2, ✖, L2, Triangle at the cheat menu.
Unlock Cigar car:
Finish in first place on Frankfurt track in arcade mode.
Unlock Driving 101 FMV sequence:
Finish all Driving 101 options to unlock the Driving 101 FMV sequence.

CITY CRISIS

Unlock Final rescue mission and time attack mode:
Complete all of the chase missions to unlock the time attack mode.
Unlock Chase car mode:
Beat an "A" rank on each mission and an "S" rank on the "Bus Chase".
Unlock Final rescue mode:
Beat an "S" rank with the Sports Car.
Unlock Disaster mode:
Beat an "S" rank in final rescue mode.

COMMANDOS 2

Bonus missions:
Collect all the brown bonus books during a mission to complete the photograph at the end and unlock a bonus mission. Note: The "Saving Private Smith" mission does not have an associated bonus mission.

CONFLICT DESERT STORM

NOTE: THESE CHEATS REQUIRE A USB KEYBOARD...
Unlock Toggle damage:
Press K during game play to toggle damage on and off.
Unlock Display debug position and rotation:
Press L during game play to display your position.
Unlock Reverse aiming:
Press Y during game play.
Unlock Pause game play:
Press ✖ to freeze the game.
Unlock Display menu:
Press \ to toggle the menu.

CONTRA: SHATTERED SOLDIER

Completion bonuses:
Successfully complete the game under the normal difficulty setting and at least a "B" rank to unlock the "Theater" option, "Database" option, and level 5 in training mode. Successfully complete the game with an "A" rank to view an alternate ending sequence and unlock level 6. Successfully complete level 6 with an "A" rank to unlock level 7 and level 6 in training mode.

CRASH BANDICOOT: THE WRATH OF CORTEX

Unlock Alternate ending sequence:
Collect all 46 gems.
Avalanche: Getting all the boxes:
While riding the snowboard and the avalanche is chasing you, do not try to get the boxes. The avalanche destroys them for you. Just keep boarding.
Bonzat Bonsat: Super belly flop power:
After acquiring the Red Gem, go to the Bonzat Bonsat level. Jump onto the Red Gem, then make your way to the end to find a gem and the super belly flop power move.

CRAZY TAXI

Unlock Secret Push Bike:
Hold L1 + R1 at the main character selection screen. Release L1, and then release R1. Hold L1 + R1 again, then release them simultaneously and then, hit ✖.
Unlock Expert mode:
Hold L1 + R1 + START at the main menu screen. Continue to hold the buttons until the main character selection screen appears, then hit ✖ to select the game mode and variation.
Disable arrow indicators:
Hold R1 + START after choosing your time limit and before the main character selection screen appears.
Disable destination indicator:
Hold L1 + START after choosing your time limit and before the main character selection screen appears.
Unlock Another Day mode:
Hit R1 at the main character selection screen, then release it. Then, hold R1 and hit ✖.
TIP: More money:
Your passenger will get very excited and into it and give you more money when you pass other drivers on the road.
Class S license:
Play the game in original mode and work for ten minutes, earn $5,000 dollars or more, you will get the Class S license.
Crazy Dash:
Hit Drive + Accelerate.
Crazy Stop:
Hit Reverse + Brake.
Crazy Drift:
Hit ⇦ or ⇨ while shifting into Reverse then into Drive while driving at a high speed.

Crazy Drift Stop:
Do a Crazy Stop immediately after a Crazy Drift.
Jump:
When driving down a straight road, build speed, then hit Drive + Brake.
Easy drive off:
When you are dropping off someone, hit ⇨ + Brake to drive off easy.
Extra speed:
Hit R1 + R2 for extra speed on the road.
Win a $99,999:
Execute a Crazy Drift, wait until you have spun 180 degrees, then hit Reverse + Drive. You can earn as much as a 450 combo and $99,999.

CRICKET 2002

Unlock Super batsmen:
Select the "Inside EA Sports" option at the main menu screen and hit R2, ●, L2, R1, SELECT. Hit L1 during in game for your new power shot this will hit a six each time.

DARK CLOUD

Invincibility:
Finish every level up to the Gallery Of Time then return to any either of the first two levels. No damage will be done to you when someone attacks. You will loose life only when you go to back levels and when you are poisoned.
Boss clues:
When fighting a Boss, use Xiao with Steve. Steve will talk and give TIP on how to defeat the Bosses.

DARK SUMMIT

Gain Extra points:
Hold SELECT + START, then hit ▲, ■, L1, ●, R1, ✖, R1, ✖ at the main menu screen.
Unlock All boarders:
Hold SELECT + START, then hit ▲, ■, L1, ●, R1, X, R1, ▲ at the main menu screen.
Unlock All Challenges completed:
Hold SELECT + START, then hit ▲, ■, L1, ●, R1, ✖, R1, ■ at the main menu screen.
Alien unlocked:
Hold SELECT + START, then hit ▲, ■, L1, ●, R1, ✖, R1, ✖ at the main menu screen.
Unlock Shoot projectile:
Hold SELECT + START, then hit ■, ●, ▲, R1 at the main menu screen.
Unlock Slow motion:
Hold SELECT + START, then hit ■, ●, ▲, L1 at the main menu screen.

DAVE MIRRA FREESTYLE BMX 2

Master code:
Hit ⇧, ⇨, ⇩, ⇦, ⇨ x2, ⇧, ⇩, ⇦, ⇨, ⇧, ⇦, ⇨ x2, ⇩, ■ at the main menu screen.
Unlock Mike Diaz:
Hit ⇧, ⇦, ⇩, ⇨ x2, ⇦, ⇧, ⇩, ⇧, ⇨, ■ at the main menu screen.
Unlock Amish guy:
Hit ⇧, ⇦, ⇩, ⇨ x2, ⇦ x2, ⇩, ⇧, ⇦, ■ at the main menu screen.
Unlock All bikes:
Hit ⇧, ⇦, ⇩, ⇨, ⇩ x2, ⇨, ⇩ x2, ⇦, ■ at the main menu screen.
Level select:
Hit ⇧, ⇩ x2, ⇦, ⇨, ⇩, ■ at the main menu screen.
Unlock All themes in park editor:
Hit ⇧, ⇦, ⇩, ⇨, ⇩, ⇧, ⇩, ⇨, ⇦ x2, ■ at the main menu screen.
Unlock All objects in park editor:
Hit ⇧, ⇦, ⇩, ⇨, ⇩, ⇧ x2, ⇩, ⇨ x2, ■ at the main menu screen.
Unlock All FMV sequences:
Hit ⇧, ⇦, ⇩, ⇨, ⇦ x2, ⇨, ⇦, ⇧, ⇩, ■ at the main menu screen.
Unlock Amish Guy moves:
Hit ⇦, ⇨, ⇧ x2, ⇨, ⇩, ⇨ x2, ■ at the main menu screen.
Unlock Colin Mackay bikes:
Hit ⇩ x2, ⇨ x5, ⇧, ■ at the main menu screen.
Unlock Colin Mackay levels:
Hit ⇧ x2, ⇨, ⇦, ⇧, ⇨ x2, ⇧, ■ at the main menu screen.
Unlock Colin Mackay moves:
Hit ⇦, ⇨ x2, ⇧, ⇦, ⇨ x2, ⇧, ■ at the main menu screen.
Unlock Colin Mackey FMV sequences:
Hit ⇦ x2, ⇨ x2, ⇩ x2, ⇨, ⇧, ■ at the main menu screen.
Unlock Colin Mackey's competition outfit:
Hit ⇧, ⇩, ⇨, ⇩, ⇧, ⇨ x2, ⇧, ■ at the main menu screen.
Unlock Dave Mirra bikes:
Hit ⇩ x2, ⇧, ⇨, ⇧, ⇨, ⇧ x2, ■ at the main menu screen.

Unlock Dave Mirra levels:
Hit ⇧ x3, ⇨, ⇧, ⇦, ⇧ x2, ■ at the main menu screen.
Unlock Dave Mirra move:
Hit ⇦, ⇨, ⇧ x2, ⇦, ⇨, ⇧ x2, ■ at the main menu screen.
Unlock Dave Mirra's competition outfit:
Hit ⇧, ⇩, ⇧, ⇩, ⇨, ⇦, ⇧ x2, ■ at the main menu screen.
Unlock Dave Mirra's FMV sequences:
Hit ⇦ x2, ⇧, ⇨, ⇧, ⇦, ⇧ x2, ■ at the main menu screen.
Unlock Joey Garcia bikes:
Hit ⇩ x2, ⇧, ⇨, ⇦ x2, ⇩, ⇨, ■ at the main menu screen.
Unlock Joey Garcia FMV sequences:
Hit ⇦ x2, ⇧ x2, ⇩, ⇨, ⇩, ■ at the main menu screen.
Unlock Joey Garcia levels:
Hit ⇧ x4, ⇩ x3, ⇨, ■ at the main menu screen.
Unlock Joey Garcia moves:
Hit ⇦, ⇨, ⇧, ⇨, ⇩, ⇧, ⇩, ⇨, ■ at the main menu screen.
Unlock Joey Garcia's competition outfit:
Hit ⇧, ⇩, ⇧, ⇦, ⇩, ⇨, ⇩, ⇨, ■ at the main menu screen.
Unlock John Englebert bikes:
Hit ⇩ x2, ⇦, ⇧, ⇦, ⇧, ⇦ x2, ■ at the main menu screen.
Unlock John Englebert levels:
Hit ⇧ x2, ⇦, ⇩, ⇨, ⇩, ⇦ x2, ■ at the main menu screen.
Unlock John Englebert moves:
Hit ⇦, ⇨, ⇦, ⇦, ⇩, ⇧, ⇦ x2, ■ at the main menu screen.
Unlock Kenan Harkin bikes:
Hit ⇩ x2, ⇦, ⇧, ⇩, ⇨, ⇩ x2, ■ at the main menu screen.
Unlock Kenan Harkin FMV sequences:
Hit ⇦ x4, ⇨ x2, ⇩ x2, ■ at the main menu screen.
Unlock Kenan Harkin levels:
Hit ⇧ x2, ⇦, ⇦, ⇩, ⇧, ⇩ x2, ■ at the main menu screen.
Unlock Kenan Harkin moves:
Hit ⇦, ⇨, ⇦, ⇩, ⇧, ⇩ x3, ■ at the main menu screen.
Unlock Kenan Harkin's competition outfit:
Hit ⇧, ⇩, ⇦, ⇩, ⇦, ⇧, ⇩, ⇧, ■ at the main menu screen.
Unlock Leigh Ramsdell bikes:
Hit ⇩ x3, ⇧, ⇦, ⇦, ⇩, ⇦, ■ at the main menu screen.
Unlock Leigh Ramsdell FMV sequences:
Hit ⇦ x2, ⇩ x2, ⇦, ⇨, ⇩, ⇦, ■ at the main menu screen.
Unlock Leigh Ramsdell levels:
Hit ⇧ x2, ⇩, ⇧, ⇦, ⇩ x2, ⇦, ■ at the main menu screen.
Unlock Leigh Ramsdell moves:
Hit ⇦, ⇨, ⇩, ⇦ x2, ⇨, ⇩, ⇦, ■ at the main menu screen.
Unlock Leigh Ramsdell's competition outfit:
Hit ⇧, ⇩ x2, ⇦, ⇩ x3, ⇦, ■ at the main menu screen.
Unlock Luc-E's competition outfit:
Hit ⇧, ⇩, ⇦, ⇩, ⇦, ⇨, ⇦ x2, ■ at the main menu screen.
Unlock Luc-E's FMV sequences:
Hit ⇦ x2, ⇨ x2, ⇩ x2, ⇨, ⇧, ■ at the main menu screen.
Unlock Mike Laird bikes:
Hit ⇩ x2, ⇨, ⇦, ⇩, ⇧ x2, ⇨, ■ at the main menu screen.
Unlock Mike Laird levels:
Hit ⇧ x2, ⇨, ⇩ x2, ⇨, ⇧, ⇨, ■ at the main menu screen.
Unlock Mike Laird move:
Hit ⇦, ⇨ x3, ⇦, ⇨, ⇧, ⇨, ■ at the main menu screen.
Unlock Mike Laird's competition outfit:
Hit ⇧ x2, ⇩ x2, ⇦, ⇨ x2, ⇦, ■ at the main menu screen.
Unlock Mike Laird's FMV sequences:
Hit ⇦ x2, ⇨, ⇧ x2, ⇨, ⇧, ⇨, ■ at the main menu screen.
Unlock Rick Moliterno bikes:
Hit ⇩ x2, ⇧, ⇦, ⇨ x2, ⇦, ⇧, ■ at the main menu screen.
Unlock Rick Moliterno FMV sequences:
Hit ⇦ x2, ⇧, ⇩, ⇨, ⇦ x2, ⇧, ■ at the main menu screen.
Unlock Rick Moliterno levels:
Hit ⇧ x3, ⇩, ⇨, ⇨, ⇦, ⇧, ■ at the main menu screen.
Unlock Rick Moliterno moves:
Hit ⇦, ⇨, ⇧ x3, ⇩, ⇦, ⇧, ■ at the main menu screen.
Unlock Rick Moliterno's competition outfit:
Hit ⇧, ⇩, ⇧ x4, ⇦, ⇧, ■ at the main menu screen.
Unlock Ryan Nyquist bikes:
Hit ⇩ x5, ⇨, ⇧, ⇩, ■ at the main menu screen.
Unlock Ryan Nyquist levels:
Hit ⇧ x2, ⇩ x2, ⇦, ⇨, ⇧, ⇩, ■ at the main menu screen.
Unlock Ryan Nyquist move:
Hit ⇦, ⇨, ⇩ x3, ⇧ x2, ⇩, ■ at the main menu screen.
Unlock Ryan Nyquist's competition outfit:
Hit ⇧, ⇩ x2, ⇦, ⇩, ⇧ x2, ⇩, ■ at the main menu screen.
Unlock Ryan Nyquist's FMV sequences:
Hit ⇦ x2, ⇩, ⇨, ⇩, ⇨, ⇧, ⇩, ■ at the main menu screen.
Unlock Scott Wirch bikes:
Hit ⇩ x2, ⇨, ⇧, ⇩ x2, ⇦, ⇨, ■ at the main menu screen.
Unlock Scott Wirch FMV sequences:

Hit ⇦ x2, ⇨, ⇧ x3, ⇦, ⇨, ■ at the main menu screen.
Unlock Scott Wirch levels:
Hit ⇧ x2, ⇨, ⇧, ⇦ x3, ⇨, ■ at the main menu screen.
Unlock Scott Wirch moves:
Hit ⇦, ⇨ x3, ⇧, ⇩, ⇦, ⇨, ■ at the main menu screen.
Unlock Scott Wirch's competition outfit:
Hit ⇧, ⇩, ⇨, ⇩, ⇧, ⇨ x2, ⇧, ■ at the main menu screen.
Unlock Slim Jim moves:
Hit ⇦, ⇨, ⇩, ⇦, ⇧, ⇦, ⇨, ⇦, ■ at the main menu screen.
Unlock Tim Mirra bikes:
Hit ⇩ x2, ⇨, ⇦, ⇩, ⇨, ⇩, ⇧, ■ at the main menu screen.
Unlock Tim Mirra levels:
Hit ⇧ x2, ⇨, ⇩, ⇨, ⇦, ⇩, ⇧, ■ at the main menu screen.
Unlock Tim Mirra moves:
Hit ⇦, ⇨ x2, ⇧, ⇩, ⇧, ⇩, ⇧, ■ at the main menu screen.
Unlock Tim Mirra's competition outfit:
Hit ⇧, ⇩, ⇨, ⇦ x2, ⇧, ⇩, ⇧, ■ at the main menu screen.
Unlock Tim Mirra's FMV sequences:
Hit ⇦ x2, ⇨, ⇧, ⇩, ⇦, ⇩, ⇧, ■ at the main menu screen.
Unlock Todd Lyons bikes:
Hit ⇩ x4, ⇦, ⇨, ⇦, ⇩, ■ at the main menu screen.
Unlock Todd Lyons' competition outfit:
Hit ⇧, ⇩ x2, ⇨, ⇧, ⇦ x2, ⇩, ■ at the main menu screen.
Unlock Todd Lyons FMV sequences:
Hit ⇦ x2, ⇩, ⇧ x2, ⇨, ⇦, ⇩, ■ at the main menu screen.
Unlock Todd Lyons levels:
Hit ⇧ x2, ⇩, ⇧, ⇨ x2, ⇦, ⇩, ■ at the main menu screen.
Unlock Todd Lyons moves:
Hit ⇦, ⇨, ⇩ x2, ⇦, ⇨, ⇦, ⇩, ■ at the main menu screen.
Unlock Troy McMurray bikes:
Hit ⇩ x2, ⇦, ⇩, ⇨, ⇦, ⇧, ⇦, ■ at the main menu screen.
Unlock Troy McMurray levels:
Hit ⇧ x2, ⇦, ⇧ x2, ⇨, ⇧, ⇦, ■ at the main menu screen.
Unlock Troy McMurray move:
Hit ⇦, ⇨, ⇦ x2, ⇧, ⇩, ⇧, ⇦, ■ at the main menu screen.
Unlock Troy McMurray's competition outfit:
Hit ⇧, ⇩, ⇦, ⇩, ⇨, ⇦, ⇧, ⇦, ■ at the main menu screen.
Unlock Troy McMurray's FMV sequences:
Hit ⇦ x3, ⇩, ⇧, ⇨, ⇧, ⇦, ■ at the main menu screen.
Unlock Zach Shaw bikes:
Hit ⇩ x2, ⇦, ⇩, ⇧, ⇨ x2, ⇩, ■ at the main menu screen.
Unlock Zach Shaw FMV sequences:
Hit ⇦ x3, ⇨, ⇦, ⇩, ⇨, ⇩, ■ at the main menu screen.
Unlock Zach Shaw levels:
Hit ⇧ x2, ⇦, ⇨, ⇩ x2, ⇨, ⇩, ■ at the main menu screen.
Unlock Zach Shaw moves:
Hit ⇦, ⇨, ⇦, ⇩, ⇦, ⇧, ⇨, ⇩, ■ at the main menu screen.
Unlock Zach Shaw's competition outfit:
Hit ⇧, ⇩, ⇦, ⇨, ⇩ x2, ⇨, ⇩, ■ at the main menu screen.

DAVID BECKHAM SOCCER

Unlock Edit Player option:
Select the Professional Player Certificate in Train With Beckham mode, and you must score at least five goals in "Free Play".
Unlock Manchester United Eleven team:
Select the Professional Player Certificate in Train With Beckham mode, now get a score of at least 20 points in "Target Free Kicks".
Unlock World All-Stars team:
Select the Professional Player Certificate in Train With Beckham mode, now get a score of at least 20 points in "Target Passing".
Unlock England Eleven team:
Select the Professional Player Certificate in Train With Beckham mode, now get a score of at least 20 points in "Target Crossing".
Unlock Classic match games:
Select the Professional Player Certificate in Train With Beckham mode, now get a score of at least 15 points in the "Target Shooting".
Unlock Bonus stadiums:
Select the Professional Player Certificate in Train With Beckham mode. Complete "Panel Bash" in under ten seconds.

DEAD OR ALIVE 2: HARDCORE

Extra options:
Hit START to pause in game , then hit ▲ + ✖.
Unlock Bayman:
Finish the game with all original characters.
Unlock Tengu:
Collect 10 stars in survival mode.
Longer credits:
Finish the game with all the characters under the very hard difficulty setting.
Unlock CG Gallery:
Win team mode with five characters.
Unlock Alternate stage time:
Hit ● when choosing the Aerial Garden or Iron Hell.
Change winning pose view:
Hit ▲ during your fighter's victory pose, you must use the D-pad to change the camera angle, hit ■ to zoom in, or ● to zoom out.

DEVIL MAY CRY

Unlock Easy difficulty:
Intentionally use continues

DEVIL MAY CRY 2

Unlock Dante's Diesel bonus level and costume:
Play Dante's mission 1, then save the game. Restart the PlayStation2 and wait for the "Press START button" then press L3, R3, L1, R1, L2, R2, L3, R3. A sound will confirm correct cheat code entry. Press START to return to the main menu. Choose the "Load game" option, press L1 or R1 to access the new costume, then click on the load a game option to play the bonus level.

Unlock Lucia's Diesel bonus level and costume:
Play Lucia's mission 1, then save the game. Restart the PlayStation2 and wait for the "Press START button" then press L3, R3, L1, R1, L2, R2, L3, R3. A sound will confirm correct cheat code entry. Press START to return to the main menu. Choose the "Load game" option, press L1 or R1 to access the new

costume, then click on the load a game option to play the bonus level.

Unlock Dante's Diesel costume:
Press R1x2 ,▲, ■, R2x2 in game.

Unlock Lucia's Diesel costume:
Press L1x2 ,▲, ■, L2x2 in game.

In-game restart:
Press START + SELECT in game to return to the title screen.

Unlock Play as Trish:
You must complete the game with Dante under the hard difficulty setting. Trish has Dante's stats and items and starts with the Sparda.

Unlock Bloody Palace mode:
You must complete the game with Dante and Lucia to unlock Bloody Palace mode.

Unlock Dante Must Die mode:
You must complete the game with Dante and Lucia under the hard difficulty setting.

Unlock Lucia Must Die mode:
You must complete the game with Lucia under the hard difficulty setting.

Unlock Hard difficulty setting:
You must complete the game with Dante and Lucia.

Unlock Level select:
You must complete the game as either character under any difficulty setting.

while completing one of the first three levels and an option for the easy difficulty setting will appear when starting then next level.
Hidden Replay bonus:
Finish the game under the easy difficulty setting and you will be able to retain all your weapons from the previous game.
Unlock hard difficulty setting:
Finish the game to unlock the hard difficulty setting.
Unlock legendary dark knight mode:
Finish the game under the hard difficulty setting.
Unlock Dante must die mode:
Finish the game in legendary dark knight mode.
Unlock Super Dante mode:
Finish the game in Dante must die mode.
Unlock All-star group photo:
Finish the game with an S rank on all missions.
Skip FMV sequences:
Hit Select during an FMV sequence.

DEUS EX: THE CONSPIRACY

Unlock Cheat mode:
Enter the Goals screen and then hit L2, R2, L1, R1 and START x3 to display another tab on this screen with the following options:

God	Full Health
Full Energy	Full Ammo
Full Mods	All Skills
Full Credits	Tantalus

DINO STALKER

Hidden Completion bonuses:
Finish the game under the easy difficulty setting to unlock the special menu and movie mode.
You Can Shoot credits!
You can use your gun to shoot the ending credits as they roll.

DONALD DUCK

Getting special moves:
Quickly collect five cogs to get one letter from the word "SPECIAL" in any level, then collect all the letters to spell "SPECIAL".
Special moves:
To execute a special move, butt stomp three consecutive enemies then quickly hit R1 followed by one of the following codes.
Unlock Bonus screen:
Complete 100% of the game to see a screen featuring the characters in the game.

DRAGON BALL Z: BUDOKAI

Unlock Android #16:
You will unlock Android #16 when you you must complete the "Aim For Perfect Form" episode.
Unlock Cell, Android #17, and Teen Gohan:
Play through "The Androids Saga" at any level.
Unlock Dodoria:
Beat Recoome with Vegeta.
Unlock Freiza, Ginyu, and Recoome:
Play through "The Namek Saga" at any level.
Unlock Mr. Satan (Hercule):
Win a World Match Tournament at the "Adept" level.
Unlock Radditz, Vegeta, and Nappa:
Play through "The Saiyan Saga" at any level
Unlock Saiyaman (Gohan's alter ego):
Win a World Match Tournament at the "Advanced" level.
Unlock Super Saiyan ability (Goku only):
Play through "The Namek Saga" at any level.
Unlock Super Saiyan ability (Vegeta only):
Play through "The Androids Saga" at any level.
Unlock Super Saiyan and Super Saiyan 2 abilities (Teen Gohan only):
Play through "The Androids Saga" at any level.
Unlock Super Vegeta:
You will unlock Super Vegeta when you you must complete the "Vegeta's Confidence" episode.
Unlock Trunks:
You will unlock trunks when you you must complete the "Perfect Form Cell You must complete" episode.
Unlock Yamcha:
You will unlock Yamcha when you you must complete the "Aim For Perfect Form" episode.
Unlock Zarbon:
You will unlock Zarbon when you you must complete the "Vegeta's Attack" episode.
View alternate costumes:
Press R1 and R2 at the Capsule change screen to view the character's alternate costumes.

DRAKAN: THE ANCIENT GATES

Unlock Invincibility:
Hold L1 + R2 + L2 + R1 and hit ✖, ⇩, ▲, ⇧, ●, ⇨, ■, ⇦ during in game ..
Unlock Full health:
Hold L1 + R2 + L2 + R1 (in order) and hit ▲, ⇩, ●, ⇦, ■, ⇨, ✖, ⇧ during in game
Unlock Extra money:

Hold L1 + R2 + L2 + R1 (in order) and hit ●, ■, ⇨, ⇦, ✖, ▲, ⇩, ⇧ during in game

DRIVEN

Unlock All cars:
Hit ⇧, ⇩, ⇨ x2, ⇦, ⇧ x2, ⇩ at the main menu screen.
Unlock All tracks:
Hit ⇧ x2, ⇦, ⇩, ⇦, ⇨ x2, ⇧ at the main menu screen.
Unlock Story mode:
Hit ⇩, ⇦, ⇧, ⇨ x2, ⇧, ⇩, ⇦ at the main menu screen.
Unlock Arcade championships:
Hit ⇨, ⇦, ⇧, ⇨, ⇩ x2, ⇦ x2 at the main menu screen.
Unlock Multi-player championships:
Hit ⇦, ⇩, ⇦, ⇧, ⇨, ⇦, ⇩, ⇨ at the main menu screen.

DRIVING EMOTION TYPE S

Unlock Bonus cars:
Win the Autocross 1, 2 and 4 to unlock the Toyota Corolla Levin, Mazda MX-5 the Mazda and the Toyota Sprinter Truno GTVand the Toyota MR2.

DROPSHIP

Unlock Invincibility:
Select the "Classified Files" option at the main menu screen and enter TEAMBUDDIES as an unlock code.
Unlock Unlimited ammunition:
Select the "Classified Files" option at the main menu screen and enter BLASTRADIUS as an unlock code.
Unlock Level select:
Select the "Classified Files" option at the main menu screen and enter KINGSLEY as an unlock code.
Unlock Bonus level 1:
Select the "Classified Files" option at the main menu screen and enter KREUZLER as an unlock code.
Unlock Bonus level 2:
Select the "Classified Files" option at the main menu screen and enter SHEARER as an unlock code.
Unlock Bonus level 3:
Select the "Classified Files" option at the main menu screen and enter UBERDOOPER as an unlock code.
Unlock Mini-game:
Enable the "Bonus level 3"code, then hold Left Analog-stick ⇧ and quickly hit ■, ▲, ●, ▲, ■, ● during the intro sequence to the level.

DYNASTY WARRIORS 2

Unlock all generals:
Hit ■, R1, ■, R2, ■, R2, ■, and R1 at the main title screen.
Unlock All Shu generals:
Hit ■ x2, R1 x2, ■ x2, and R2 x2 at the main title screen.
Unlock All Wei generals:
Hit ■ x4, R2 x2, and R1 x2 at the main title screen to unlock.
Unlock All Wu generals:
Hit ■ x2, R2 x2, R1 x2, and ■ x2 at the main title screen.

DYNASTY WARRIORS 3

Unlock All generals:
Highlight the "Free Mode" icon at the main menu screen and then, hit R2 x3, L1, ▲, L2 x3, R1, ■.
Unlock All Shu generals:
Highlight the "Free Mode" icon at the main menu screen and then, hit L1, ■, ▲, R2, L1, L2, L2, R1, ■, and L1.
Unlock All Wei generals:
Highlight the "Free Mode" icon at the main menu screen and then, hit L2, L1, ■, ▲, L1, L2, R1, R2, L1, and L2.
Unlock All Wu generals:
Highlight the "Free Mode" icon at the main menu screen and then, hit ▲ x2, L1, ■, R1, R2, L1, L2 x3.
Unlock Free mode side selection:
Highlight the "Free Mode" icon at the main menu screen and then, hit R1, R2, L2, L1, ■, L1, L2, R2, R1, and ▲.
Unlock All FMV sequences:
Highlight the "Free Mode" icon at the main menu screen and then, hit ▲, L1, ▲, R1, ▲, ■, L2, ■, R2, ■.

ECCO THE DOLPHIN: DEFENDER OF THE FUTURE

Have Unlimited air:
Hold L1 + L2 + R1 + R2 and hit ■ x2, ▲, ✖, ● at the main title screen.
Unlock Unlimited health:
Hold L1 + L2 + R1 + R2 and hit ▲, ✖ x2, ⇧ x2, ⇩ at the main title screen.
Unlock Level select:
Hold L1 + L2 + R1 + R2 and hit ⇧ x2, ⇩ x2, ▲, ✖ x2 at the main title screen.
Dolphin Soccer Mini Game:

Go to the Powers of Levitation level and make your way to the room where the clan General is located. Swim through the side of the wall that looks like jelly and on the floor near one of the orange lights is a soccer ball, grab it. You must return to the main menu screen to play this mini game.
Unlock Bonus levels:
Finish the game under the hard difficulty setting. The Up & Down level will wobble and you can now access both 2D bonus levels from the old MegaDrive game.

ESCAPE FROM MONKEY ISLAND

Unlock Murrayball mini-game:
Go to the Palace Of Prostheses, using the filing system enter "Monkey-Pumpkin-Bunny" as the code to get the Ryan J. Danzwithwolves file. Look at the file, pause in game , then select the "Bonus stuff" option to access it.
View hidden sequence:
Finish the game and wait until all the credits complete to see a new FMV sequence.

ESPN INTERNATIONAL TRACK AND FIELD

Hidden Athlete interviews:
Win five bronze, five silver, five gold, or ten gold medals in trial or championship mode.
Unlock Bonus Rhythmic Gymnastics song:
Win a gold medal for all three rhythmic gymnastics songs in trial or championship mode.
Hidden Sound Effects:
Win the gold medal in all events in trial or championship mode.

ESPN INTERNATIONAL WINTER SPORTS 2002

Unlock Bear costume:
Win all gold medals in the men's events in championship mode. Hit L1 or R1 at the main character selection screen to access the costume.
Unlock Penguin costume:
Win all gold medals in the women's events in championship mode. Hit L1 or R1 at the main character selection screen to access the costume.
Unlock Robot costume:
Win all gold medals in the men's and women's events in trial mode. Hit L1 or R1 at the main character selection screen to access the costume.

ESPN WINTER X GAMES: SNOWBOARDING

Unlock Bonus levels:
Win a gold medal in all X Games competitions to unlock the Deep Freeze Mountain, Grind Or Die, Halfpipe Winter Style, and more Slopestyle Events.
Hidden Night levels:
Finish all events in X Games mode to unlock Big Air and Super Pipe at night.
Unlock Hard mode:
Unlock all 36 licenses in arcade mode under the normal difficulty setting, then hit Circle at the level selection screen.

ESPN X GAMES SKATEBOARDING

Unlock Level select:
Hit ⇧ x3, ⇩ x3, ⇧, ⇩ x3, L1, R1 at the main title screen.
Unlock Big head mode:
Hit ⇧ x3, ⇩ x3, ⇦, ⇨ x3, L1, R1 at the main title screen.
Unlock Extra characters:
Hold R1, R2, L1, or L2 at the main character selection screen.
Unlock new arcade mode:
Get all 36 licenses in arcade mode, and then hit Circle at the stage selection screen.

ETERNAL RING

Unlock The Master code:
Hit ●, ✖, ▲, ■ x2, ●, ▲ at the main title screen.

EVE OF EXTINCTION

Unlock Bonus modes:
Finish the game under any difficult setting to unlock the "Survival" and "3 Minute Attack" options.
Unlock Bonus weapon:
Finish the game under any difficulty setting, save your game and restart from this save point.

EVIL TWIN

Unlock Unlimited lives:
Enter ✖, ■, ▲, ✖, ● as the code.
Unlock Super shots cheat:
Enter ●, ▲, ▲, ■, and ✖ as the code.
Unlock Rapid-fire cheat:
Enter ■, ▲, ✖, ▲, ● as the code.
Unlock Sniper mode:
Enter ■, ●, ✖, ▲, ● as the code.

EXTERMINATION

Unlock Secret mode:
Finish the game having found all fifteen dog tags

and Roger's knife and save the game. Replay the game from this save point to begin with 300 bullets, 50 shotgun shells, 99 grenade shells, 1000-flame thrower capacity, 25 recovery unit type A, 5 type B, 5 MTS vaccines, 5 booster shot type A, 3 booster shot type B, 25 missiles and the AT-6 Grenade Launcher.

EXTREME-G 3

Unlock Unlimited shields:
Pause in game and hit L1+R1, L2 + R2, L1 + L2, R1 + R2.
Unlock Unlimited turbo:
Hit L1 + R1, L2 + R2, L1 + R1, L2 + R2 at the main menu screen.
Unlock Unlimited shields and turbos:
Hit L1 + R1, L2 + R2, L1 + L2, R1 + R2 at the main menu screen.
Unlock Unlimited ammunition:
Hit L2, R2, L1, R1, L2 + R2, L1 + R1 at the team selection screen or the screen with the League Race and XG Mall options.
Unlock All tracks:
Hit L1 x2, L2 x2, R2 x2, R1 x2, L1 + R1 + L2 + R2 at the main menu screen.
Always win XG career mode races:
Hit R2 + L2 + R1 + L1, R2 + L2, R1 + R2, R2 + R1 + L2 + L1 at the main menu screen.
Double Your prize money:
Hit L1, L2, R2, R1, R1, R2, L2, and L1 at the main menu screen.
Start with extra money:
Begin a new career, select a driver, then hit L1 x5, L2 x5, R1 x5, R2 x5, L1 + R1 + L2 + R2.
Unlock Extreme lap challenge:
Hit L1, L2, L1, R1, L1, R2, L1 + R1, L2 + R2 at the main menu screen.
Unlock StarCom team:
Hit L1, L2, R2, R1, R1, R2, L2, L1 at the main menu screen.
Quick start:
To get a jump-start when you begin a race, hold Forward during the countdown without hitting Accelerate until "Go" appears.

FANTAVISION

Unlock Cheat mode:
Hold L1 + L2 + R1 + R2 and hit ✖, ⇧, ✖, ⇧, ⇩, ■ at the options screen.
Unlock Extra option:
Finish and save the game under the normal difficulty setting.
Unlock Extra 2 option:
Finish and save the game under the hard difficulty setting.

FIFA 2002

Unlock Bonus tournaments:
Win the following World Cup qualifications to unlock the following corresponding bonus tournaments, show below:
AFC: Asians Nations Cup
CONCEBOL: Gold Cup
CONCACAF: Copa America
UEFA: European Championships (Euro 2004)
Special moves:
Hurdle: Tap L2.
Shimmy: Tap R2.
Drag-Back: Tap L2 x2.
Flick-Over: Tap R2 x2
Keep-ups: Stand still and hold L2 + R2 + Triangle.
Monster kick: Tap L2 then tap Square or Circle

FIFA 2003

Open Up The Seoul stadium:
Win the International Cup to unlock the Seoul stadium.
Open Up The Stade de France stadium:
Win the Club Championship to unlock the Stade de France stadium.

FINAL FANTASY X

Airship Coordinates
Use the following coordinates on the airship world map, then press ✖ when you've found the spot. These coordinates are approximates, so move the cursor around a little and press ✖ repeatedly to find a hidden areas.
Baaj Temple — X:14 Y:60 (find Lulu's Onion Knight and Anima)
Sanubia Desert: X:15 Y:41 (find Tidus's Ascalon)
Omega Ruins: X:74 Y:36 (battle Ultima Weapon, steal items, and find spheres)
Besaid Falls: X:31 Y:73 (find Kihmari's Dragoon Lance)
Mi-I'hen Ruins: X:34 Y:58 (find Rikku's Sonar)
Battle Site: X:42 Y:57 (find Lulu's Phantom Bangle)

Airship Passwords
You can also input passwords to uncover secret locations. These passwords are hidden throughout the game in Al Bhed, but if you can't read it, here they are (they all have to be entered in capitals).
GODHAND — Lets you go to lower Mushroom Rock Road where you will find Rikku's legendary weapon.
VICTORIOUS — Enter this to access a secret area in the ruins of Besaid. Climb the tree to get your hands on Rikku's powerful Victorious armor.
MURASAME — Another secret area in the ruins of Besaid. You will find Auron's Murasame here.

Hidden Aeons
Don't stop with Bahamut. There are three more aeons that you can find in Final Fantasy X that are not required to finish the game, but make beating tough fiends a whole lot easier.

Yojimbo
Save up at least 200,000 Gil before you go hunting for Yojimbo. To find him, head to the Calm Lands, go to the northeastern exit and pass underneath the bridge to go the area at the end of the gorge. Here, you will find a save point and the entrance to the Cavern of the Stolen Fayth. Walk deep into the cavern until you bump into the ghost of a dead summoner who will call upon the aeon Yojimbo. Defeat him using your aeons (in overdrive) and your most powerful magic attacks. Before you leave the cavern, use the warp pads to the left and right to get your hands on some helpful items, such as the Flexible Arm and X-Potions. When you're done, go to the Chamber of the Fayth. Talk to Yojimbo and you will find out that he doesn't work for free. Answer "To defeat the most powerful of enemies" to his question to get the lowest asking price, then offer Yojimbo half of what he's asking for plus 1 Gil. He will make a new offer and you should respond by raising your bid. Do this until he accepts your offer. Don't worry if Yojimbo turns you down, you can always repeat the procedure. If you are feeling rich, you can get some valuable Teleport Spheres from Yojimbo if you offer him triple his asking price. Useful for powering up your characters on the sphere grid.

Anima
First, make sure that you have solved all the destruction sphere puzzles in each of the previous five Halls of Trials. If you're unsure whether you left some of them unsolved, go back and do them now. Note that the monks won't let you into the temples unless you have spoken to Maester Mika on High Road. If you've solved all the puzzles, enter the coordinates for Baaj temple in the airship and make your way to the underwater temple entrance. Geosgaeno awaits. This can be a tough fight, so be sure to equip anti-stone/death armour if you have it or stock up on Soft items if you don't. Use elemental magic and OverDrives to win the battle, then enter the temple. You will find six statues that correspond to the six Cloisters of Trials in Spira. Five of them will now activate, but you still need the last one. To get it, go to Zanarkand Dome and look for the square white floor panels. Step on all seven of them (there are three in the first room and four in the large hall) to open up a Destruction Sphere in the first room. Grab it and put it into the hole in the large room right next to the monitor to make it blow up. You will get the Magistral Rod as a reward. It's time to go back to Baaj Temple. All six statues are now active and you can enter the Chamber of the Fayth to claim the incredibly powerful Anima.

Magus Sisters
First, get your hands on the above two aeons, then complete the Monster Arena side quest in the Calm Lands and capture all the fiends from Mt. Gagazet. You will receive the Blossom crown as a reward. Next, go to Remiem Temple, which is hidden in the mountains east of the Calm Lands. Here, you can challenge Belgemine and fight against any aeon that you have unlocked so far. Beat her Bahamut and you will get the Flower Sceptre. You must still defeat Yojimbo and Anima. Once you have beaten all the aeons, use your Blossom Crown and Flower Sceptre to open the locked door ahead and get the final aeon in FFX.

Ultimate Weapons
Each character in FFX can get his or her hands on an all-powerful weapon that makes defeating fiends easy. You also need to find two items that unlock each weapon's true powers and removes its "No AP" ability. Once you have found both items for a weapon, go to

Macalania Woods and use the Celestial Mirror to upgrade the weapon to its full power. To open treasure boxes containing legendary weapons, you will need the Celestial Mirror, so complete the mirror sidequest first:
Cloudy Mirror: Go to Remiem Temple in the mountains east of the Calm Lands using a Chocobo on the feather on the ground. Follow the path, which leads to Remiem Temple. Go to the left side of the temple, examine the sphere and then enter the chocobo race by talking to the chocobo to the right. Use as many shortcuts as you can to win the Cloudy Mirror.
Celestial Mirror: Now head back to Macalania Woods to get the Celestial Mirror. Look for the mother and son close to the save spot in the south of the woods. They will tell you that they're looking for daddy. You can find the man at the campsite you started at earlier in the game. Talk to him to reunite him with his family, then head south to find a path made from glowing fog and light. Go up to find the son standing in front of a large crystal. Talk to him, and then use the Cloudy Mirror on the crystal to change it into the Celestial Mirror.

Caladbolg
Character: Tidus
Required items: Sun Crest, Sun Sigil
Go to the Calm Lands and become a Chocobo trainer by talking to the female Chocobo rider (leave the area and come back in on foot if she's not there). You will have to complete four training exercises. Win the final race and you can access the northwestern end of the Calm Lands where you can get your hands on Tidus's legendary weapon, Cadalbolg. Caladbolg causes more damage when Tidus's HP is at maximum.
Sun Sigil: Getting the Sun Sigil is tough and may take some time. To get this item, you have to win the Catcher Chocobo challenge with a total time of 0,0,0 (concentrate on the balloons).
Sun Crest: Go back to the Zanarkand Ruins. You will find the Sun Crest in Zanarkand Dome where you originally fought Yunalesca.
Nirvana
Character: Yuna
Required items: Moon Crest, Moon Sigil
To get Nirvana, talk to the owner of Monster Arena in the eastern portion of the Calm Lands. He will ask you to catch his escaped fiends. Walk around the Calm Lands and capture at least one of each type (using the weapons the arena owner sells you) and once you have all nine, return to claim your prize. Once upgraded, Nirvana will do more damage when Yuna's MP are at maximum and it enables Valefor to cause higher damage than 9,999.
Moon Crest: Go to the Isle of Besaid. Swim east from the beach and look for a small alcove on the map. You will find the Moon Crest inside the treasure chest on that beach.
Moon Sigil: Once you have gotten all aeons (including the Magus Sisters), go back to Remiem Temple (in the mountains east of the Calm Lands) and challenge Belgemine. Defeat all of the aeons and send Belgemine to win the Moon Sigil necessary to upgrade Yuna's legendary weapon.

FREEKSTYLE

Unlock Master code:
Enter LOKSMITH as the code.
Unlock All characters:
Enter POPULATE as the code.
Unlock All costumes:
Enter YARDSALE as the code.
Unlock All tracks:
Enter TRAKMEET as the code.
Unlock All bikes:
Enter WHEELS as the code.
Unlock No bike:
Enter FLYSOLO as the code.
Unlock Bike always has flames from back:
Enter FIRESALE as the code.
Unlock Slow motion effect:
Enter WTCHKPRS as the code.
Unlock Low gravity:
Enter FTAIL as the code.
Unlock Freekout Time always active:
Enter ALLFREEK as the code.
Unlock Clifford Adoptante:
Enter COOLDUDE as the code.
Unlock Mike Jones:
Enter TOUGHGUY as the code.
Unlock Jessica Patterson:
Enter BLONDIE as the code.
Unlock Greg Albertyn:
Enter GIMEGREG as the code.
Unlock Rider wears a helmet:
Enter HELMET as the code.
Unlock Burn It Up track:
Enter CARVEROK as the code.

Unlock Gnome Sweet Gnome track:
Enter CLIPPERS as the code.
Unlock Let It Ride track:
Enter BLACKJAK as the code.
Unlock Rocket Garden track:
Enter TODAMOON as the code.
Unlock Crash Pad FreeStyle track:
Enter WIDEOPEN as the code.
Unlock Burbs FreeStyle track:
Enter TUCKELLE as the code.
Unlock Brian Deegan's Dominator bike:
Enter WHOZASKN as the code.
Unlock Brian Deegan's Heavy Metal bike:
Enter HEDBANGR as the code.
Unlock Brian Deegan's Mulisha Man bike:
Enter WHATEVER as the code.
Unlock Brian Deegan's Muscle Bound costume:
Enter RIPPED as the code.
Unlock Brian Deegan's Commander costume:
Enter SOLDIER as the code.
Unlock Clifford Adoptante's Gone Tiki bike:
Enter SUPDUDE as the code.
Unlock Clifford Adoptante's Hang Loose bike:
Enter STOKED as the code.
Unlock Clifford Adoptante's Island Spirit bike:
Enter GOFLOBRO as the code.
Unlock Clifford Adoptante's Tiki costume:
Enter WINGS as the code.
Unlock Clifford Adoptante's Tankin' It costume:
Enter NOSLEEVE as the code.
Unlock Greg Albertyn's Champion bike:
Enter NUMBER1 as the code.
Unlock Greg Albertyn's National Pride bike:
Enter PATRIOT as the code.
Unlock Greg Albertyn's The King bike:
Enter ALLSHOOK as the code.
Unlock Greg Albertyn's Sharp Dresser costume:
Enter ILOOKGUD as the code.
Unlock Greg Albertyn's Star Rider costume:
Enter COMET as the code.
Unlock Jessica Patterson's Charged Up bike:
Enter LIGHTNIN as the code.

FUR FIGHTERS: VIGGO'S REVENGE

Unlock Big head mode:
After defeating Rico's wife, go back to Rico's house to play a game of snake and get a score of 3,100.
Unlock Fish eye mode:
After defeating Bungalow's wife return to his house and play the bear game, you must score 20,100.
Rotate cam:
Put the slider puzzle together in under 60 seconds to unlock the rotate cam cheat.

GAUNTLET: DARK LEGACY

Unlock Invincibility:
Enter INVULN as a name.
Unlock Always invisibility:
Enter 000000 as a name.
Unlock Always x-ray vision:
Enter PEEKIN as a name.
Unlock Always full turbo:
Enter PURPLE as a name.
Unlock Always triple shot:
Enter MENAGE as a name.
Unlock Always have nine potions and keys:
Enter ALLFUL as a name.
Unlock Win 10,000 gold per level:
Enter 10000K as a name.
Unlock All FMV sequences:
Hold ✖ while the game loads. All FMV sequences in the game will begin to play after the copyright screen. Hit ✖ to advance to the next sequence.

(TOM CLANCY'S) GHOST RECON

God Mode For You
Pause the game and press L1, R2, L2, R1, SELECT.
Unlock All Missions
On the title screen and press ✖, L2, ▲, R2, SELECT.
Unlock All Special Features
Press L1, L2, R1, R2, ✖, SELECT at the title screen.

GIANTS: CITIZEN KABUTO

Unlock Cheat menu:
Enter ALPUN as the code.
Unlock Cheat shop:
Enter LILBUDY as the code, then hit SELECT + ⇧ during in game .
Unlock Invincibility:
Enter MOLITOR as the code.
Unlock Level select:
Enter MBP4UJP as the code.

Unlock Unlimited ammunition:
Enter FALLOUT as the code.
Unlock Unlimited jet pack fuel:
Enter 38HK as the code.
Unlock Unlimited Mana:
Enter BGDA as the code.

GRANDIA 2

Alternate game:
Finish the game once, then play again and new items will appear.
Book Of War:
To get the Book Of War, win the Walnut game six times.

GRAND THEFT AUTO 3

Unlock Tank:
Hit ● x6, R1, L2, L1, ▲, ●, ▲ during in game.
Unlock Flying car:
Hit ⇨, R2, ●, R1, L2, ⇩, L1, R1 during in game.
Unlock No wanted level:
Hit R2 x2, L1, R2, ⇧, ⇩, ⇧, ⇩, ⇧, ⇩ during in game.
Unlock Higher wanted level:
Hit R2 x2, L1, R2, ⇦, ⇨, ⇦, ⇨, ⇦ during in game.
Unlock All weapons:
Hit R2 x2, L1, R2, ⇦, ⇩, ⇨, ⇧, ⇦, ⇩, ⇨, ⇧ during in game.
Unlock Full health:
Hit R2 x2, L1, R1, ⇦, ⇩, ⇨, ⇧, ⇦, ⇩, ⇨, ⇧ during in game.
Unlock Full armor:
Hit R2 x2, L1, L2, ⇦, ⇩, ⇨, ⇧, ⇦, ⇩, ⇨, ⇧ during in game.
Unlock More money:
Hit R2 x2, L1, L1, ⇦, ⇩, ⇨, ⇧, ⇦, ⇩, ⇨, ⇧ during in game.
Unlock Destroy all cars:
Hit L2, R2, L1, R1, L2, R2, ▲, ■, ●, ▲, L2, and L1.
Unlock Better driving skills:
Hit R1, L1, R2, L1, ⇦, and R1 x2, ▲ during in game.
Unlock Increased gore:
Hit ■, L1, and ●, ⇩, L1, R1, ▲, ⇨, L1, and ✖ during in game.
Unlock Fog:
Hit L1, L2, R1, R2 x2, R1, L2, ✖ during in game.
Unlock Overcast skies:
Hit L1, L2, R1, R2 x2, R1, L2, ■ during in game.
Unlock Rain:
Hit L1, L2, R1, R2 x2, R1, L2, ● during in game.
Unlock Normal weather:
Hit L1, L2, R1, R2 x2, R1, L2, ▲ during in game.
Unlock Invisible cars:
Hit L1 x2, ■, R2, ▲, L1, ▲ during in game.
Unlock Faster in game:
Hit ▲, ⇧, ⇨, ⇩, ■, L1, and L2 during in game.
Unlock Slower in game :
Hit ▲, ⇧, ⇨, ⇩, ■, R1, and R2 during in game.
Speed up time:
Hit ● **x3,** ■ **x5, L1,** ▲, ●, ▲ during in game.
Unlock Different costume:
Hit ⇨, ⇩, ⇦, ⇧, **L1, L2,** ⇧, ⇦, ⇩, ⇨ during in game.
Unlock Pedestrians riot:
Hit ⇩, ⇧, ⇦, ⇧, ✖, R1, R2, L2, L1 during in game.
Unlock All pedestrians have weapons:
Hit R2, R1, ▲, ✖, L2, L1, ⇧, ⇩ during in game.
Unlock Pedestrians attack you:
Hit ⇩, ⇧, ⇦, ⇧, ✖, R1, R2, L1, L2 during in game.

THE GETAWAY

Skip intermission sequences:
Press R3 to skip some intermission sequences.
Free Roam mode:
You must complete all standard missions to unlock the "Free Roam" option.
Double health:
Press ⇧ x2 , ⇦ x2 , ⇨ x2 , ● x2, ⇩ during the FMV sequence that plays before the main menu appears.
Armored car weapon:
Press ⇧, ⇩, ⇦, ⇨, ■, ▲, ● during the FMV sequence that plays before the main menu appears.

GRAND THEFT AUTO: VICE CITY

Unlock Weapons (1):
Press R1, R2, L1, R2, ⇦, ⇩, ⇨, ⇧, ⇦, ⇩, ⇨, ⇧

during game play.
Unlock Weapons (2):
Press R1, R2, L1, R2, ⇦, ⇩, ⇨, ⇧, ⇦, ⇩ x2, ⇦ during game play.
Unlock Weapons (3):
Press R1, R2, L1, R2, ⇦, ⇩, ⇨, ⇧, ⇦, ⇩ x3 during game play..
Unlock Health:
Press R1, R2, L1, ●, ⇦, ⇩, ⇨, ⇧, ⇦, ⇩, ⇨, ⇧ during game play.
Unlock Armor:
Press R1, R2, L1, ✖, ⇦, ⇩, ⇨, ⇧, ⇦, ⇩, ⇨, ⇧ during game play.
Unlock Raise wanted level:
Press R1 x2, ●, R2, ⇦, ⇨, ⇦, ⇨, ⇦, ⇨ during game play.
Unlock Lower wanted level:
Press R1 x2, ●, R2, ⇧, ⇩, ⇧, ⇩, ⇧, ⇩ during game play.
Unlock Bloodring Banger (1):
Press ⇧, ⇨ x2, L1, ⇨, ⇧, ■, L2 during game play.
Unlock Bloodring Banger (2):
Press ⇩, R1, ●, L2 x2, ✖, R1, L1, ⇦ x2 during game play.
Unlock Caddy:
Press ●, L1, ⇧, R1, L2, ✖, R1, L1, ●, ✖ during game play.
Unlock Hotring Racer (1):
Press R1, ●, R2, ⇨, L1, L2, ✖ x2, ■, R1 during game play.
Unlock Hotring Racer (2):
Press R2, L1, ●, ⇨, L1, R1, ⇨, ⇧, ●, R2 during game play.
Unlock Love Fist Limousine:
Press R2, ⇧, L2, ⇦ x2, R1, L1, ●, ⇨ during game play.
Unlock Rhino tank:
Press ● x2, L1, ● x3, L1, L2, R1, ▲, ●, ▲ during game play.
Unlock Romero's Hearse:
Press ⇩, R2, ⇩, R1, L2, ⇦, R1, L1, ⇦, ⇨ during game play.
Unlock Sabre Turbo:
Press ⇨, L2, ⇩, L2 x2, ✖, R1, L1, ●, ⇦ during game play.
Unlock Trashmaster:
Press ●, R1, ●, R1, ⇦ x2, R1, L1, ●, ⇨ during game play.
Unlock Aggressive traffic:
Press R2, ●, R1, L2, ⇦, R1, L1, R2, L2 during game play.
Unlock Pink traffic:
Press ●, L1, ⇩, L2, ⇦, ✖, R1, L1, ⇨, ● or ✖ during game play.
Unlock Increase your vehicle's top speed:
Press ⇨, R1, ⇧, L2 x2, ⇦, R1, L1, R1 x2 during game play.
Unlock flying car:
Press ⇨, R2, ●, R1, L2, ⇩, L1, R1 during game play.
Unlock Flying boats:
Press R2, ●, ⇧, L1, ⇨, R1, ⇨, ⇧, ■, ▲ during game play..
Unlock Car floats on water:
Press ⇨, R2, ●, R1, L2, ■, R1, R2 during game play.
Unlock Change wheel size:
Press R1, ✖, ▲, ⇨, R2, ■, ⇧, ⇩, ■ during game play.
Unlock Destroy cars:
Press R2, L2, R1, L1, L2, R2, ■, ▲, ●, ▲, L2, L1 during game play.
Unlock Better driving skills:
Press ▲, R1 x2, ⇦, R1, L1, R2, L1 during game play.
Unlock Pedestrians riot:
Press ⇩, ⇦, ⇧, ⇦, ✖, R2, R1, L2, L1 during game play.
Unlock Pedestrians attack you:
Press ⇩, ⇧ x3, ✖, R2, R1, L2 x2 during game play.
Unlock Pedestrians have weapons:
Press R2, R1, ✖, ▲, ✖, ▲, ⇧, ⇩ during game play.
Unlock Candy Suxxx costume:
Press ●, R2, ⇩, R1, ⇦, ⇨, R1, L1, ✖, L2 during game play.
Unlock Hilary King costume:
Press R1, ●, R2, L1, ⇨, R1, L1, ✖, R2 during game play.
Unlock Ken Rosenberg costume:
Press ⇨, L1, ⇧, L2, L1, ⇨, R1, L1, ✖, R1 during game play.
Unlock Lance Vance costume:
Press ●, L2, ⇦, ✖, R1, L1, ✖, L1 during game play.
Unlock Love Fist musician 1 costume:
Press ⇩, L1, ⇩, L2, ⇦, ✖, R1, L1, ✖ x2 during game play.
Unlock Love Fist musician 2 costume:
Press R1, L2, R2, L1, ⇨, R2, ⇦, ✖, ■, L1 during game play.
Unlock Mercedes costume:
Press R2, L1, ⇧, L1, ⇨, R1, ⇨, ⇧, ●, ▲ during game play.
Unlock Phil Cassady costume:
Press ⇨, R1, ⇧, R2, L1, ⇨, R1, L1, ⇨, ● during game play.
Unlock Ricardo Diaz costume:
Press L1, L2, R1, R2, ⇩, L1, R2, L2 during game play.
Unlock Sonny Forelli costume:
Press ●, L1, ●, L2, ⇦, ✖, R1, L1, ✖ x2 during game play.
CHEAT: Unlock Instant Suicide:
Press ⇨, L2, ⇩, R1, ⇦ x2, R1, L1, L2, L1 during game play.
Unlock Slower game play:
Press ▲, ⇧, ⇨, ⇩, ■, R2, R1 during game play.
Unlock Faster game play:
Press ▲, ⇧, ⇨, ⇩, L2, L1, ■ during game play.

Unlock Faster game clock:
Press ● x2, L1, ■, L1, ■ x3, L1, ▲, ●, ▲ during game play..
Unlock Normal weather:
Press R2, ✖, L1 x2, L2 x3, ⇩ during game play.
Unlock Sunny weather:
Press R2, ✖, L1 x2, L2 x3, ▲ during game play.
Unlock Rainy weather:
Press R2, ✖, L1 x2, L2 x3, ● during game play.
Unlock Foggy weather:
Press R2, ✖, L1 x2, L2 x3, ✖ during game play.
Unlock Overcast skies:
Press R2, ✖, L1 x2, L2 x3, ■ during game play.
Unlock Bikini women with guns:
Press ⇨, L1, ●, L2, ⇦, ✖, R1, L1 x2, ✖ during game play.
Unlock Tommy groupies:
Press ●, ✖, L1 x2, R2, ✖ x2, ●, ▲ during game play.

GRAN TURISMO CONCEPT

Unlock Ace mode:
Highlight the "Hard" selection on the difficulty selection screen. Hold L1 + R1 until it changes to "Ace".
Unlock All licenses:
Finish the Toyota Pod Event.
Unlock Extra credits for Gran Turismo 3 A-spec:
Complete 50% of the races to unlock a saved game file with 1,000,000,000 credits for Gran Turismo 3 A-spec.
Unlock Bonus FMV sequences:
Complete 100% of the races to unlock two FMV sequences.

GRAVITY GAMES

Master code:
Enter LOTACRAP at the cheat code screen under the options menu.
Maximum stats for all riders:
Enter MAXSTATS at the cheat code screen under the options menu.
All bikes:
Enter PIKARIDE at the cheat code screen under the options menu.
Dennis McCoy's stats:
Enter DMCDMAN at the cheat code screen under the options menu.
Bobby Bones:
Enter BONEGUY at the cheat code screen under the options menu.
Bird Brains:
Enter FLYAWAY at the cheat code screen under the options menu.
Hotty Babe:
Enter BADGIRL at the cheat code screen under the options menu.
Angus Sigmund:
Enter SIGMAN at the cheat code screen under the options menu.
Ramp Granny:
Enter OLDLADY at the cheat code screen under the options menu.
Oil Refinery level:
Enter OILSPILL at the cheat code screen under the options menu.
Train Depot level:
Enter CHOOCHOO at the cheat code screen under the options menu.
Museum District level:
Enter ARTRIDER at the cheat code screen under the options menu.
Museum District Competition:
Enter ARTCOMP at the cheat code screen under the options menu.
Fuzzy's Yard level:
Enter FUZYDIRT at the cheat code screen under the options menu.
Mount Magma level:
Enter VOLCANO at the cheat code screen under the options menu.
Gravity Games Street level:
Enter PAVEMENT at the cheat code screen under the options menu.
Gravity Games Vert level:
Enter GGFLYER at the cheat code screen under the options menu.
Gravity Games Dirt level:
Enter MUDPUDLE at the cheat code screen under the options menu.
Andre Ellison's FMV sequence:
Enter ANDFMV at the cheat code screen under the options menu.
Dennis McCoy's FMV sequence:
Enter DMCFMV at the cheat code screen under the options menu.
Jamie Bestwick's FMV sequence:
Enter JAMFMV at the cheat code screen under the options menu.
Leigh Ramsdell's FMV sequence:
Enter LEIFMV at the cheat code screen under the options menu.
Mat Berringer's FMV sequence:
Enter MATFMV at the cheat code screen under the options menu.
Reuel Erikson's FMV sequence:
Enter REUFMV at the cheat code screen under the options menu.
Fuzzy Hall's FMV sequence:
Enter FUZFMV at the cheat code screen under the options menu.

THE GETAWAY

Listen up geezer, if you want to be a face in this manor but don't want to end up in the slammer, you wanna be reading our bleedin' guide to the baddest gangster game this side of Vice City. You'd be a muppet not to!

MARK HAMMOND'S MISSIONS

01 – THE FRIGHTENER

EPISODE 1 – THE CHASE TO THE WAREHOUSE

After watching your wife die and your son being snatched, you jump in your car ready to give chase. The villain's car is the Red Rover 75 turning the corner at the end of the road. Get after it as quickly as possible making sure you don't lose sight of it for more than 45 seconds, or they will get away. Whilst making sure you stay on their tail is important, try not to crash more than a couple of times. Your car will take damage quickly, and if your axel breaks or you catch fire, you will almost certainly lose them. If you do lose sight of the target car, keep a careful eye on your indicators, as they will tell you which way to go. Once you reach the warehouse, jump out of the car and pull out your gun (Triangle).

EPISODE 2 – THE SHOOTOUT IN THE WAREHOUSE

Once at the warehouse, your objective is to get to Charlie's office. First though, you will need to take out all of the villains in between. Before walking through the brown gate, shoot anyone you can see using the auto target (R1). As soon as you do get through the gate, use free aim (R2) to target and shoot the barrels under the fire escape. This will take out the guy at the top and hopefully anyone coming through the doorway ahead. When the yard is clear, head inside through the green doorway. You may be able to collect the AK-47 the guy on the fire escape drops, but the wreckage might block it. Either way, make sure you pick up a second pistol and rest to regain some health before entering. Blast your way through the first room, checking the rooms on the right for

a shotgun or two, before making for the door in the far right corner. Shoot your way through this second room and again make your way to the door in the corner. Head up the stairs and sneak to the door at the top. Carefully aim for the red barrels around the corner and shoot them to take out the guys in this area. Follow the corridor through the offices, killing anything that moves, until you reach Charlie's office.

02 – BURNING BRIDGES

EPISODE 1 – THE DRIVE TO THE RESTAURANT

After receiving instructions from Charlie, head out of the yard in the Range Rover and follow the car's indicators to find the restaurant. It is quite a distance and you

will need to avoid a few police roadblocks. It is also worth following the rules of the road to avoid attracting passing police. When you reach the Republic Restaurant, your hazard lights will flash, telling you to stop and get out.

EPISODE 2 – SETTING THE RESTAURANT ALIGHT

Make your way into the restaurant and take out the gangsters on the ground floor. Work your way up to the top floor, clearing out each floor in between. On the first floor you can get a shotgun from the bloke behind the bar. Continue up the next flight of stairs and carefully take out the

remaining villains on the top floor. An easy way to get them all out of the room and out of their hiding places is to shoot one of the lamps and wait for the smoke to overpower them. Next you need to shoot the rest of the lamps to set the place ablaze. As soon as the alarm goes off, head back down the stairs.

EPISODE 3 – GETAWAY FROM THE RESTAURANT

Shoot the villain on the stairs and the cop at the bottom. If you hang around at the top of the stairs too long, the smoke from

the fire will affect your health. Once outside, shoot any cops in your way and jump in the Rover (or another car close by). You now need to get out of Soho and lose the police tail for at least five seconds. Before you think about abandoning your car, remember that you need to be in a motor to complete this episode.

03 – ART APPRECIATION

EPISODE 1 – THE DRIVE TO THE GALLERY

Follow the car's indicators and head to the Reptilian Art Gallery. On your way you will

encounter both cops and the Soho gang, who will not hesitate to lean out of the windows and blast you with AK's. Do your best to avoid them by weaving in and out of traffic and practicing some evasive driving. When you reach the gates of the art gallery, make sure you don't have a tail and head inside.

EPISODE 2 – STEALING THE DRUGS

Park up and make sure your gun is hidden before heading inside. Head towards the stairs to the left of the entrance and knock

out the guy at the bottom. If you are careful you can do this without alerting the guards. Cross to the other side of the gallery on the 1st floor, using walls and plinths as cover to take out any gangsters. Once you reach the stairs, head down and quickly take out the villains waiting for you. Kill all the bad guys guarding the back of the basement and then approach the crate with the Chinese characters to complete the mission.

EPISODE 3 – THE GETAWAY FROM THE GALLERY

Jump in the nearest car and high tail it out of the gallery grounds. There will be several Triad cars and blokes with guns trying to stop you so change cars on the main road if your tyres are shot. You need to get to Reggie's Pub near Trafalger Square. The

Triads will chase you hard so some aggressive driving will be needed. You will also certainly attract the attention of some cops, who also need to be avoided.

04 – AIDING AND ABETTING

EPISODE 1 – RAM THE VAN

Your work for Jolson is not yet done, he wants you to help break out a friend of his from a prison van. Jump in the Lexus parked outside the pub and wait for Eyebrows to get in before speeding off. Follow your indicators to reach the Old Bailey before the time runs out. Once you get close to the convey of cars, your car will slow down automatically and the hazard lights will flash. Once the ambush is over, you will regain control of the car a must chase the escaping prison van. Ram the van hard repeatedly until it bursts into smoke and eventually come to a stop. Hitting the van from the side seems to do more damage. Eventually the van will crash and Jake will escape.

EPISODE 2 – GETAWAY TO THE WAREHOUSE

Once Jake has blown up the prison van, he will jump into the back of your car and tell you to drive. You need to make sure both Jake and Eyebrows are with you at all times, so changing cars is not really an option. This means that quick but careful driving is needed to avoid the chasing police. Use the traffic and various lampposts etc to shake them off. You are heading for Charlie's Depot in Southwark so follow the indicators to take the quickest route.

05 – TAXI FOR MR CHAI?

EPISODE 1 – SNEAK INTO CHARLIE'S OFFICE

There are several ways to complete this mission, but we found the following way to be the best. The moment the first guy turns around, grab him from behind and break his neck. Go through the door, turn right and then left. Run forwards with the crate on your left and the wall on your right until you get to the end. Turn left and head towards the stairs. Take out the villain before the stairs by breaking his neck or pistol whipping him. Run behind the stairs and hide while the guy comes down them.
Wait for him to leave the room before heading up the stairs to the next floor. Use stealth by the doorway and watch the badguys walk down the hallway before moving into the room. Once the last guy has turned his back, run out and crouch behind the low wall. Shuffle to the left end of the wall to see a conversation between 2 guys.
One of them will come back down towards you to look at Johnny Chai. Wait where you are until

the 2 guys finish their conversation, and then run through the small room. Turn left and break the guy's neck from behind. Enter the next room and do the same for the second chap. Walk through into the adjoining room and out the other side. Run across the corridor into Charlie's office to finish the mission.

EPISODE 2 – DRIVE TO CHINATOWN

Once the Bethnal Green boys have tied poor Johnny into the passenger seat, drive the Honda Accord out of the yard. Follow you indicators, being careful not to attract any unwanted police attention, until you reach Chinatown. Try your best to avoid any rival gang cars, although you will almost certainly meet some of the Soho gang along the way. Johnny obviously cannot get out of the car, so you need to take good care of it and avoid any major crashes.

06 – OUT OF THE FRYING PAN

EPISODE 1 – LURING THE TRIADS

The Triads are understandably upset that you have just delivered one of their men dead and will immediately start to chase you in their powerful Honda's. You need to lure them to the Yardie drug factory in Holywell, getting there any way you can.

The indicators will guide you along the most direct route, but don' be afraid to use some side roads to shake off your pursuers. It is impossible to lose your tail so just keep driving as well as you can until you reach your destination.

EPISODE 2 – ESCAPE FROM THE DRUG FACTORY

Lead the Triads under the arch with the wrecked car, taking out the single guard. Don't hang around in the open for very long or you will have both the Yardies and the Triads taking shot at you. Find yourself a relatively safe hiding place (behind the burnt out car or the yellow skip are good places) and only take out villains who are coming directly towards you. The best thing to do is not to get involved as much as possible and allow the gangs to kill themselves. Once everything has died down, run into the rubbish room in the building and kill the final Yardie inside. Run out of the courtyard and into the street for mission success.

07 – FILTHY BUSINESS

EPISODE 1 – LOCATE THE BT VAN

To get inside the police station, you will need to disguise yourself as a BT engineer. To do this, you first need to find the BT van parked in Grosvenor Place. This is a timed mission, so don't hang around to admire the sights of London. Follow your indicators to find the most direct route as always and jump in the van once you have spotted it parked in a lay-by.

EPISODE 2 – DRIVE TO THE POLICE STATION

Next you need to locate the real BT technician and ram him off the road within the time limit. Follow the van's indictors to find the van on Oxford Street. As soon as you see the real BT van, it will drive off. You must stop it before it reaches the police station or the mission is failed. To do this, you need to ram the van repeatedly (from the side is best) until it starts to smoke and eventually stop. The engineer will get out and you can take him out if you wish. Now get back into your BT van and follow the indicators to the nearby cop shop. Park in the lay-by and stroll through the open doors.

EPISODE 3 – THE ASSASSINATION OF MCCORMACK

This might seem like a foolish thing to do, surely walking into a police station means instant pain, death or worse. Luckily, your simple disguise fools the stupid plod and they will happily let you walk around the ground floor. You do however, need to follow a few rules if you are to complete this mission. Follow the cop at the entrance and let him lead you to the phone room. As soon as he leaves, run out to the

main corridor and follow the signs to the first floor (through the Custody Area). Once upstairs, use the increasingly handy signs to make straight for the Evidence room. Pick up the pistol inside and put it in your pocket before turning around, get too close to the door with the gun drawn and you will be spotted by the camera. Walk back out the room and turn right, where you should see McCormack with another cop. Wait for them to move off and then follow at a safe distance. When they get into the Computer Room, wait for McCormack to leave before walking around the back of the computers and breaking the cop's neck. Follow McCormack out through the other door, through the offices and back downstairs to the interview rooms. Once there, kill McCormack (who takes quite a beating) and step into Interview Room 3 to finish the mission.

EPISODE 4 – GETAWAY TO THE DEPOT

You first problem now is fighting your way back out of a police station where every cop is armed and after your blood. A SWAT team has also arrived and uses gas grenades to block your escape routes. Your second problem is protecting Yasmin along the way. Follow the signs for the exit, making sure you stay in front of Yasmin to protect her. The front exit is now locked so you need to get out the back door. As soon as you step outside, the big gate will start to close. To stop it you need to shoot the

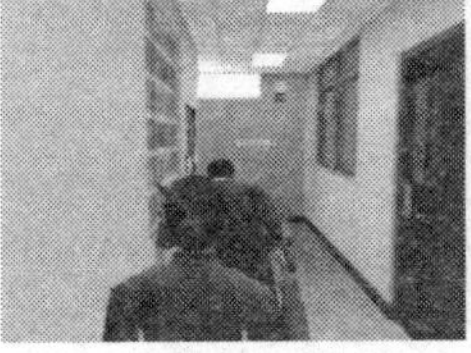

yellow power box on the gate. If you fail to do this, you will need to run back inside the station and exit via the front entrance, otherwise, take a car and follow the indicators to Charlie's depot, avoiding the police as best you can. Yasmin will follow you if you change cars but she may need a honk of the horn to get her moving.

08 – A TOUCH OF CLASS

EPISODE 1 – DRIVE TO THE LAP DANCING BAR

Once you have received your orders from Charlie, get a car and follow the indicators to the Lap Dancing bar. If you drive sensibly, you should avoid police attention, although you may attract some gang cars along the way. Yasmin will help you out by leaning out of the window and shooting at them. It is quite a long drive but there is no timer to worry about.

EPISODE 2 – SHOOTOUT AT THE LAP DANCING BAR

Your hazard lights will flash to tell you that you are outside the club. There will also be a guard outside who needs to be taken out before entering. Head downstairs into the bar and shoot all of the bad guys using the auto aim. As well as the main room, there are also several smaller rooms at the back which may hide gangsters. Make sure you clear them all before heading into the room with the shower. Upon entering, Layla, the dancer you were sent to collect, will be shot. Luckily, Yasmin has a plan.

09 – THE COWGIRL AND THE CASH

EPISODE 1 – DRIVE TO THE MANSION

With Yasmin dressed up in the cowgirl outfit, drive her to Charlie's mansion following the indicators. Drive as carefully as you can and avoid any gang cars and cops. When you reach the mansion, Yasmin will get out of the car and run inside.
You now need to speed off to the Yardie Crackhouse on Rivington Street, again avoiding the gang cars and cops as best you can.

EPISODE 2 – SHOOTOUT AT THE CRACKHOUSE

The Yardie Crackhouse looks like a fairly normal house so keep an eye on your hazard lights to tell you when to stop. You access the house through the hole in the wall. As soon as you are through the hole, get your gun/s out and be ready to blast the guards outside the back door. With the doorway cleared, head inside and make your way up the stairs, clearing each room as you come to it. If the deafening music is putting you off, you can shoot the decks to

turn it off. Whenever you clear a room, take a rest to regain your health before continuing. Shoot everyone in sight until you reach the room containing the drug money.

10 – CAT IN A BAG

EPISODE 1 – DRIVE TO CHARLIE'S DEPOT

After hiding the cash, a large group of Yardies arrive to teach you lesson. Take out any in your way and get into a car fast. The cops will also arrive around this time so that is another headache for you. Lose them if you can or just avoid them all and follow the indicators back to Charlie's Depot.

EPISODE 2 – SHOOTOUT AT CHARLIE'S DEPOT

Your first problem once the cut scene has finished, is the fact that there are three men in front of you who want you dead. Turn around and head towards the left corner of the room, where you can find a large stack of boxes to give you cover. Sparky (the bold one in the white top) takes quite a few hits to kill, so it is handy to be able to duck around a corner and catch your breath between bouts of firing. Keep at it and he will eventually bite the bullet. Now move towards the two raised shelving sections and kill the guard on top of them. You now need to work your way across the room until you can follow Jake up onto the balcony. In the centre of the room is an ammo dump guarded by four men with large guns. Take them out in one go by shooting the ammo from a safe distance. Use stealth and caution to reach the large stack of crates closest to the balcony and repeat the ammo shooting trick to clear it. Jake is up on the balcony with one other guard. Shoot the guard and Jake will flee, allowing you to follow. Once up on the balcony go through the door and downstairs into the main reception area. Find the back room where Jake is hiding and go inside.

11 – THE PRODIGAL SON

EPISODE 1 – SHOOTING OUT OF THE WAREHOUSE

Unfortunately, it seems you are not as tough as you thought and end up in a cell with Jasmin. Listen to the conversations and then just wait for Jasmin to work her magic and get a gun. Once she has killed the first guard, grab the gun he drops and try to get in front of Jasmin. She has a nasty habit of running into rooms all guns blazing, and if she dies the mission is failed. Grab a second pistol and then a more powerful shotgun or AK-47 as soon as you can. Make your way up the steps into the warehouse, taking out guards as you see them and doing your best to protect Jasmin. Be aware that if you shoot Jasmin by mistake too many times, she will turn on you and shoot you until you are dead. Get out of the warehouse as quickly as possible to find a getaway car.

EPISODE 2 – DRIVE TO CHARLIE'S MANSION

Nothing too taxing here, just follow the indicators through the London traffic until you reach Charlie's mansion. You will no doubt be chased by gang cars and cops so deal with them in the usual way i.e. driving aggressively through traffic, between lamp posts and any other obstacles. As usual your hazards will flash to let you know when you are outside the correct house. The entrance is through a small iron gate and down some steps.

EPISODE 3 - SHOOTOUT AT CHARLIE'S MANSION

Almost as soon as you enter the house you come across the thing that is going to make this mission tough, laser trip wires. The first set can be avoided by using the laser to the left of the couches and then roll and stealth onto the wall to the right where you can see a gap. Use stealth past the vertical lasers and then go back out onto the landing. Kill any guards that appear and head up to the next floor. Again, Yasmin will get trapped outside. Turn right and stealth pass the vertical lasers against the wall. Come off the wall and roll under the horizontal lasers over the snooker table. Roll back under the lasers on the opposite side of the snooker

stealth against the wall. They will switch off as soon as you are past (as do nearly all of them). Approach the next door and more lasers will appear, so turn to the left and enter the kitchen. Kill the gangster and continue into the next room. Continue through the cellars, killing guards as they appear until you reach more lasers on the

stairs. Shoot the guys at the top before using stealth to get past. Another couple of guards wait at the top, with a third on the balcony. Once inside the house, Yasmin will be trapped outside. Continue to the next lasers and roll under them (X while moving forwards). Wait for Jasmin to catch up and then head upstairs. Head into the room to the right and Yasmin will be trapped outside again. In the main room, roll under

table and go through the door. Turn left and roll and stealth onto the wall by the door. Stealth up to the door way and then roll under the lasers just inside the next room. Continue upstairs and head into the back room. Roll under the lasers on either side of the bed, shoot the guy who comes in and go through the bathroom. Roll under the horizontal laser in front of you and turn left 90 degrees and walk down the room. Roll under the laser again from the other side. Leave the room and go upstairs. Finally, walk into the room directly in from of you at the top of the stairs to finish this tough mission.

12 – ABOARD THE SOL VITA

EPISODE 1 – THE DRIVE TO THE CARGO SHIP

After that hellish mission, comes a nice relaxing drive...or not. This is probably the toughest drive yet with the cops and gangsters chasing you relentlessly. Unless you are a particularly skilled (or lucky) driver you will almost certainly have to change cars several times as you plough through the heavy city traffic. This brings

its own problems, as Jasmin will fight rather than just follow you to the nearest fast car. Help her take out any nearby enemies and then beep your horn to get her in the car. Follow the car's indicators as usual and head to the cargo ship, Sol Vita.

EPISODE 2 – SHOOTOUT AT THE CARGO SHIP

There are 2 ways to get onto the cargo ship; the first is via the gangplank and the second via the crane. Heading up the gangplank is risky, as Jasmin will often die because she wades into fights without you. Instead climb the crane and gain entry to the wheelhouse. Kill any guards and head down into the engine room while Yasmin guards the top. Once in the engine room, turn right through the door and blast any guards that appear. Head toward the front of the ship, but before you get to the last set of stairs, turn left into the room full of crates. A crate should fall right in front of you here and it is worth knowing that Harry is controlling the crane to try to crush you with the boxes. Head towards the balcony to your left, climb the steps and cross to the other side. Go down the steps and turn right, towards a second crate room. Take out the forklift by shooting the gas canister on the front and then shoot Harry on the balcony. Mark's story is now complete and you get to play as the cop, Frank Carter.

FRANK CARTER'S MISSIONS

13 – BARGAIN BASEMENT

EPISODE 1 – SHOOTOUT AT THE BROTHEL

When you get to Joe inside the brothel, turn left down the corridor. Joe will run up the stairs to the right and the stairs will collapse behind him. To find another route, head straight down the corridor, shooting the guy who ambushes you througfh a hole through the wall. Turn left and then immediately right. Walk under the collapsed ceiling and then up the stairs. Clear the area at the top of the stairs, then use stealth to get pass the collapsed floor. Follow the red light to the next set of stairs going up and then use stealth to get past the second collapsed floor. Here you will find an injured Joe who urges you on. Go up stairs and wait for SO19 back up. Follow the two SO19 members down the corridor and then watch 4 other SO19 members fall through the floor (you

shouldn't laugh). Use stealth to get past the newly collapsed section and follow the two SO19 members into the room at the end, where they will arrest Jake.

EPISODE 2 – RUSHING JOE TO THE HOSPITAL

Run to the nearest car and wait for poor Joe to hobble over to it and get in. Once Joe gets into a car with you, he will not get out again; so treat it with care if you want to complete the mission. Follow the indicators and take Joe to UCL Hospital within the time limit (i.e. before he dies). If the traffic is bad, turn on the police sirens, the traffic should give way.

14 – SHOW SOME REMORSE

EPISODE 1 – DRIVE TO THE RIVERSIDE DELIVERY DEPOT

Take the nearest car and head out of the gates and onto the streets. Your destination is the Riverside Delivery Depot of St. Saviour's dock. It is a fairly long drive and using your sirens will make navigating the busy streets much easier. Follow the car's indicators and get to the delivery depot within the ample time limit.

EPISODE 2 – SHOOTOUT AT THE RIVERSIDE DELIVERY DEPOT

Once out of your car, maker your way in amongst the shipping containers and take out any patrolling Yardies. There are massive cranes working in this area, so be sure to check where they are before moving through the piles of containers. The small gaps, which connect the lanes, are safe havens from the massive machinery. Work your way forwards and right until you pass the crane area and emerge out into an open area. Once in the open, SO19 will come to your aid and help you clear the area of smugglers. The suspects you are looking for are in the white van in the far corner of the yard. Approach the van to finish the mission.

15 – DISTURBANCE IN SOHO

EPISODE 1 – DRIVE TO THE RESTAURANT

This is a tough drive if you do not know the best route. Although you have the indicators to help you, there are a couple of places where the directions are a bit dodgy. If you see your indicators flashing very fast, stop and turn around as this means you are going in the wrong direction. You are heading for the Republic Restaurant, the same one you visited as Mark Hammond. There is a time limit, so try to keep your car intact to avoid wasting time grabbing another. When you reach the restaurant, all hell is breaking loose.

EPISODE 2 – MAKING ARRESTS AT THE RESTAURANT

The road the restaurant is on is a mess of police vehicles, ambulances and fire engines. There is also a good deal of smoke coming from the restaurant itself (wonder who started that?). Get out of your car and run past the fire engine and ambulances at the end of the road. Shoot any gang members in range and then jump in the first police car parked across the road. You can use this to drive down the street and run down many of the

gangsters. Then get out of the car and clear the rest with your guns. Some gang members will surrender and you can arrest them (if you are feeling kind).
Once the street is cleared of fighting, the fire crews can move in.

16 – PAINTING THE TOWN RED

EPISODE 1 – DRIVE TO CHINATOWN

It seems there is no rest for the wicked, because as soon as the cut scene ends you will need to race to Chinatown to stop another mass disturbance. There is only one clear entrance into Chinatown as the others have been sealed off to contain the violence.

Carefully follow the car's indicators to get there in the given time. Luckily it is fairly close the restaurant. On Gerrard Street (the main street to Chinatown), there is a large gang fight taking place. To clear the street, you need to shoot/ arrest/ run over all the gang members. Once this is done, continue to the end of the street to find the NCP car park where several gang members have holed up.

EPISODE 2 – SHOOTOUT AT THE NCP

Make your way down the slope carefully and take out the numerous gangsters at the bottom. You will get a bit of help from a single SO19 officer at this point and it is a good idea to let him do a fair share of the fighting. Use the numerous cars and pillars to make your way along the parking area safely. Towards the end, a pillar will collapse and you will need to take the stairs on the left. Make your way down to the next floor and clear the area as before.
As you continue to descend, several more SO19 officers will arrive to back you up and you may even find a useable car (many have no tyres) to run over some bad guys. Make your way down to basement level 3 (3B) and shoot everyone there to finish the mission.

17 – ESCORT DUTY

EPISODE 1 – PROTECTING THE PRISON VAN

You start this mission already in a car and moving behind the prison van. You are held back at a certain distance until you see a Range Rover ram the van and speed off. Following orders, you need to leave the convoy and chase the fleeing Rover. Some very, very good driving is needed to both keep up with the Range Rover and catch up enough to ram it three or four times. The traffic is fairly light but still heavy enough to cause you problems if you are not aware of it. The Range Rover will make sudden turns to shake you so have you finger on the handbrake, ready to slide around corners after it. The route it takes is the same each time you try, so failing a couple of times will really help you learn the places you can gain ground. If you have not

caught it when it reaches a certain road, it will speed away however hard you accelerate after it and the mission will end in failure. Ram it enough to stop it and the mission is a success.

EPISODE 2 – DRIVE BACK TO THE PRISON VAN

With the Range Rover stopped, you now need to get back to the prison van and the rest of the convoy. Along the way you will see the wreckage of many cars caused by Mark Hammond. Follow the car's indicators and get back to the van within the time limit. Unfortunately, however fast you drive you will not be fast enough to reach the van in time, and the silver car you saw crash in Hammond's mission turns out to be you.

18 – THE VIGILANTE

EPISODE 1 – DRIVE TO THE DRUG FACTORY

This is a fairly short and easy drive to the Yardie Drug Factory. There is a time limit but you shouldn't need to worry about it unless you are terrible driver. Follow the car's indicators as usual and get to the Yardie Drug Factory in time. Easy.

EPISODE 2 – RESCUING THE COPS

You arrive at the Drug Factory around the same time as the gang fight in Mark's mission, but you enter the building from an alternate entrance. Shoot the yardies guarding the back entrance and gain access to the factory. Go upstairs carefully and shoot everyone in the growing room. On the next floor is the lab, where you can shoot the gas canisters to help you clear the room. Make sure you get out of the doorway before they blow or you will go with them. Once the lab is clear, walk through to the back room to find a couple of cops tied up.

19 – STALKING McCORMACK

EPISODE 1 – TAILING MCCORMACK

After hearing what the tied up cop has to say, head back down stairs and shoot your way out of either exit. Take a car (preferably a fast one) and follow the indicators to the police station. Once there, your car will automatically slow down and you should see McCormack's car (An unmarked police Vectra) pull out from the car park.

Follow the car but don't get too close. Your hazards will flash to warn you when you are in danger of being spotted. However, don't stay so far behind that you lose sight of it for 45 consecutive seconds or you will fail the mission. McCormack's car will eventually come to a stop at Charlie's depot.

EPISODE 2 – SNEAKING INTO CHARLIE'S DEPOT

There are many ways to complete this mission. Here is one example. Follow McCormack through the reception and

watch as he stops to have a conversation with the guy just inside the main loading area. Wait for them to finish the conversation and then move into the room after them. Keep to the left hand side of the depot and only move when McCormack moves on to the next point. Keep checking to see where the other men in the room are. Before he reaches his third pause point, you need to get to the top left corner of the room (or the other guy will turn around and may see you). Now follow McCormack back down the other side of the room and up the stairs to the balcony.

EPISODE 3 – DRIVE TO THE HOSPITAL AND FINDING JOE

Listening into the conversation in the next room reveals that your partner Joe is a target for a hit. There is no time to lose; you must get to the hospital before the gangsters do. Grab the fastest car you can see on the street (or the powerful Lexus in the car park) and follow the indicators to the hospital. Once there, get out of the car and go through the front entrance on the street. Run straight up to the second floor and turn right into the wards. Follow the corridor along until you see a policeman outside a room. Joe is, luckily, safely inside.

20 – DO THE WORLD A FAVOUR

EPISODE 1 – SHOOTOUT AT THE HOSPITAL

Step out of Joe's room and you will immediately come under fire from thugs in the corridor. Take them all out and move down the corridor, clearing all of the side rooms as you go. Make your way down one floor and repeat the process of clearing all the areas. On this floor you will meet up with Big Walter, who is the leader of this pack of thugs. Walter will take more of a beating than the normal guys and will also run away to other areas. Chase him down and kill him. When the hospital is clear of all bad guys, you will hear a message telling you so.

EPISODE 2 – DRIVE TO MCCORMACK'S LOCKUP

Leave the hospital and jump in the nearest police car. Switch on your sirens and make your way to the lock up by following your indicators. You will certainly be attacked by the Bethnal Green gang along the way, and there will also be several cars waiting for you outside the lockup. Use your car to ram them and then jump out to finish them off. Grab a AK or shotgun and head inside the garage.

EPISODE 3 – SHOOTOUT AT THE LOCKUP

Head into the lock up and take out any gangsters in sight. You can use the cars and other debris to get some cover from

their return fire. Look out for the guy in the pit. Once the first area is clear, head through the doorway on the right and clear the second room of villains. In the far right corner of the room is the guy with the files you need to retrieve. Kill him and walk up to his body to finish the mission.

21 – THE JOLSON FILES

EPISODE 1 – DRIVE TO THE WAREHOUSE

The first episode of this mission is a nice easy drive back to the Charlie's Warehouse. Grab one of the gang cars outside the lock up and follow your indicators as usual. There is a time limit, but it is fairly generous and you shouldn't have any trouble beating it. If any gang cars get in your way, use your evasive driving skills to shake them off.

EPISODE 2 – SNEAKING INTO THE WAREHOUSE

You need to enter the warehouse via the entrance on the main road. Stealth by the entrance and watch the two guys in the yard. When they move off, grab the guy who standing next to the car and knock him out. Go inside the warehouse and knock out the second guy looking at the notice board. Go up the steps and stealth by the doorway looking into the main warehouse area. Wait there until one of the three guys wanders into the room you are in. Stay still in stealth mode by the doorway and he will miss you. Run into the warehouse and stealth onto the left hand side of the crate of beers. Two guys will start walking in the direction of the player and have a conversation. Again wait for them to move off before walking to the

door on your left. The moment the two guys on the right move off, grab the slowest one and knock him out. Run down the room and hide behind the moving crate, getting closer to the two guys near the basement. One guy will walk down into the basement, grab the other guy and arrest him. Make your way down into the basement, and stealth against the wall when you get to the bottom to observe a conversation between two guys.
Once one moves off to watch TV, run pass him and knock out the second guy. Then head through the opening into the next section for mission success.

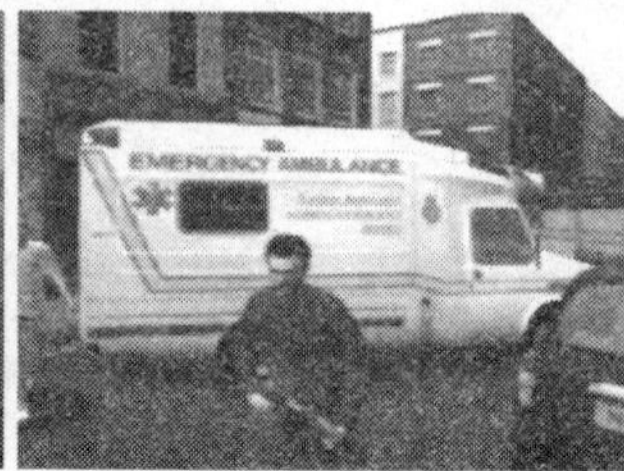

22 – MEET MARK HAMMOND

EPISODE 1 – SHOOTING OUT OF THE WAREHOUSE

You now need to get out of the basement safely. This is tough, as there is a huge number of bad guys waiting for you. Take it slowly and clear one area at a time, making sure you pick up a second pistol and a heavier weapon as soon as you can. Use the crates to regain health as and when you can, but be aware of gangsters

creeping up on you. When you can, take either exit to leave the warehouse. Leaving by the one you entered by allows you to grab a very cool and fast car.

EPISODE 2 – DRIVE TO CHARLIE'S DEPOT

In your cool car, drive out of the yard and follow your indicators back to Charlie's depot. Gang cars will almost certainly chase you, but you should be able to out-run and out-manoeuvre them by now.

EPISODE 3 – SNEAKING INTO CHARLIE'S DEPOT

Go into the depot via the main entrance (through the reception), once the two badguys have moved away. Follow the guy who goes upstairs into the meeting room and arrest him. Go into the main loading area and down the stairs. Once the faster guy has moved away, arrest or knock out the slower guy. Continue towards the centre of the warehouse, using the crates as cover. Make sure no one is watching before crossing open spaces. You need to get to the area where the large cache of ammo was piled in a previous mission to finish the mission.

23 – SHOWDOWN WITH JAKE

EPISODE 1 – DRIVE TO THE CARGO SHIP

Once the cut scene ends, shoot the remaining villains in the warehouse and run outside. Grab a Lexus or other fast car and head out of the gates. Follow your indicators to the docks and the cargo ship, the Sol Vita. You will need to enter via the main gate, rather than the alley down which Mark entered.

EPISODE 2 –SHOOTOUT AT THE CARGO SHIP

Head straight for the boat house, shooting anyone in the way. Once inside, head

upstairs. On each floor of the boathouse, there are several guards with heavy weapons. Fight your way through each floor, resting on each one, until you get to the top, then go out onto the balcony. Jake now tries to make his escape on the crane, but you can stop him here if you are quick enough. If not, run back downstairs after him and head to the front of the ship for a final shootout with Jake. Jake is a tough cookie, so don't be afraid to run away and regain health if you need to.

24 – LAND OF HOPE AND GLORY

EPISODE 1 – ESCAPE FROM THE CARGO SHIP

After the long and entertaining cut scene, you have just three minutes to get back onto the deck before the whole ship explodes.

Run down the stairs you start on and straight down the corridor, shooting any bad guys in your way. Go up the stairs at the far end of the corridor and head onto the balcony of the loading area. Run straight to the end and down the steps. Shoot any lurking villains as you make your way right, towards the open door. Shoot the barrels outside the door to clear the area outside and then head through. Turn left and run to the end of the corridor. Kill any bad guys around the steps to the engine room before climbing them and heading through the door. Clear ALL the enemies in this room BEFORE climbing the two sets of steps to safety.

And that's it. You have completed the game and unlocked the Free Roam mode.

GRAND THEFT AUTO 3

This guide is for the GTA fans amongst you who want to get that little bit more out of this fantastic game. Be warned, this is not a beginners guide, we will not be telling you how to drive the cars or how to do mission 10.

Extra Missions

There are a large number of extra missions to do either when you have finished the main story missions or while you still have some to do. Some of the rewards for these missions can be very useful.

Ambulance Missions

Steal an ambulance (you can always whack a few pedestrians if you can't find one) and press R3 to start the ambulance missions. You have to find a patient (they show up as pink dots on your radar) pick them up and deliver them to the hospital in a set time. If you drive to recklessly your patient may die on route so be careful. You will have to deliver 1 patient on level 1, 2 patients on level 2 and so on. The ambulance can only carry 3 patients so on the later levels you will have to make more than one trip.

Reward

If you save 50 patients you will receive Health at your hideout. If you save 100 patients you will receive Adrenalin pills at your hideout. Complete level 12 (to h but possible) and you will unlo infinite run.

Taxi Missions

Find/steal a Taxi or Cabbie (the Taxi is the safer option as it is less prone to tipping over) and press the R3 button to start the missions. Simply find a fare (they have a large blue arrow above their head and show up as a green dot on your radar) pull over and wait for them to get in. Once they have got in drive them to there destination which shows up as a pink dot on the radar, being careful not to crash to many times or your passenger will flee in terror. When you have arrived at their destination, a blue marker will tell you where to drop them off. Try and keep your vehicle in good condition or the fares will not get in.

Reward

The amount of money you receive is dependent on the length of the journey and the amount of time it took you to get there. Deliver 100 fares (don't worry it does not have to be consecutively) and you will have access to a new type of cab, the Borgnine, which can be found in the car park of Head Radio in Harwood.

Fire Truck Missions

Start off by stealing a fire truck (torch a few cars if you can't find one) and press R3 to begin the missions. You will have set amount of time to find the fire (red dots on radar) and put it out using the hose. The O button operates the hose. Don't get too close to the burning vehicles or you may find it hard to put the fires out. The fire truck is prone to tipping over so be careful.

Reward

For every fire you put out consecutively you earn double the money. When you have put out roughly 20 fires in each part of town, Shoreside Vale, Staunton Island and Portland the flame-thrower will appear at your hideout. This is the only non-cheating way to get the flamethrower apart from collecting hidden packages.

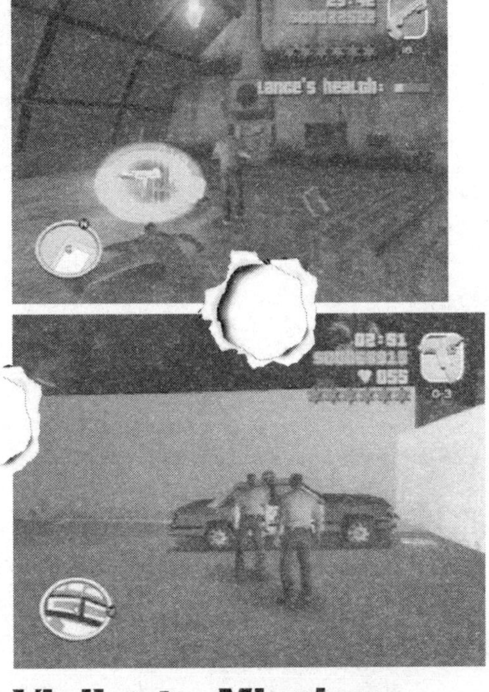

Fire truck locations

If you cannot find a fire truck you can always locate one at the fire stations that are dotted around.

PORTLAND: Head south out of the Porter tunnel, take the first left and you should see one.

STAUNTON ISLAND: On the eastern highway that runs along the shoreline with Shoreside opposite.

SHORESIDE VALE: Drive down the road that leads in to the rear of the airport. You will find the fire engine on the left opposite a car park.

Vigilante Missions

First of all steal any law enforcement vehicle (including the Rhino) and press R3 to start the missions. You will have a set time to hunt down the criminals (green dots on the radar) and eliminate them by destroying their vehicle, or alternatively making them abandon the vehicle and simply running the criminals over or shooting them. You will find this a lot easier if you use the Rhino although it can be tricky getting one without cheating.

Reward

When you have eliminated roughly 40 criminals in each part of town, you will receive 2 Police Bribes at your hideouts.

Vehicle Cranes

In various parts of the city there are cranes to be found that will take certain vehicles off your hands. Each crane has a list of vehicles that it will take. You will receive quite large amounts of money if you complete the lists.

Emergency Vehicle Crane

At a certain point in the game you will receive a pager message that the crane in Portland Harbour will now take Emergency Vehicles. The crane can be found near the ship next to some stacked containers. Park your vehicle in the marked area under the magnet, get out of the vehicle and the crane will do its job.

The required vehicles:

Fire-Truck:
Found: Parked in the fire stations or attending fires.

Enforcer:
Found: In the car park of Staunton Island Police Station.

Ambulance
Found: Parked in the hospitals or attending traffic accidents.

Police Car:
Found: Can be found anywhere in Liberty City.

Barracks OL:
Found: Northeast of the Stadium on Staunton Island. In Phil Cassidy's hideout behind some camouflaged buildings.

Rhino:
Found: After the "Exchange" mission it can be found in the same place as the Barrack OL above. Alternatively, use the Rhino cheat.

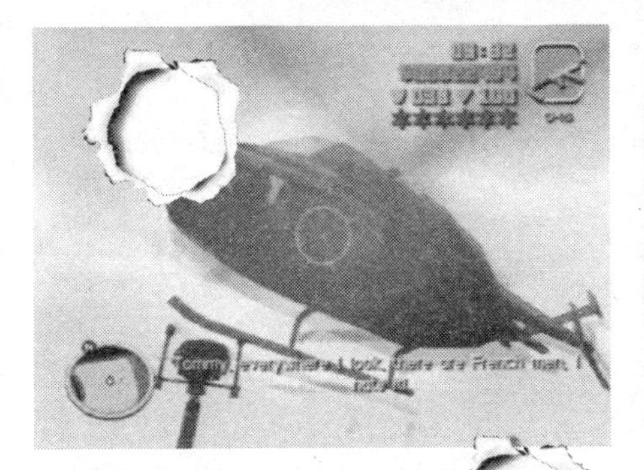

Reward

You will receive $1,500 for every vehicle, and when you have delivered every vehicle on the list you will receive $200,000, along with seven GTA3 pick-ups for each one of the vehicles collected. You can return to these pick-ups at any time to collect the vehicle of your choice.

Industrial Import/Export Garage

To find this garage enter Portland Harbour from the road and head left through the car park area. Drive through the narrow alley and head right upon exiting to find a blue garage with a list to the left.

The required vehicles:

Moonbeam:
Found: There is one in the car park of Head Radio in Portland.

Coach:
Found: On the streets of Portland.

Flatbed:
Found: Staunton Island.

Linerunner:
Found: Parked in the coach park, near the entrance to Portland harbour

Trashmaster:
Found: Start a Vigilante Mission and it will be used as a getaway vehicle.

Patriot:
Found: Everywhere.

Mr. Whoopee:
Found: Start a Vigilante Mission and it will be used as a getaway vehicle.

Blista:
Found: Staunton Island and Shoreside Vale.

Bobcat:
Found: Portland and Staunton Island.

Yankee:
Found: Portland and Staunton Island.

Pony:
Found: Can be found anywhere in Liberty City.

Rumpo:
Found: Staunton Island and Shoreside Vale.

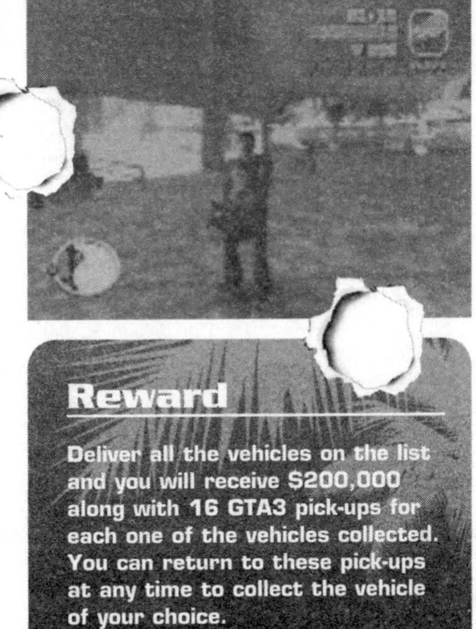

Reward

Deliver all the vehicles on the list and you will receive $200,000 along with 16 GTA3 pick-ups for each one of the vehicles collected. You can return to these pick-ups at any time to collect the vehicle of your choice.

Suburban Import/Export Garage

This garage can be found in Shoreside Vale, on the corner of the Cochrane Dam. The garage is part of the Fudge Packing Corp and the list is to the left of a rusty coloured garage door.

The required vehicles:

Sentinel:
Found: Shoreside Vale.

Cheetah:
Found: Staunton Island and Shoreside Vale.

Banshee:
Found: In the showrooms of Easy Credit Autos in Portland.

Stinger:
Found: Staunton Island and Shoreside Vale.

Infernus:
Found: Staunton Island and Shoreside Vale.

Esperanto:
Found: Can be found anywhere in Liberty City.

Taxi:
Found: Can be found anywhere in Liberty City.

Stretch:
Found: Staunton Island and Shoreside Vale.

Perennial:
Found: Can be found anywhere in Liberty City.

Landstalker:
Found: Staunton Island and Shoreside Vale.

Manana:
Found: Staunton Island and Shoreside Vale.

Idaho:
Found: Can be found anywhere in Liberty City.

Stallion:
Found: Can be found anywhere in Liberty City.

BF injection:
Found: Parked outside Misty's Flat in Hepburn Heights (Portland) near the El Burro phone in the park between 22:00 and 5:00 on the game clock.

Deliver all the required vehicles and you will receive $200,000 along with 16 GTA3 pick-ups for each one of the vehicles collected. You can return to these pick-ups at any time to collect the vehicle of your choice.

Securicar Garage

This garage is in Portland Harbour. When you enter the harbour area there are three parked cars one of these being a Kuruma. Behind the Kuruma there are a row of blue garages with numbers on. Drive a Securicar in to the one that is not numbered to receive $50,000. You will receive $5,000 less for every subsequent Securicar you deliver.

RC Toyz Missions

Throughout Liberty city there are blue vans with the "RC TOYZ" logo on them. When you enter the van you gain control of small remote control vehicles that are rigged with explosive. Use these to destroy real vehicles (O button to detonate the cars).

Mafia Massacre

Location: In an alley in St. Mark's, Portland, across the street from Toni Cipriani's Restaurant.
Objective: Try and destroy as many Mafia Sentinels as you can in 2 minutes. You receive $1,000 for every one you destroy.

Diablo Destruction

Location: In Portland, just around the corner from the Hepburn Heights El Train Station.
Objective: Try and destroy as many Diablo Stallions as you can in 2 minutes. You receive $1,000 for every one you destroy.

Casino Calamity

Location: In a car park in Torrington, Staunton Island, across the street and west of the casino.
Objective: Try and destroy as many Yakuza Stingers as you can in 2 minutes. You receive $1,000 for every one you destroy.

Rumpo Rumpage

Location: Behind your hideout in Wichita Gardens, Shoreside Vale. The van is in a corner behind two billboards. This van is a dark grey colour.
Objective: Try and destroy as many Hoods Rumpo XLs as you can in 2 minutes. You will receive $1,000 for every one you destroy.

4x4 Missions

Dotted around Liberty City there are four vehicles that allow you to test your driving skills against the clock. You are given a specific amount of time, which starts from when you pass through the first checkpoint. The checkpoints can be collected in any order you wish. You will receive $30,000 each time you complete one of these missions.

Patriot Playground

Location: Portland View, Portland, there is a Patriot in the car park of the "Supa Save!" Store in Portland View.
Objective: You have five minutes to collect the fifteen checkpoints. Every checkpoint adds twenty seconds to the clock.

Multi-Story Mayhem

Location: Staunton Island, park a Stallion just outside of the multi story car park in Newport, then exit and re-enter the vehicle.
Objective: You have two minutes to collect twenty checkpoints. Every level has four checkpoints. The final checkpoint can be found just beyond the ramp in the corner of the upper level. Remember to build up enough speed to collect it.

A Ride in the Park

Location: Belleville Park, Staunton Island, there is a Landstalker in the actual park area of Belleville Park, near the cottage.
Objective: You have two minutes to collect twelve checkpoints. Every checkpoint adds ten seconds to the clock.

Gripped!

Location: Shoreside Vale, head northeast from your hideout until you come to a dirt road. Follow the dirt road until you find the Patriot.
Objective: You have five minutes to collect twenty checkpoints. Every checkpoint adds fifteen seconds to the clock.

The Hooker Trick

First of all, this trick will not work if you are in a police car or a wreck of a car. All you have to do is pull up next to a hooker (they wear skimpy pink or brown clothes) and she should walk up to your window and talk to you for a brief moment before getting in the car. Drive to a secluded location and wait for the action to start. The car will start rocking, your health will go up and your money will go down. The best thing about this trick is you can get your health up to a maximum of 125. When the hooker finishes and gets out of the car you can simply shoot her to get your money back (nasty). Use a convertible and your health will go up as soon as you park up.

GTA III Cheats

Tank (Rhino):
Press ● x6, R1, L2, L1, ▲, ●, ▲ during the game. The tank will drop from the sky. This cheat can be repeated as many times as necessary.

Flying car (low gravity):
Press ⇨, R2, ●, R1, L2, ⇩, L1, R1 during the game. Accelerate and press ⇧ to fly.

No wanted level:
Press R2 x2, L1, R2, ⇧, ⇩, ⇧, ⇩, ⇧, ⇩ during the game. Saving the game will make the effects of this code permanent.

Higher wanted level:
Press R2 x2, L1, R2, ⇦, ⇨, ⇦, ⇨, ⇦ during the game. Saving the game will make the effects of this code permanent.

All weapons:
Press R2 x2, L1, R2, ⇦, ⇩, ⇨, ⇧, ⇦, ⇩, ⇨, ⇧ during the game. Repeat this code for more ammunition.

Full health:
Press R2 x2, L1, R1, ⇦, ⇩, ⇨, ⇧, ⇦, ⇩, ⇨, ⇧ during the game. Entering this cheat while in a vehicle will repair any damage to it.

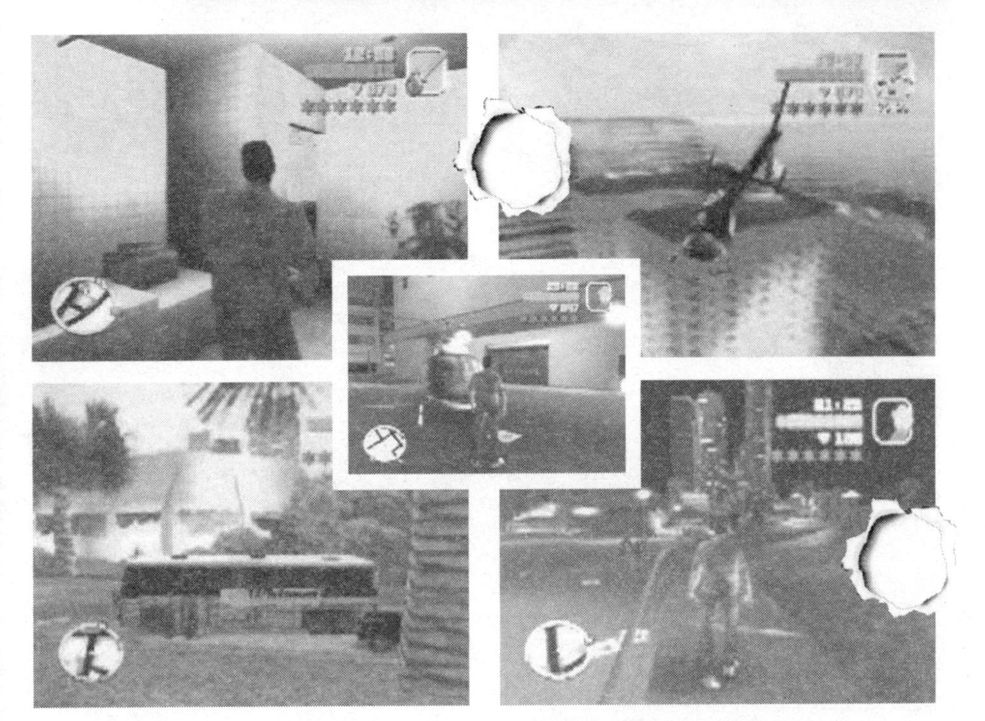

Full armor:
Press R2 x2, L1, L2, ⇦, ⇩, ⇨, ⇧, ⇦, ⇩, ⇨, ⇧ during the game.

More money:
Press R2 x2, L1, L1, ⇦, ⇩, ⇨, ⇧, ⇦, ⇩, ⇨, ⇧ during the game.

Destroy all cars:
Press L2, R2, L1, R1, L2, R2, ▲, ■, ●, ▲, L2, L1 during the game.

Better driving skills:
Press R1, L1, R2, L1, ⇦, R1 x2, ▲ during the game. Press L3 or R3 to jump while driving. Saving the game will make it so your car will never tip over.

Increased gore:
Press ■, L1, ●, ⇩, L1, R1, ▲, ⇨, L1, ✖ during the game.

Fog:
Press L1, L2, R1, R2 x2, R1, L2, ✖ during the game.

Overcast skies:
Press L1, L2, R1, R2 x2, R1, L2, ■ during the game.

Rain:
Press L1, L2, R1, R2 x2, R1, L2, ● during the game.

Normal weather:
Press L1, L2, R1, R2 x2, R1, L2, ▲ during the game.

Invisible cars:
Press L1 x2, ■, R2, ▲, L1, ▲ during the game. Only your vehicle's wheels will be visible.

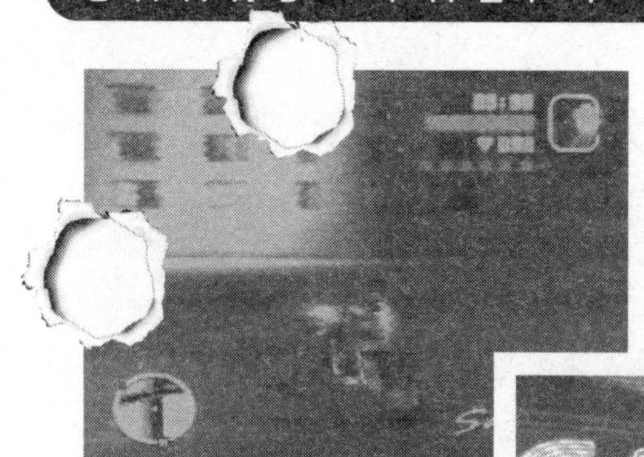

Different costume:
Press ⇨, ⇩, ⇦, ⇧, L1, L2, ⇧, ⇦, ⇩, ⇨ during the game. Repeat the code for different costumes.

Pedestrians riot:
Press ⇩, ⇧, ⇦, ⇧, ✖, R1, R2, L2, L1 during the game. Saving the game will make the effects of this code permanent.

Faster game play:
Press ▲, ⇧, ⇨, ⇩, ■, L1, L2 during the game. Repeat this code to increase its effect.

All pedestrians have weapons:
Press R2, R1, ▲, ✖, L2, L1, ⇧, ⇩ during the game. Some pedestrians will throw bombs or shoot at you if you steal their car. Saving the game will make the effects of this code permanent.

Slower game play:
Press ▲, ⇧, ⇨, ⇩, ■, R1, R2 during the game. This also continues the effect of an adrenaline pill.

Speed up time:
Press ● x3, ■ x5, L1, ▲, ●, ▲ during the game. Repeat this code to increase its effect.

Pedestrians attack you:
Press ⇩, ⇧, ⇦, ⇧, ✖, R1, R2, L1, L2 during the game. Saving the game will make the effects of this code permanent.

SECRETS

GTA: VICE CITY

Hours of exhaustive playing and trial and error have allowed us to bring you a guide packed with tips, tricks and cool secrets. Our Vice City guide will help you not only to be the Don of the city, but also help you to have the most fun possible.

SECRETS

Throughout Vice City there are many secrets and Easter eggs, some of which are more immediately obtainable than others. But we do recommend that you read the headers first if you haven't yet completed the game and don't want to spoil the story for yourselves as there are a few minor spoilers dotted about.

BLACK CARS

A rather pointless cheat this, unless you like black cars. All you have to do is enter the Black Cars Cheat to turn every car in the game black. When you place a car in one of your garages all of the other cars will revert to normal.

PINK CARS

Another rather pointless cheat, unless of course you like pink cars. Just enter the Pink Cars Cheat to turn every car in the game pink. When you place a car in one of your garages all the other cars will revert to normal.

100% COMPLETION!

Upon completing 100% of the game you will be rewarded with the following gifts.

INFINITE AMMO

3 Bodyguards (found in Vercetti's Mansion)
Frankie Costume (that say's 'I completed Vice City and all I got was this lousy T-Shirt')
Cars take double damage
200 Health
200 Armour

HEALING VEHICLES

To restore your vehicles back to a pristine state just enter the Health Cheat whilst inside a car. Your car will be as good as new.

HELICOPTERS WITH WHEELS

If you can manage to manoeuvre a helicopter in to a Pay N' Spray it will come out complete with wheels. Not that useful but fun none the less.

TURBO CHARGED MOTORCYCLES

When you are at top speed on a motorcycle, press up and Tommy will stand up causing a slight increase in speed.

INFINITE RUN

There are two ways to get infinite run. The hardest is to complete level 12 of the Paramedic Missions. The second and easier one is start running and get up to full speed and then tap the X button as quickly as possible. It probably won't last forever but is still useful.

FREE PAINT JOB

Before you enter a Pay N' Spray input the Health Cheat and your car will be re-sprayed for nothing. Nice.

TAXI SERVICE

When you have been killed or busted during a mission you may notice a taxi hanging around outside of the Hospital or Police Station. If you hop in you will be driven to the start of the mission you have just failed (for a $9 fee).

FAILED ARREST

When behind the wheel of a coach you can't be arrested even if the police manage to get inside. If the police do manage to get in the coach you will just lose control. To regain control, exit the coach and get back in.

LOSE YOUR WANTED LEVEL

If your wanted level is too high and you can't get to a Pay N' Spray don't panic. All you have to do is save your game and reload it. Your wanted level will have disappeared.

GETTING TO LITTLE HAVANA PART 1

Before the second Island is available there is a way to get there early. All you have to do is enter the Cars Float On Water Cheat and drive across the river to Little Havana.

GETTING TO LITTLE HAVANA PART 2

There is another way to get to the second island. Make your way onto the bridge between Prawn Island and Washington Beach where you'll notice boats passing under the bridge. Wait until a boat passes beneath you and carefully drop down onto it. The driver will panic and leap into the water leaving the boat free for you. All you have to do is drive over there.

GETTING TO LITTLE HAVANA PART 3

Steal a PCJ-600 and head for the bridge with the barrier barring access to Little Havana. Drive in to the barrier at full speed and you should fly over the barrier losing some health in the process. You are now free to explore the second island at you leisure.

Enter Leaf Link's Golf Course Fully Armed

Steal yourself a boat and just drive up onto the course or alternatively fly a helicopter onto the course.

HOVERING HELICOPTERS

Enter the Cars Hover Cheat and then get into a helicopter and head for the sea. You can now land your helicopter on the water without it sinking.

EXTRA ARMOUR

If you find yourself short on armour and can't find any, head for any Police Station

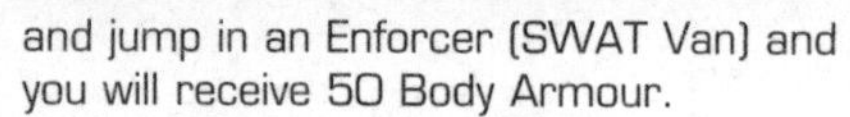

and jump in an Enforcer (SWAT Van) and you will receive 50 Body Armour.

EXTRA HEALTH

If you find yourself short on health and can't find any, head for any Hospital and jump in an Ambulance and you will receive 50 Health.

FREE SHOTGUN

To get yourself a free shotgun, jump into a Police car and you will receive a fully loaded shotgun.

FREE MONEY

Should you be really short of cash, just steal a taxi and jump in and you will receive some cash.

TAXI TIMER

If the Taxi missions are too difficult for you, drop a customer off when the timer hits exactly 0:00 and the timer will disappear leaving you as much time as you want to complete the missions.

SHOOT THE MOON

Shoot the moon using a sniper rifle and you will notice that it gets bigger and smaller in a similar style as it did in GTA III.

UNLIMITED WHEELIES

Steal a Sanchez (the best bike for this trick) and find a long stretch of road. When you are at a fairly high speed pull back on the left analog stick to perform a wheelie and let go of the X button remembering to hold back on the left analog stick. With a bit of practice you should be able to wheelie almost indefinitely. The same method can be used for stoppies.

INCREASE YOUR ACCURACY

You will need a gum with a large amount of ammo for this. First of all find yourself a tank or a burnt out car. Shoot the vehicle (in third-person view) constantly and over a long period of time your accuracy will increase.

NATURAL AQUARIUM

You will a sniper rifle for this one. Head for the beach and enter the water to about waist deep. Kneel down so you are fully submerged, don't worry you will not drown. Use the zoom to look under the water and you should be able to see a multitude of marine animals.

ARCADE FEVER

You may have noticed the Pogo the Monkey and Degenatron arcade machines in the Pizza Restaurants and Kaufman Cabs. Unfortunately you can't play these machines but maybe next time.

DIRTY MINDS

When walking or driving around Little Haiti you may notice a coloured lady wearing a jumper and yellow bandana. Use the sniper rifle to shoot her and then use the scope to look up her skirt and you will see she is going commando.

GTA III

In your apartment in the Ocean View Hotel there is a poster of the main character from GTA 3 on the wall.

BOOM SHINE
When you have completed all of Phil Cassidy's missions, head for your apartment in the Ocean View Hotel and you will discover a barrel of Boom Shine in there.

MIAMI VICE
When your wanted level reaches 3 stars you will have noticed the undercover police in the Cheetahs. Take a closer look at the passengers; one is black while the other is white. Crockett and Tubbs?

CHILDS PLAY
When you have completed the "Demolition Man" mission for Avery Carrington make your way back to the Vercetti Mansion and you will discover a box full of RC toys.

BROWN THUNDER
When you have unlocked the Hunter (awesome) if you press R3 you will start a vigilante mission called "Brown Thunder". If you were watching TV in the 80's you may remember a programme called Blue Thunder, which has obviously inspired this.

TROPHY
When you have completed any of the races at the Stadium or the Shooting Range in the Downtown Ammunation you receive a trophy. If you look in the lounge of the Vercetti Mansion you will see that each trophy appears on top of the TV. Cool.

CANDY SUXXX
When you complete the Film Studio missions for Steve Scott you will find a huge poster of Candy Suxxx and various photos of her in Tommy's office at the Vercetti Mansion

SCREW DIAZ
When you have acquired the Vercetti Mansion, look in the office and you will discover that the picture of Ricardo Diaz has been vandalised. Who could of done that?

PHONE NUMBERS
Some of the telephone numbers that the radio station give out actually work.

1-866-9-save-me	**Pastor Richards**
1-866-pillage	**Thor**
1-866-9-bury-me	**Funeral Home**

SOMEONE CALL A CLEANER
When you acquire the Vercetti Mansion, walk in to the mansion and take a look to

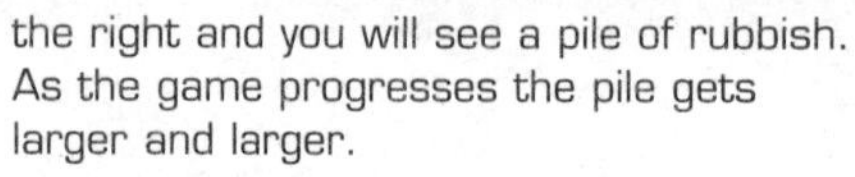

the right and you will see a pile of rubbish. As the game progresses the pile gets larger and larger.

HEADLESS BIKER

During one of the cut scenes with Mitch Baker keep looking on the ground and you will see a decapitated head.

GTA III CUT-OUT-SHOOT-OUT

During the "Shootist" mission when you are in the urban target zone, two of the cut-outs may appear familiar. That's because they are Misty and Luigi from GTA3

TAKE THE KIDS FOR A SPIN

Take a look a t the front of the Gang Burrito's that drive around on the second island. Most of them have a teddy bear strapped to the front. Aaah, they're big softies really.

GAINING ENTRANCE TO THE STADIUM.

The stadium is only open from 20:00 hrs until 23:59 hrs.

BYPASSING THE AIRPORT METAL DETECTORS

If you want to gain entrance to the Airport with all your weapons use this trick. Steal/find a car and park it so the bonnet is facing the metal detectors. All you have to do now is jump on the bonnet and using the extra height jump over the railings. Simple.

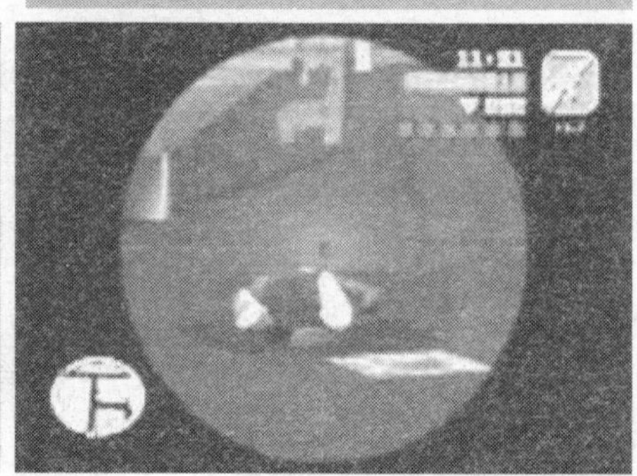

FAST LOAD

To gain the Fast Load ability you need to have completed the "Shootist" mission. Enter the shooting range in the Downtown Ammunation and get a score of 45 or over and you will be rewarded with this ability.

EASY MONEY

If you want some easy money look for the parking meters south of the Hyman Condo. Knock over the meters and you will receive between $200-$400 for each one.

SAVING ANY HELICOPTER AT HYMAN CONDO

If you want to save another helicopter (the Hunter?) at the Hyman Condo instead of the Maverick this is what you have to do. Ram the Maverick of the helipad and land the helicopter you wish to save directly on the H pad. Get out and save the game. The game will think that your helicopter is the Maverick. This may not work first time so keep trying.

EASTER EGG

You will need a helicopter to make your way to the top of the of the Vice City News building. Stand by the news helicopter and turn to the building on the right and you will see a hollow wall. Jump through the closest window to access this wall and you will discover a chocolate Easter Egg.

SCARFACE

Make your way to the apartment to the right side of the Pay N' Spray in Ocean Beach. Walk up the stairs and go through the open door. You will find yourself in an apartment reminiscent of the apartment scene from Scarface. If you enter the bathroom you will find blood-soaked shower curtain along with a chainsaw.

FAMILIAR FACES

Find the row of shops in Ocean Beach and look in the window of Rockstar Games. You will see cardboard cutouts of some familiar faces from GTA3.

HIDDEN SUBMARINE

Using the map that came with Vice City make your way to grid 5A (you will need a

boat or helicopter) and you will see a submarine.

SUNKEN SHIPS
Around the waters of Vice City there are three sunken ships. Here is a list of where to find them.
In between both islands in line with the boat yard.
Under the bridge near the Vice City News building.

BIKINI POOL
If you find yourself flying above Starfish Island have a look at the pool on the north side of the island, which looks like the body of a woman.

Y.M.C.A.
If you look in the Malibu Club on the podium you will see five men who look suspiciously like the Village People.

CEMENT BOOTS?
Get yourself a boat and drive from the Leaf Links Golf Course towards the second island until you come across a small group of rocks under the water. Stop the boat and look down in to the water. You will see a man who has obviously got on the wrong side of someone.

IT LOOK LIKE A GIANT...
Head for the Malibu Club and take a look at the lights that shine from the hotel across the street. If you get at the right angle the lights form the shape of a penis. It needs to be night for this to work.

WONDERFUL WHITE STUFF
When you have completed the game head on over to the Ocean View Hotel and enter your room. Near the mini-bar you will see a large bag of cocaine spilt on the floor

ROCKSTAR TOWELS
Take a stroll on the beach and look out for a beach towel. Look down and you will see the Rockstar logo in the corners.

RED LIGHT DISTRICT
When you acquire the Film Studio take a walk down the street set and you will discover it is a replica of the Red Light District from GTA 3

ROCK STARS
As night falls in Vice City take the chance to do a bit of stargazing. You will see the Rockstar logo in the form of a constellation.

UNHYGIENIC!
Take a look through the window of the butchers shop in Little Havana and you will see a severed arm on the counter.

UNTOUCHABLE CASH
When you have completed "The Job" mission head back to your room at the Ocean View Hotel. On the bed you will see a bag full of lovely cash. Unfortunately you can't collect it.

ROCKSTAR LOGO
Yes, another Rockstar logo, this time in the shape of a swimming pool. Fly over Starfish Island and take a look.

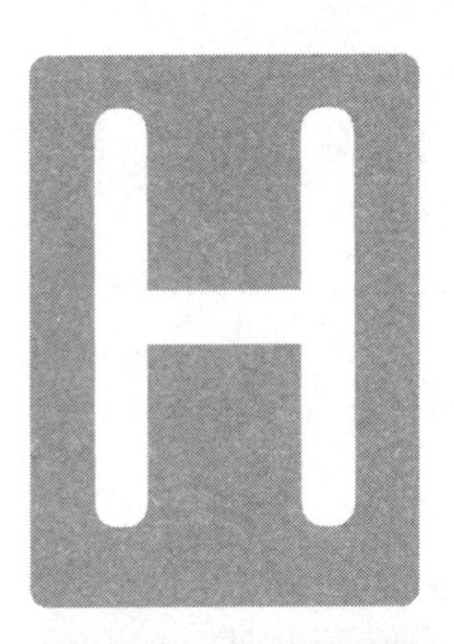

HALF-LIFE

Unlock Invincibility:
Hit ⇦, ■, ⇧, ▲, ⇨, and ●, ⇩, ✖ at the cheat selection screen.

Unlock Unlimited ammunition:
Hit ⇩, ✖, ⇦, ●, ⇩, ✖, ⇦, ● at the cheat selection screen.

Unlock Slow motion mode:
Hit ⇨; ■, ⇧, ▲, ⇨, ■, ⇧, ▲ at the cheat selection screen.

Unlock Invisibility:
Hit ⇦, ■, ⇨, ●, ⇦, ■, ⇨, ● at the cheat selection screen.

Unlock Alien mode:
Hit ⇧, ▲, ⇧, ▲, ⇧, ▲, ⇧, ▲ at the cheat selection screen.

Unlock Xen gravity:
Hit ⇧, ▲, ⇩, ✖, ⇧, ▲, ⇩, ✖ at the cheat selection screen.

Unlock Bonus levels:
Hit ▲, ■, ⇦, ⇨, ●, ✖, ⇧, ⇩ at the cheat selection screen. Choose the "Extras" at the options screen to load new levels found from other discs.

HAVEN: CALL OF THE KING

Refill Health
To refill your health during gameplay, press R2, L2, R1, ●, ▲, and L2, ✖, ■.

HEADHUNTER

Unlock Debug mode:
Hold R1 + ■ and hit START during in game .

Unlock Expert mode:
After completing the game for the first time, and when asked to save, hit "and when asked to save, hit "Yes" restart from this save point to unlock this new mode.

Door password:
To unlock the room on the

HARRY POTTER AND THE CHAMBER OF SECRETS

Famous Witches and Wizard
There are 101 famous witches and wizards cards to be collected in the game. Every 10 you find will raise your stamina bar. Make sure you check all the chests and other nooks and crannies throughout the game.

Bertie Bott's Beans
You can find these Jelly Beans everywhere in the game. Collect all the beans you can so you can trade them with Fred and George once you reach Hogwarts. Beans can be traded for mini games, items and spells.

Learning Spells
Of course, learning spells is the whole point of being a wizard. There are 8 level 2 spells to learn before your year at Hogwarts is complete.

Owls Treats
Throughout the game you will find and be able to buy Owl treats. These can be fed to Hedwig (your owl) and other owls to get them to do favours for you. This might be taking a message for you or opening a previously unreachable area.

Defeating the Gytrashes
Almost as soon as you step into the mist, several Gytrashes appear and lurch towards you. Quickly cast your Lumos spell and use the patch of light to hit the advancing spirits. If the bean of light touches a Gytrash, it will howl and back off. Continue to do this until the bar at the bottom of the screen is empty, and the Spirits have all been banished.

Fred and George's Shop
Approach an item in the shop and press A to find out the price in beans. Your total number of beans appears in the bottom left corner of the screen. There are loads of important things for sale here, so be sure to come back often.

Unlock the Nimbus 2000 Broomstick
On the second day of school, go to the Quidditch practice. You must complete the training with a "B" or better rank to get the Nimbus 2000 flying broomstick. You will now fly anywhere around the school during the day. Note: You will only land on grass and cannot fly inside the school.

Gain Easy Bertie Blotts Every Flavor Beans
When you exit of the Gryffindor Tower check out the object in the corner. Hit it with Flipendo to make three Beans appear. Go around the corner and walk at least three steps away. Return and cast Flipendo again to get three more Beans. Repeat this to get as many Beans as needed.

COMPLETE THE EXPELLIARMUS CHALLENGE

Room 1
No sooner has the lesson started, when Lockhart tells Harry he is going to have to do the Expelliarmus Challenge to find the Expelliarmus Spell. Upon reaching the large room with the shiny floor, fire Flipendo at the two green hand symbols to release three spiked balls from each side. You need to destroy all of the balls to progress. To do this, approach the balls until one or more chases you, then dodge and fire Flipendo at them as they return. Repeat this two or three time for each ball to destroy it for good. You can then use the blocks that the balls appeared from to climb up onto the ledges. Climb the ledge left of the entrance (if facing into the room) and use Lumos

in the alcove. Push the hidden door and continue through the second door. Inside this room is a Wiggenweld Potion Cauldron. Fill up if you need to and then head back out and climb the ledge on the other side of the room. Use the Severing spell to remove the tapestry and open the door behind it.

Room 2
Use the slope to get as high as possible a look at the nearest spiked ball. Use the Severing spell to cut the rope holding the ball and the wall blocking your path will drop...revealing a nasty Imp. Flipendo the imp and throw it over the edge. You now need to repeat this process all the way around the room until you reach the door. As you progress, more and more imps will appear and the ones you have thrown over the edge will follow you around the path. In the last alcove before the door, you can find a Cauldron Cake to help you recover some stamina.

Room 3
In the next room is yet more trouble. The path you need to follow is blocked by two huge spinning balls. To slow them down enough to dodge past them you are going to have to Sever the ropes holding the two blocks on either side of the padlocked door.

However, doing this releases more Imps for you to deal with. Your best bet is to just cut both ropes, stun both imps and run past the balls as soon as you can. You can rest between the first and second ball but be sure it is not going to hit you.

Room 4
The next area contains a Pumpkin Pasty in the chest and a couple of nasty Fire Crabs. Run to the very end of the path, hitting the fire crabs with Flipendo to stun them and then climb up onto the lowest wall. The Fire Crab statue will spit flame at you just as happily as the real thing so stay away from it. The statues are on pivots and can be flipped up, making them harmless for a few vital seconds and allowing you to run past. Timing is also essential as the flames keep burning even though they are pointed up in the air. The two chests along the way both contain tasty Pumpkin Pasties so be sure to collect them.

Room 5
This room contains yet another massive spiked ball, along with a couple of Cauldron Cakes in the chests. Thankfully, cutting the rope on the ball simply opens up the room containing the Expelliarmus Spell book. Walk carefully across the narrow path to grab it. Unfortunately, this triggers a battle with a huge winged statue (we thought that last room was a bit easy). This gives you a chance to try out your new spell, by blocking and rebounding the statues' spells. This can be a bit like tennis as the statue can also rebound spells. Four good hits should see the end of this creature and you can climb out of the room and return to class.

second floor of the bikers' hideout, enter "1993" as a password.

Killing silently:
Sneak up behind someone and hit R1 + ✖ to will break your foe's neck.

HERDY GERDY

Unlock Cheat mode:
Hit L2, L1, L2, L1, Up, R1, R2, R1, and R2, Down, Select at the main title screen.

HIDDEN INVASION

Unlock Easy mode:
Quickly hit ⇧, ⇩ x 2, ⇧, ⇦ x 2, ⇧, ⇨ x 2, ⇧ x 3 at the main title screen.

Unlock Big head mode:
Quickly hit ⇦ x 2, ⇧ x 2, ⇨ x 2, ⇩ x2 at the main title screen.

Unlock Oogie Boogie mode:
Quickly rotate the Left Analog-stick counter-clockwise four times at the main title screen.

HITMAN 2: SILENT ASSASSIN

Unlock Level select:
Press R2, L2, ⇧, ⇩, ■, ▲, ● at the main menu.

Unlock Level skip:
Press R2, L2, ⇧, ⇩, ✖, L3, ●, ✖, ●, ✖ during game play.

Unlock God mode:
Press R2, L2, ⇧, ⇩, ✖, R2, L2, R1, L1 during game play.

Unlock All weapons:
Press R2, L2, ⇧, ⇩, ✖, ⇧, ■, ✖ during game play.

Unlock Full heal:
Press R2, L2, ⇧, ⇩, ✖, ⇧, ⇩ during game play.

Unlock Lethal charge:
Press R2, L2, ⇧, ⇩, ✖, R1, R1 during game play.

Unlock Slow motion:
Press R2, L2, ⇧, ⇩, ✖, ⇧, L2 during game play.

Unlock Nailgun mode:
Press R2, L2, ⇧, ⇩, ✖, L1x2 during game play. Weapons will pin people to walls when this code is activated.

I

ICO

Finding Yorda:
When in the last level, go towards the left following the shore of the beach to find Yorda.

Avoid losing Yorda:
As soon as you release Yorda, hit R1 and hold her hand.

ISS PRO EVOLUTION SOCCER

Unlock Brazil Classic team:
Win the American Cup as Brazil.

Unlock Argentina Classic team:
Win the American Cup as Argentina.

Unlock World All-Star team:
Win the International Cup as any team.

Unlock European All-Star team:
Win the International Cup as France.

Unlock European Classic team:
Win the European Cup as England.

Unlock Holland Classic team:
Win the European Cup as Holland.

Unlock Germany Classic team:
Win the European Cup as Germany.

JAMES BOND 007: AGENT UNDER FIRE

Unlock Golden gun:
Finish the Trouble In Paradise level with a "Gold" rank.

Unlock Golden gun in multi-player mode:
Finish the Precious Cargo level with a "Platinum" rank and all 007 icons.

JAMES BOND 007: NIGHTFIRE

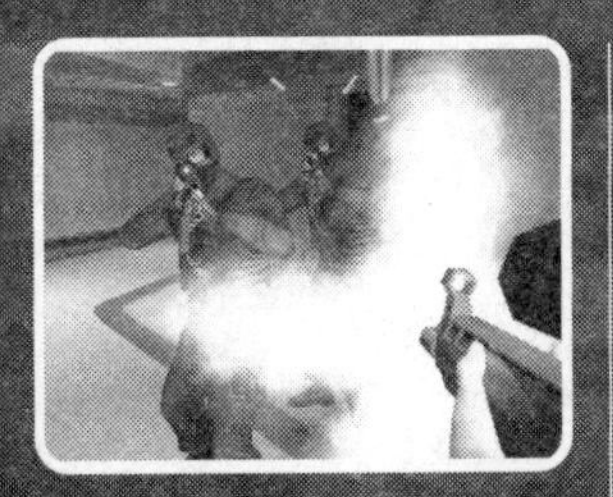

Drive a Shelby Cobra:
Begin the Enemies

Vanquished level and then pause the game, hold L1 and press d x2, a x2, w, and now release L1.

Unlock Level select:
Enter PASSPORT as a profile name.

Unlock Uplink mode:
Enter TRANSMIT as a profile name.

Unlock Demolition mode:
Enter TNT as a profile name.

Unlock Protect mode:
Enter GUARDIAN as a profile name.

Unlock Multi-player mode explosive scenery:
Enter BOOM as a profile name.

Unlock Multi-player mode assassination option:
Enter SCOPE as a profile name.

Unlock Multi-player mode Team King Of The Hill option:
Enter TEAMWORK as a profile name.

Unlock Multi-player mode GoldenEye Strike:
Enter ORBIT as a profile name.

Unlock Golden CH-6:
Finish the Precious Cargo level with a "Gold" rank.

Unlock Golden accuracy power-up:
Finish the Bad Diplomacy level with a "Gold" rank.

Unlock Golden clip power-up:
Finish the Cold Reception level with a "Gold" rank.

Unlock Golden grenade power-up:
Finish the Night Of The Jackal level with a "Gold" rank.

Unlock Golden bullet power-up:
Finish the Poseidon level with a "Gold" rank.

Unlock Golden armor power-up:
Finish the Forbidden Depths level with a "Gold" rank.

Unlock Unlimited Golden gun ammunition:
Finish the Evil Summit level with a "Gold" rank.

Unlock Unlimited car missiles:
Finish the Dangerous Pursuit level with a "Gold" rank.

Unlock Rocket Manor multi-player level:
Finish the Trouble In Paradise level with a "Platinum" rank and all 007 icons.

Unlock Stealth Bond skin in multi-player mode:
Finish the Dangerous Pursuit level with a "Platinum" rank and all 007 icons.

Unlock Guard skin in multi-player mode:
Finish the Cold Reception level with a "Platinum" rank and all 007 icons.

Unlock Alpine guard skin in multi-player mode:
Finish the Streets Of Bucharest level with a "Platinum" rank and all 007 icons.

Unlock Cyclops Oil guard skin in multi-player mode:
Finish the Poseidon level with a "Platinum" rank and all 007 icons.

Unlock Poseidon guard skin in multi-player mode:
Finish the Mediterranean Crisis level with a "Platinum" rank and all 007 icons.

Unlock Carrier guard multi-player skin:
Finish the Evil Summit level with a "Platinum" rank and all 007 icons.

Unlock Rapid fire power-up:
Finish the Fire And Water level with a "Gold" rank.

Unlock Regenerative

armour power-up:
Finish the Mediterranean Crisis level with a "Gold" rank.

Unlock Calypso gun in multi-player mode:
Finish the Fire And Water level with a "Platinum" rank and all 007 icons.

Unlock Full arsenal in multi-player mode:
Finish the Forbidden Depths level with a "Platinum" rank and all 007 icons.

Unlock Gravity boots in multi-player mode:
Finish the Bad Diplomacy level with a "Platinum" rank and all 007 icons.

Unlock Viper gun in multi-player mode:
Finish the Night Of The Jackal level with a "Platinum" rank and all 007 icons.

Unlock Lotus Esprit car:
Finish the Streets Of Bucharest level with a "Gold" rank.

JAX AND DAXTER: THE PRECURSOR LEGACY

Alternate ending:
Finish the game after collecting 101 Power Cells.

Faster credits:
When the names of the Naughty Dog staff have disappeared off the screen, hold ✖ or ●.

Faster Zoomer:
Hold L1 + R1 to go faster on the Zoomer.

Shoot Your cannon farther:
To make the cannons shoot farther, hold ■ or ● + ✖.

Perform Super jump:
Hit L1 + ✖.

Avoiding fall damage:
Hit Circle to spin kick just before you hit the ground when falling.

JERRY McGRATH SUPER CROSS WORLD

Unlock Moon gravity:
Hit ⇧ x 4, R1, ■, ● at the main menu screen.

Unlock Unlimited turbo:
Hit R2, L1, ■, ● x3 at the main menu screen.

Unlock All bikes:
Finish the hardcore part of career mode.

Do An Endo:
Hold L2 + ■ at a good speed and you will ride on your front wheel.

JOJO'S BIZARRE ADVENTURE 2

Completion bonus:
Successfully complete the game in super story mode to unlock another story mode and the picture gallery.

KENGO: MASTER OF BUSHIDO

Unlock Play as a student:
Hold R1 + R2 + L1 + L2 when selecting a character.

Unlock Final Character:
When you complete the tournament, the Ninth fighter will be unlocked, but you cannot see his face. To play as him, hold L1 + R1 + R2 + L2 then hit ✖.

Unlock All hidden characters:
To unlock all the hidden characters in Versus and Tournament mode, defeat all the Dojos in single player mode.

KESSEN

Unlock Play as the West:
Finish the game as the East.

Unlock Battle mode option:
Finish the game as the East and the West.

KESSEN 2

Unlock Select side:
Finish the game with the Lui Bei or Cao Cao.

KINGDOM HEARTS

Alternate ending sequence:
Successfully complete the game with all keyholes, all 99 Dalmatians, and also the Hades Cup to unlock a new end sequence.

KLONOA 2: LUNATEA'S VEIL

Play as Mometsuto:
Finish the game to unlock Mometsuto as a playable character.

Boss battle arena:
Finish the fairground levels to unlock a new area that allows you to battle previously defeated Bosses.

Picture gallery:
Finish the fairground levels to unlock an option for a picture gallery.

Music test:
Complete the either bonus level to unlock songs in the music box.

KNOCKOUT KINGS 2001

Unlock Ashy Knucks:
Enter MECCA as your player namefor a created boxer in career mode.

Unlock Barry Sanders:
Enter MRBARRY as your player namefor a created boxer in career mode.

Unlock Bernardo Osuna:
Enter OSUNA as your player namefor a created boxer in career mode.

Unlock Chuck Zito:
Enter ZITO as your player namefor a created boxer in career mode.

Unlock Charles Hatcher:
Enter HATCHER as your player namefor a created boxer in career mode.

Unlock David Bostice:
Enter BOSTICE as your player namefor a created boxer in career mode.

Unlock David Defiagbon:
Enter DEFIAGBN as your player namefor a created boxer in career mode.

Unlock David DeMartini:
Enter DEMART as your player namefor a created boxer in career mode.

Unlock Jason Giambi:
Enter JGIAMBI as your player namefor a created boxer in career mode.

Unlock Joe Mesi:
Enter BAILEY as your player namefor a created boxer in career mode.

Unlock John Botti:
Enter JBOTTI as your player namefor a created boxer in career mode.

Unlock Junior Seau:
Enter JRSEAU as your player namefor a created boxer in career mode.

Unlock Muhammad Ali:
Enter SBATISTE as your player namefor a created boxer in career mode.

Unlock Owen Nolan:
Enter OWNOLAN as your player namefor a created boxer in career mode.

Unlock Ray Austin:
Enter AUSTIN as your player namefor a created boxer in career mode.

Unlock Steve Francis:
Enter STEVEF as your player namefor a created boxer in career mode.

Unlock Trevor Nelson:
Enter NELSON as your player namefor a created boxer in career mode.

KNOCKOUT KINGS 2002

Unlock Cheat mode:
Use a created character to Finish the game to unlock one of five cheat modes.

LE MANS 24 HOURS

Unlock all tracks:
Enter SPEEDY as your player namein championship mode, and then return to the main menu screen.

Unlock all cars:
Enter ACO as your player namein championship mode, and then return to the main menu screen.

Unlock all championships:
Enter NUMBAT as your player namein championship mode, and then return to the main menu screen.

Unlock Le Mans mode:
Enter WOMBAT as your player namein championship mode, and then return to the main menu screen.

View credits:
Enter HEINEY as your player namein championship mode, and then return to the main menu screen.

LEGACY OF KAIN: BLOOD OMEN 2

Unlock Cheat mode:
Hit L1, R1, L2, R2, ■, Circle, Triangle at the main menu screen. Start a new game to begin with the Soul Reaver and Iron Armour.

Sneaking up on enemies:
Hold L2 during in game to be able to creep up on enemies and attack them.

LEGACY OF KAIN: SOUL REAVER 2

Unlock Bonus materials:
Hit ⇦, ▲, ⇨, ▲, ⇩, ●, ✖ at the main menu screen

Unlock Fire Reaver:
Pause in game , then hold R1 and hit ⇩, ●, ▲, ⇧, ⇨, ●.

Perform a Low kick:
Hold R1 + L2 + ■ when facing an enemy and Raziel will kick them in the leg.

LEGENDS OF WRESTLING

Unlock All wrestlers:
Hit ⇧ x2, ⇩ x2, ⇦, ⇨, ⇦, ⇨, ▲ x2, ■ at the main menu screen.

Unlock Alternate costumes:
Hit Circle instead of ✖ at the main character selection screen.

Unlock Captain Lou Albano:
Finish career mode with a wrestler in the "Hated" category.

Unlock David Von Erich:
Finish career mode as Kevin Von Erich.

Unlock Dory Funk:
Finish career mode as Terry Funk.

Unlock Fritz Von Erich:
Finish career mode as Kerry Von Erich.

Unlock Ivan Koloff:
Win the versus tournament.

Unlock Jimmy Hart:
Finish career mode with a wrestler in the "Loved" category.

Unlock King Kong Bundy:
Win the Southeast Territory in career mode.

Unlock Michael Von Erich:
Finish career mode as David Von Erich.

Unlock Mr. Fuji:
Win the Tag Belts in tournament mode.

Unlock Robert Gibson and Ricky Morton:
Win the tag tournament.

Unlock Sabu:
Finish career mode as The Sheik.

Unlock Bonus arenas:
Finish the game in career mode to unlock the Back Lot, Gym, Beach Resort, and Casino arenas in exhibition mode.

LEGENDS OF WRESTLING 2

Unlock Andy Kaufman:
Select career mode and choose Jerry Lawler as your wrestler the beat Andy Kaufman to unlock him at the shop.

Unlock Big John Studd:
Select career mode and choose any wrestler then beat Big John Studd to unlock him at the shop.

Unlock British Bulldog:
Select career mode and choose Dynamite Kid then you must complete career mode to unlock British Bulldog at the shop.

Unlock Bruno Sammartino:
Select career mode and choose Hulk Hogan then you must complete career mode to unlock Bruno Sammartino at the shop.

Unlock Owen Hart:
Select career mode and choose Bret Hart. You must complete career mode to unlock Owen Hart at the shop.

LEGO RACERS 2

Unlock Martian:
Hit ⇨, ⇦, ⇨, ⇧, ⇩, ⇦, ⇨, ⇧ x2 at the main menu screen.

Unlock Mars tracks:
Pause in game then hit ⇦ x2, ⇨ x2, ⇦ x2, ⇨ x2, ⇩, ⇦, ⇨.

Unlock Wide-angle mode:
Pause in game then hit ⇦ x3, ⇨ x3, ⇧ x3, ⇩ x3, ⇦ x3, ⇨ x3.

LMA MANAGER 2002

Unlock More money:
Enter MINTED as your name.

Unlock Auto-select tactics:
Enter NO BRAINER as your name.

Unlock 90% skill:
Enter AWESOME as your name.

Unlock Run fast:
Enter HYPERACTIVE as your name.

Unlock Aggressive players:
Enter WHO WANTS SOME as your name.

Unlock Win every game:
Enter RUN OF FORM as your name.

Unlock Buy any player:
Enter FANTASY as your name.

Unlock Fast stadium construction:
Enter QUICK DRY as your name.

Unlock Quick healing:
Enter HEALING HANDS as your name.

Unlock Blind referee:
Enter MUST BE BLIND as your name.

Unlock Always Good Weather:
Enter SUN BURN as your name.

Unlock Always Bad Weather:
Enter UMBRELLA as your name.

THE LORD OF THE RINGS: THE FELLOWSHIP OF THE RING

Unlock Endless Coins.
On the East Road just out of Hobbiton on the ledge above the stumps that summon the elves is a house. Enter it and walk up to the bookcase. Press Action and a gold coin will appear leave and repeat this to get loads of coins.

THE LORD OF THE RINGS: THE TWO TOWERS

Unlock Restore health:
Pause game play, then hold L1 + L2 + R1+ R2 and press ▲, ⇩, ✖, ⇧. The sound of a sword clash will confirm correct code entry.

Unlock Restore ammunition:
Pause game play, then hold L1 + L2 + R1+ R2 and press ✖, ⇩, ▲, ⇧. The sound of a sword clash will confirm correct code entry.

Unlock Add 1000 experience points:
Pause game play, then hold L1 + L2 + R1+ R2 and press ✖, ⇩ x3. The sound of a sword clash will confirm correct code entry.

Unlock Level 2 skills:
Pause game play, then hold L1 + L2 + R1+ R2 and press ●, ⇨, ●, ⇨. The sound of a sword clash will confirm correct code entry.

Unlock Level 3 skills:
Pause game play, then hold L1 + L2 + R1+ R2 and press ▲, ⇧, ▲, ⇧. The sound of a sword clash will confirm correct code entry.

Unlock Level 4 skills:
Pause game play, then hold L1 + L2 + R1+ R2 and press ■, ⇦, ■, ⇦. The sound of a sword clash will confirm correct code entry.

Unlock Level 5 Skills:
Pause game play, then hold L1 + L2 + R1+ R2 and press ✖ x2, ⇩ x2. The sound of a sword clash will confirm correct code entry.

Unlock Invincibility:
Pause game play, then hold L1 + L2 + R1+ R2 and press ▲, ■, ✖, ●. The sound of a sword clash will confirm correct code entry.

Unlock Unlimited missile weapons:
Pause game play, then L1 + L2 + R1+ R2 and press ■, ●, ✖, ▲. The sound of a sword clash will confirm correct code entry.

Unlock Devastating attacks:
Pause game play, then hold L1 + L2 + R1+ R2 and press ■ x2, ● x2. The sound of a sword clash will confirm correct code entry. Hold ▲ during battles to do devastating attacks.

Unlock All combo upgrades:
Pause game play, then hold L1 + L2 + R1+ R2 and press ▲, ●, ▲, ●. The sound of a sword clash will confirm correct code entry.

Unlock Small enemies:
Pause game play, then hold L1 + L2 + R1+ R2 and press ▲ x2, ✖ x2. The sound of a sword clash will confirm correct code entry.

Unlock Slow motion:
Pause game play, then hold L1 + L2 + R1+ R2 and press ▲, ●, ✖, ■. The sound of a sword clash will confirm correct code entry.

Easy money:
On the East Road look upon the ledge located above the stumps that summon the elves and you will notice a small house. Enter it and press action on the bookcase to make a gold. Leave the house and re-enter and repeat this porcess to get as many coins as you need.

LOTUS CHALLENGE

Unlock Cheat mode:
Enter CRAIGSAYS as driver name to unlock all cars and tracks.

Ending bonus:
Finish all challenges for Jack and Zoe and finish in first place in all championship races to unlock all cars and a reverse mode.

Switch On Headlights:
Hit R1 during a race to turn on your headlights.

MAD MAESTRO

In-game reset:
Hold L1 + L2 + R1 + R2 and hit START + SELECT during in game .

MADDEN NFL 2001

Unlimited creation points:
Create a player, then go to "Edit Player" at the roster screen. Hit ⇧ or ⇩ to choose the player you want to edit and then hit ⇨ to get to the speed category. Now hit ✖, and then hit ✖ again.

Always win coin toss:
Hit START before anything appears on the coin toss screen.

MADDEN NFL 2002

Always Win the coin toss:
Repeatedly hit L1 + R1 + START before the coin toss screen appears.

Unlock Houston Texans:
After the first season in franchise mode, do the expansion draft for the Houston Texans.

Unlimited creation points:
Go the Create a player screen, then "Edit Player" on the roster screen, now hit ⇧ or ⇩ to choose the player you want to edit then hit ⇨ and hit ✖ x2.

Thanksgiving commentary:
Set the system date to the third Thursday in November.

Christmas commentary:
Set the system date to December 25.

New Year's commentary:
Set the system date to January 1.

MADDEN NFL 2003

Unlimited creation points:
Go to "Rosters", and then choose "Edit Player". Select the players that you want to be rated 99. Go to his attributes, and then increase everything.

Unlock Cheerleader Cards and game CHEAT:
Get a gold rank in any event on the All Pro, Pro and Rookie levels.

Unlock Deion Sanders:
Get a gold rank in the DB Swat drill in mini-camp mode under the All-Madden level.

Unlock Gale Sayers:
Get a gold rank in the RB Ground Attack drill in mini-camp mode under the All-Madden level.

Unlock Kevin Butler:
Get a gold rank in P-Coffin Corner Punt under the All-Madden level.

Unlock Mike Singletary:
Get a gold rank in the LB Chase and Tackle drill in mini-camp mode under the All-Madden level.

Unlock Reggie White:
Get a gold rank in All-Madden DL-Trench Fight under the All-Madden level.

MAT HOFFMAN'S PRO BMX 2

Unlock Level select:
Hit ■, ⇨ x2, ▲, ⇩, ■ at the "Hit START" screen.

Unlock Boston level in road trip mode:
Hit ■, ⇧, ⇩ x2, ⇧, ■ at the "Hit START" screen.

Unlock Chicago level in road trip mode:
Hit ■, ⇧, ▲, ⇧, ▲, ■ at the "Hit START" screen.

Unlock Las Vegas level in road trip mode:
Hit ■, **R1**, ⇦, **L1**, ⇨, ■ at the "Hit START" screen.

Unlock Los Angeles level in road trip mode:
Hit ■, ⇦, ▲ x2, ⇦, ■ at the "Hit START" screen.

Unlock New Orleans level in road trip mode:
Hit ■, ⇩, ⇨, ⇧, ⇦, ■ at the "Hit START" screen.

Unlock Portland level in road trip mode:
Hit ■, ✖ x2, ▲ x2, ■ at the "Hit START" screen.

Unlock Cory Nastazio's FMV sequences:

Hit **R1**, ■, ● x2, ■ x3, **R1** at the "Hit Start" screen.

Unlock Joe Kowalski's FMV sequences:
Hit **R1**, ⇧, ✖, ▲, ⇩, **R1** at the "Hit Start" screen.

Unlock Kevin Robinson's FMV sequences:
Hit **R1**, ✖, ▲, ⇩, ⇧, **R1** at the "Hit Start" screen.

Unlock Mat Hoffman's FMV sequences:
Hit **R1**, ⇦, ●, ⇦, ●, ⇦, **R1** at the "Hit Start" screen.

Unlock Mike Escamilla's FMV sequences:
Hit **R1**, ●, ✖ x2, ●, ✖ x2, **R1** at the "Hit Start" screen.

Unlock Nate Wessel's FMV sequences:
Hit **R1**, ⇩, ▲, ●, ⇩, ▲, ●, **R1** at the "Hit Start" screen.

Unlock Ruben Alcantara's FMV sequences:
Hit **R1**, ⇦, ⇨, ⇦, ⇨, ⇦, ⇨, **R1** at the "Hit Start" screen.

Unlock Rick Thorne's FMV sequences:
Hit **R1**, **L1**, ⇨, **R1**, ⇦, and **R1** at the "Hit Start" screen.

Unlock Seth Kimbrough's FMV sequences:
Hit **R1**, ⇧, ⇧, ● x3, **R1** at the "Hit Start" screen.

Unlock Simon Tabron's FMV sequences:
Hit **R1**, **L1** x2, **R1**, **L1** x2, **R1** at the "Hit Start" screen.

Unlock All music tracks:
Hit **L1**, ⇦ x2, ⇨ x3, ✖ x2 at the "Hit Start" screen.

Unlock Mime: Find all of the gaps in the game.

CHARACTER'S SPECIALS:

BIGFOOT
Backflip No Footer: Hit ⇨, ⇦, ●.
Superman One Hander: Hit ⇦, ⇨, ■.
Decade Air: Hit ⇦, ⇧, ●.

CORY NASTAZIO
Back Flip Tabletop X-Down: Hit ⇧, ⇦, ■.
Back Flip Tailwhip: Hit ⇨, ⇦, ●.
Half Barspin Tailwhip: Hit ⇦, ⇨, ■

DAVE SMITH
Back Flip One Footer: Hit ⇦, ⇨, ■.
Decade Air: Hit ⇨, ⇦, ●.
Pendulum: Hit ⇦, ⇩, ■

JOE KOWALSKI
Half Barspin Tailwhip: Hit ⇧, ⇦, ●.
No Footed Candybar One Hander: Hit ⇨, ⇦, ■.
Superman One Hander: Hit ⇦, ⇨, ●

KEVIN ROBINSON
Pendulum: ⇦, ⇨, ■.
Rocket One Footer Candybar: ⇨, ⇦, ●.
No Handed Backflip: ⇩, ⇨, ■

MAT HOFFMAN
Back Flip Tailwhip: Hit ⇨, ⇩, ■.
Barhop: Hit ⇨, ⇦, ●.
Peacock: Hit ⇦, ⇧, ●

MIKE ESCAMILLA
Back Flip No Footer: Hit ⇦, ⇨, ●.
Body Varial: Hit ⇨, ⇧, ■.
Decade Air: Hit ⇨, ⇦, ■

NATE WESSEL
Back Flip No Footer: Hit ⇨, ⇦, ●.
Pendulum: Hit ⇦, ⇨, ■.
Superman Double Seat Grab: Hit ⇩, ⇦, ■

RICK THORNE
No Hander Backflip: Hit ⇩, ⇨, ■.
One Handed Swing Leg: Hit ⇨, ⇦, ●.
Rocket One Footer Candybar: Hit ⇨, ⇦, ●

RUBEN ALCANTARA
Decade Air: Hit ⇦, ⇨, ●.
Double Tailwhip: Hit ⇩, ⇦, ●.
Superman One Hander: Hit ⇨, ⇦, ■

SETH KIMBROUGH
Barhop: Hit ⇦, ⇨, ■.
Superman Seat Grab Truckdriver: Hit ⇨, ⇩, ■.
Swing Leg: Hit ⇦, ⇨, ●

SIMON TABRON
900: Hit ⇦, ⇩, ■.
Double Front Peg Grab: Hit ⇨, ⇦, ■.
Swing Leg: Hit ⇦, ⇨, ●

VANESSA
Barhop: Hit ⇧, ⇦, ■.
Rocket One Footer Candybar: Hit ⇦, ⇨, ●.
Swing Leg: Hit ⇨, ⇦, ■

VOLCANO
Back Flip No Footer: Hit ⇦, ⇨, ■.
One Hander Swing Leg: Hit ⇩, ⇨, ■.
Rocket One Foot Candybar: Hit ⇨, ⇦, ●

MAX PAYNE

Unlock Level select: Complete Subway A1 and return to the main menu screen and hit ⇧, ⇩, ⇦, ⇨, ⇧, ⇦, ⇩, ●.

Unlock Unlimited health:
Hit START to pause in game , then hit **L1** x2, **L2** x2, **R1** x2, **R2** x2.

Unlock Invincibility:
Hit START to pause in game , then hit **L1** x2, **L2** x2, **R1** x2, **R2** x2, ▲, ●, ✖, ■.

Unlock All weapons and full ammunition:
Hit START to pause in game , then hit **L1, L2, R1, R2, ▲, ●, ✖, ■.**

Unlock Unlimited bullet time:
Hit START to pause in game , then hit **L1, L2, R1, R2, ▲, ✖** x2, **▲.**

Unlock Slow motion sounds:
Hit START to pause in game , then hit **L1, L2, R1, R2, ▲, ■, ✖, ●.**

Unlock Start With 8 Pain Killer Pills:
Hit START to pause in game , then hit **L1, L2, R1, R2, ▲, ●, ✖, ■.**

Unlock Last Challenge bonus level:
Finish the game under the "Dead On Arrival" difficulty setting.

MDK2 ARMAGEDDON

Unlock Invincibility:
Hit START to pause in game , hold L2 + R2 and hit ⇧ x2, ⇩ x2, ⇦ x2, ⇨ x2, ■, ▲, ■, ▲, then hold SELECT.

Unlock Slow motion:
Begin in game as Max, and then hold R2 and hit ⇧ x4.

Unlock Kurt in boxer shorts:
Hold L2 + R2 and hit ■ x2, ▲, ■ at the main menu screen.

Unlock Mixed character:
Hit Start to pause in game , then hold L2 + R2 and hit ⇧, ⇩, ⇨, ⇦, ✖, ▲, ●, ■, ■ + START to play as a character that is part Kurt, Max, and Doctor Hawkins.

Unlock Panning camera view:
Hit START to pause in game , then hold L2 + R2 and hit ●, ✖, ●, ✖.

Unlock Crazy camera view:
Hit START to pause in game , then hold L2 + R2 and hit ✖, ●, ✖, ●.

Unlock Fixed camera view:
Hit START to pause in game , then hold L2 + R2 and hit ●, ✖, ●, ▲.

Make Doctor Hawkins Fart:
Begin in game as Doctor Hawkins, then hit L2 + R2 + ⇦ + ✖.

MEDAL OF HONOR: FRONTLINE

Unlock Invincibility:
Pause in game , then hit **■, L1, ●, R1, ▲, L2, Select, R2.**

Unlock Unlimited ammunition:
Pause in game , then hit **●, L2, ■, L1, Select, R2, ▲, Select.**

Unlock Bullet shield:
Pause in game , then hit **●, Select, R2** x2, **R1** x2, **L1, R1.**

Unlock Master code:
Enter DAWOIKS at the Enigma Machine.

Unlock Silver bullet mode:
Enter WHATYOUGET at the Enigma Machine.

Unlock Rubber grenade mode:
Enter BOING at the Enigma Machine.

Unlock Snipe-O-Rama mode:
Enter LONGSHOT at the Enigma Machine.

Unlock Bullet shield mode:
Enter BULLETZAP at the Enigma Machine.

Unlock Mission 2 (A Storm in the Port):
Enter ORANGUTAN at the Enigma Machine.

Unlock Mission 3 (Needle in a Haystack):
Enter BABOON at the Enigma Machine.

Unlock Mission 4 (Several Bridges Too Far):
Enter CHIMPNZEE at the Enigma Machine.

Unlock Mission 5 (Rolling Thunder):
Enter LEMUR at the Enigma Machine.

Unlock Mission 6 (The Horten's Nest):
Enter GORILLA at the Enigma Machine.

Unlock Perfectionist mode:
Enter URTHEMAN at the Enigma Machine.

Unlock Mohton torpedoes:
Enter TPDOMOHTON at the Enigma Machine.

Unlock Achilles' head mode:
Enter GLASSJAW at the Enigma Machine.

Unlock Invisible enemies:
Enter WHERERU at the Enigma Machine.

Unlock Men with hats:
Enter HABRDASHR at the Enigma Machine.

Unlock Making Of D-Day FMV sequence:
Enter BACKSTAGEO at the Enigma Machine.

Unlock Making Of Needle In A Hay Stack FMV sequence:
Enter BACKSTAGER at the Enigma Machine.

Unlock Making Of Several Bridges Too Far FMV sequence:
Enter BACKSTAGEF at the Enigma Machine.

Unlock Making Of The Horten's Nest FMV sequence:
Enter BACKSTAGES at the Enigma Machine.

Unlock Making Of Storm In The Port FMV sequence:
Enter BACKSTAGET at the Enigma Machine.

Unlock Making Of Rolling Thunder FMV sequence:
Enter BACKSTAGEI at the Enigma Machine.

Unlock Paintball FMV sequence:
Enter MAGGOTAHOY at the Enigma Machine.

Unlock Animation reel:
Enter ANIMREEL at the Enigma Machine.

Complete current mission with Gold Star:
Enter MONKEY at the Enigma Machine.

METAL GEAR SOLID 2: SUBSTANCE

Unlock Sunglasses:
After completing the game two times, Snake and Raiden will be wearing sunglasses.

Unlock Boss survival mode:
You must complete Sons Of Liberty under any difficulty setting.

Unlock Photograph mode:
You must complete bomb disposal mode, press and hold up mode (alternative missions), and eliminate mode to unlock photograph mode in the VR Missions.

Unlock Casting theater option:

You must complete Sons Of Liberty under any difficulty setting.

Unlock Ninja Raiden:
You must complete 50% of the VR missions as Raiden to unlock Ninja Raiden in the VR Missions.

Unlock Raiden X:
You must complete 100% of the VR missions as Raiden and Ninja Raiden.

Unlock Pliskin:
You must complete 50% of the VR missions as Snake.

Unlock Tuxedo Snake:
You must complete 100% of the VR missions as Pliskin.

Unlock Metal Gear Solid 1 Snake:
You must complete 100% of the VR missions as Snake, Pliskin, Tuxedo Snake, Raiden, Ninja Raiden, and Raiden X.

Unlock Alternate ending sequence:
You must complete a Snake Tale to unlock the M9. Begin game play and use M9 to stun the Bosses instead of killing them to view an alternate ending sequence.

Complete previous mission with Gold Star:
Enter TIMEWARP at the Enigma Machine.

MEN IN BLACK 2: ALIEN ESCAPE

Unlock Invincibility:
Hit ⇨, ✖, R1, ▲, ⇧, L2, ✖, ⇦, L1, ●, ✖, R2 at the "Hit Start" screen.

Unlock All weapons:
Hit ⇧, ⇩, ✖, ■, R1, ▲ x2, ⇦, ●, L1 x2, ⇨ at the "Hit Start" screen.

Unlock Level select:
Hit R2, ▲, ⇦, ●, ■, L2, ⇦, ⇧, ✖, ⇩, L2, ■ at the "Hit Start" screen.

Unlock Full bolt:
Hit ⇦, ⇨, ⇧, ⇩, L1, ●, ▲, R2, ⇦, ⇩, ■ x2 at the "Hit Start" screen.

Unlock Full spread:
Hit L2, R1, ●, L2, ⇩, ⇧, L1, ⇨, ⇦, ✖ at the "Hit Start" screen.

Unlock Full homing:
Hit ⇨, ⇧, ■, L1, ⇦ x2, L1, ⇦, ●, ⇦ at the "Hit Start" screen.

Unlock Full beam:
Hit ⇦, ●, ▲, ⇨, L1, ■, ⇦, R1 x2, ▲ at the "Hit Start" screen.

Unlock Full area effect:
Hit ⇦, ✖, ▲, ⇧, ✖, ⇩, ■, L2, ⇦, R2 at the "Hit Start" screen.

Unlock No power-up drops:
Hit ⇩, ⇧, ✖, ■, ⇩, ⇧, ✖, ■, L1, L2, ■, ● at the "Hit Start" screen.

Unlock Boss mode:
Hit R1, ▲, ⇩ x2, ✖, L2, ⇦, ■, ⇨, ▲, R2, L1 at the "Hit Start" screen.

Unlock Training missions:
Hit ■, ⇧, L2, ⇦, ▲, ✖, R2, ●, ⇨, R1, ■, ● at the "Hit Start" screen.

Unlock Boss mode:
Hit R1, ▲, ⇩ x2, ✖, L2, ⇦, ■, ⇨, ▲, R2, L1 at the "Hit Start" screen.

Unlock Agent data:
Hit ⇧, ⇩, ●, R2, ⇦, L2, ⇨, ✖, R2, ■, ⇧, R1 at the "Hit Start" screen.

Unlock Alien data:
Hit ■, L1, ●, L2, ⇩, ▲, R1, ⇨, ✖, ⇦, R2, ▲ at the "Hit Start" screen.

Unlock "Making Of" feature:
Hit ●, R2, L2, ●, ▲, ⇩, ■, ✖, ⇨, L1, ✖, ⇧ at the "Hit Start" screen.

MIDNIGHT CLUB: STREET RACING

Unlock Manhattan police:
Finish Manhattan level 10 in Head-2-Head mode.
Unlock London police:
Finish London level 10 in Head-2-Head mode.

Unlock All Cruseros:
Finish Manhattan levels 1, 4, and 7 in Head-2-Head mode.

Unlock All Jones:
Finish Manhattan levels 2, 5, and 8 in Head-2-Head mode.

Unlock All Piranha:
Finish Manhattan levels 3, 6, and 9 in Head-2-Head mode.

Unlock All PTs:
Win the First, Fourth, and Seventh Head-2-Head races.

Unlock All Modicums:
Win the Third, Sixth, and Ninth Head-2-Head races.

Unlock All Ascents:
Win the Second, Fifth, and Eigth Head-2-Head races.

MIKE TYSON HEAVYWEIGHT BOXING

Unlock Master code:
Hit ■, ●, L2, R2 when "Hit Start" appears at the main title screen.
Unlock All created boxer items:
Hit L1, R1, ✖ x2, ▲, ✖ when "Hit Start" appears at the main title screen.
Unlock Big heads:
Hit ■, ●, ⇧, ⇩ when "Hit Start" appears at the main title screen.
Unlock Small heads:
Hit ■, ●, ⇩, ⇧ when "Hit Start" appears at the main title screen.
Unlock Random sized boxers:
Hit ■, ⇦, ⇧, ▲ when "Hit Start" appears at the main title screen.
Unlock Flat mode: Hit ⇩, ⇧, ●, ■ when "Hit Start" appears at the main title screen.
Unlock View full credits:
Hit ✖, ▲, ■, ● when "Hit Start" appears at the main title screen.
Unlock Mike Tyson Challenge:
Defeat Mike Tyson and win the Gold belt to unlock the undisputed champ mode.
Unlock Fight as Mike Tyson:
Win the Gold Belt to unlock

Mike Tyson in single player mode.
Unlock Fight as Iron Mike: Win the Mike Tyson Challenge to unlock Iron Mike, the early version of Mike Tyson.

MINORITY REPORT

Unlock Invincibility: Enter LRGARMS as a cheat code.
Unlock Level select: Enter PASSKEY as a cheat code.
Unlock Level skip: Enter QUITER as a cheat code.
Unlock All combos: Enter NINJA as a cheat code.
Unlock All weapons: Enter STRAPPED as a cheat code.
Unlock Maximum ammunition: Enter MRJUAREZ as a cheat code.
Unlock Maximum damage: Enter SPINACH as a cheat code.
Unlock Extra health: Enter BUTTERUP as a cheat code.
Unlock Play as Clown: Enter SCARYCLOWN as a cheat code.
Unlock Play as Convict: Enter JAILBREAK as a cheat code.
Unlock Play as GI: Enter GNRLINFANTRY as a cheat code.
Unlock Play as Lizard: Enter HISSSS as a cheat code.
Unlock Play as Moseley: Enter BIGLIPS as a cheat code.
Unlock Play as Nara: Enter WEIGHTGAIN as a cheat code.
Unlock Play as Nikki: Enter HAIRLOSS as a cheat code.
Unlock Play as Robot: Enter MRROBOTO as a cheat code.
Unlock Play as Superhero: Enter SUPERJOHN as a cheat code.
Unlock Play as Zombie: Enter IAMSODEAD as a cheat code.
Unlock Free aim: Enter FPSSTYLE as a cheat code.
Unlock Pain arenas: Enter MAXIMUMHURT as a cheat code.
Unlock Armor: Enter STEELUP as a cheat code.
Unlock Baseball bat: Enter SLUGGER as a cheat code.
Unlock Rag doll: Enter CLUMSY as a cheat code.
Unlock Slow motion button: Enter SLIZOMIZO as a cheat code.
Unlock Bouncy men: Enter BOUNZMEN as a cheat code.
Unlock Cluttered locations: Enter CLUTZ as a cheat code.
Unlock Dramatic finish: Enter STYLIN as a cheat code.
Unlock Ending sequence: Enter WIMP as a cheat code.
Unlock Concept art: Enter SKETCHPAD as a cheat code.
Unlock All FMV sequences: Enter DIRECTOR as a cheat code.

MISTER MOSQUITO

Unlock In-game reset: Hold L1 + L2 + R1 + R2 and hit START + SELECT during in game.

Unlock Mother Mosquito: Hold L1 and hit ⇧, ⇨, ⇦, ⇩, ■ x2, R1 x3 at the main character selection screen.

Unlock Father Mosquito: Enable the "Mother Mosquito" code. Then, hold L2 and hit ⇧, ⇨, ⇦, ⇩, ■ x2, R2 x3 at the main character selection screen.

MORTAL KOMBAT: DEADLY ALLIANCE

FATALITIES:
Bo Rai Cho (Belly Flop): Press Away x3, ⇩, ●
Johnny Cage (Brain Ripper): Press Away, Towardx2, ⇩,▲
Kano (Heart Grab): Press Toward, ⇧ x2, ⇩, ■
Kenshi (ETelekinetic Crush): Press Toward, Away, Toward, ⇩, ✖
Kung Lao (Hat Throw): Press ⇩, ⇧, Away, ✖
Li Mei (Crush Kick): Press Toward x2, ⇩, Toward, ●
Mavado (Kick Thrust): Press Away x2, ⇧ x2, ■
Quan Chi (Neck Stretch): Press Away x2, Toward, Away, ✖
Scorpion (Spear): Press Away x2, ⇩, Away +●
Shang Tsung (Soul Steal): Press ⇧, ⇩, ⇧, ⇩, ▲
Sonya (Kiss): Press Away, Towardx2, ⇩,▲
Sub Zero (Spine Rip): Press Away, Towardx2, ⇩,✖
Cyrax (Smasher): Press Toward x2, ⇧, ▲
Drahmin (Iron Bash): Press Away, Towardx2, ⇩,✖
Frost (Freeze Shatter): Press Toward, Away, ⇧,⇩,■
Hsu Hao (Laser Slice): Press Toward, Away, ⇩,⇩,▲
Jax (Head Stomp): Press ⇩, Toward x2, ⇩, ▲
Kitana (Kiss of Doom): Press ⇩, ⇧, Toward x2, ▲
Nitara (Blood Thirst): Press ⇧ x2, Toward, ■

Raiden (Electrocution):
Press Away, Toward, Toward x2, ✖
Reptile (Acid Shower):
Press ⇧ x3, Toward, ✖

MOTO GP

Unlock Race as Klonoa:
Win Challenge 22 to unlock Klonoa as a rider.
Time trial password:
Select the "Save/Load" option at the main menu screen. Select "High scores screen", then "Time Trial". Hold L1 + L2 + R1 + R2 and hit SELECT to convert each of your time trial high scores screen into passwords that can be entered at: http://www.namco.co.jp/home/cs/ps2/motogp/ranking-world/

MOTO GP 2

Unlock Legends mode:
Unlock Challenges 62 through 66 and Challenge 67 will unlock the legends mode.

MOTOR MAYHEM

Unlock Shield:
First enable the "Instant Combo" option at the CHEAT screen, now hold R1 and hit ▲, ■, ▲, ■ when in in game mode.
Weapon eject:
Hold L1 and hit ✖ x2, Square during in game .
City Canal level:
Finish the Death match level under the normal difficulty setting to unlock the City Canal level.
Downtown level:
Finish the Eliminator levels under the normal difficulty setting to unlock the Downtown level.
Unlock Santa hats:
Set the system date to December 21 through December 25.

MTV MUSIC GENERATOR 2

Unlock Hidden skin:
Go to block 999 of the song and select the option to enter the author's name as JESTER.
Unlock Gorillaz's music video:
Enter the options menu, then select "Video Palette" and select the Gorillaz video.

THE MUMMY RETURNS

Unlock Invincibility:
Play as Rick O' Connell, pause in game and hit ⇧, ⇩, ⇦, R1, R3, ▲.

MX 2002 FEATURING RICKY CARMICHAEL

Unlock Level select:
Start the game in two player mode whilst having player one hold R1 + L2 and then Player One hits ⇧, ⇩, ⇦, ⇨, ▲, then player two holds down ▲ + L2 + R2 + ✖ together.
Bail:
Hit R1 + R2 + L1 + L2 to bail.
SPECIAL TRICK MOVES:
180/360/ Bar
Turn while in the air using the Analog-stick.
Bar Hop:
Hold Trick and hit ▲ x2.
Can Can:
Hold Trick and hit ■ x2.
Cat Nac:
Hold Trick and hit ✖, ● x2.
Catwalk:
Hold Trick and hit ■, ▲.
Cliff Hanger:
Hold Trick and hit ●, ▲.
Coffin:
Hold Trick and hit ▲, ●.
Cordova:
Hold Trick and hit ●, ▲ x2.
Disco Can:
Hold Trick and hit ■ x3.
Heart Attack:
Hold Trick and hit ✖, ▲.
Heel Clicker:
Hold Trick and hit ▲.
Helicopter:
Hold Trick and hit ✖, ▲ x2.
Indian Air:
Hold Trick and hit ✖.
Kiss Of Death:
Hold Trick and hit ● x2.
La-Z-Boy:
Hold Trick and hit ●, ✖.
McMetz:
Hold Trick and hit ▲ x3.
Mulisha Air:
Hold Trick and hit ✖, ■.
Nac Nac:
Hold Trick and hit ■.
No Hander:
Hold Trick and hit ●.
Nothing:
Hold Trick and hit ●, ■ .
Pendulum:
Hold Trick and hit ■, ●.
Rocket Air:
Hold Trick and hit ✖, ●.
Rodeo Air:
Hold Trick and hit ▲, ✖.
Saran Wrap:
Hold Trick and hit ▲, ■.
Seat Grab:
Hold Trick and hit ✖ x2.
Superfly:
Hold Trick and hit ✖ x2, ▲
Superman Indian:
Hold Trick and hit ✖ x3.
Surfer:
Hold Trick and hit ■, ▲ x2.
Switchblade:
Hold Trick and hit ■, ✖.

MORTAL KOMBAT DEADLY ALLIANCE

All the moves, all the fatalities and all the secret characters and bonus from the best Mortal Kombat game yet!

FATALITIES QUICK GUIDE

What better way to start things off than a quick guide to ALL the Fatalities in the game!

Moves KEY:

S - Square	**U** - Up
T - Triangle	**D** - Down
X - X	**B** - Back
O - Circle	**F** - Forward

Bo' Rai Cho
FATALITY - Belly Flop: B, B, B, D, O
Johnny Cage
FATALITY - Brain Ripper: B, F, F, D, T
Kano
FATALITY - Open Heart Surgery: F, U, U, D, S
Kenshi
FATALITY - Telekinetic Crush: F, B, F, D, X
Kung Lao
FATALITY - Splitting Headache: D, U, B, X
Li Mei
FATALITY - Super Crush Kick: F, F, D, F, O
Mavado
FATALITY - Kick Thrust: B, B, U, U, S
Quan Chi
FATALITY - Neck Stretcher: B, B, F, B, X
Scorpion
FATALITY - Spear Head: B, B, D, B, O
Shang Tsung
FATALITY - Soul Steal: U, D, U, D, T
Sonya Blade
FATALITY - Kiss of Death: B, F, F, D, T
Sub-Zero
FATALITY - Skeleton Rip: B, F, F, D, X
Cyrax
FATALITY - Claw Smasher: F, F, U, T
Drahmin
FATALITY - Iron Bash: B, F, F, D, X
Frost
FATALITY - Ice Shatter: F, B, U, D, S
Hsu Hao
FATALITY - Laser Slicer: F, B, D, D, T
Jax Briggs
FATALITY - Head Stomp: D, F, F, D, T
Kitana
FATALITY - Kiss of Doom: D, U, F, F, T
Nitara
FATALITY - Blood Thirst: U, U, F, S
Raiden
FATALITY - Electrocution: B, F, F, F, X
Reptile
FATALITY - Acidic Shower: U, U, U, F, X

Let Kombat Begin...

Prepare for combat, full moves for every character in Mortal Kombat: Deadly Alliance.

SHANG T'SUNG

Bio:

- **Status:** Sorcerer
- **Alignment:** Evil
- **Weight:** 250 lbs.
- **Height:** 5'8"
- **Styles:** Snake and Crane
- **Weapon:** Straight Sword

Controls KEY:

Walk Forward
Directional Button Right
Walk Backward
Directional Button Left
Walk Out
Directional Button Up
Walk In
Directional Button Down
Jump Forward
Directional Buttons Up and Right
Jump Backward
Directional Buttons Up and Left
Attack 1 - Square
Attack 2 - Triangle
Attack 3 - X
Attack 4 - Circle
Special Attack - R1
Block - R2
Change Fighting Style - L1

SNAKE MOVE LIST:
Bai She Tu Xin: S
Cross Fang: Back - S
Low Palm: Down - S
Viper Strike: T
Gut Buster: Back - T
Twin Fang: Down - T
Qing She Chu Dong: Up - T
High Snap Kick: X
Twin Cobra: Down - X
Mid Kick: O
Quick Bite: Down - O
Eagle Pecking: Back - O
Back Flip: R1
Throw: Toward – R1
Combos:
Spiritual Snake Tail: T - X
Blinding Strike: T - Back - S
Soul Catcher: T - Back - O
Serpent Touch: O - Back - T
Thrusting Fang: S - S - S
Rattle Snake: S - S - X
Hissing Strikes: S - S - T - X
Cold Blooded: S - S - T - SM
Poisonous Snake: S - S - T - T
Lethal Venom: S - S - T - Back - O
Snake Eyes: S - S - T - Back - S
Cobra Revenge: S - S - O - Back - T

CRANE MOVE LIST:
Chin Punch: S
Crane Neck: Down - S
Crane Wing: T
Strong Knee: Back - T
Back Fist: Down - T
Flapping Wing: X
Hop Sidekick: Back - X
Low Peck: Down - X
Spinning Sidekick: O
Spinning Crane Kick: Up - O
Sweeping Crane: Down - O
Reversal: SM
Throw: Toward – R1
Combos:
Crazy Wings: X - X - T
X-Hit Wings: X - X - X
Sidewinder: X - X - O
Triple Chin Punch: S - S - S
Death Bed: S - S - S – L1
Raging Beak: S - S - S - Up - O
Final Withdrawal: X - X - X - S - S - S – L1
Hunt Down: X - X - X - S - S - S - Up - O

STRAIGHT SWORD MOVE LIST:
Front Swipe: S
Lifting Swing: Up - S
Shin Slash: Down - S
Rising Slice: T
Lunge: Toward - T
Low T-Hit Swipe: Down - T
Back Hand Lunge: Up - T
Foot Sword: X
Cross Strike: Back - X
Chest Slice: Down - X
Spinning Slice: O
Low Stab: Back - O
Sweeping Strike: Down - O
Impale: SM
Combos:
Deadly Blade: S - S
Ancient Strike: O - T
Soul Sucker: Toward - T - S
Pain: X - Back - X
Master's Edge: O - T - X - Back - X

SPECIAL MOVES LIST:
X-D Fire: (Far) Back - Toward - S
X-D Fire: (Close) Toward - Back - S
Straight Fire: Down - Back - S
Soul Steal: Down - Back - X

FATALITY: Up - Down - Up - Down - T

BO' RAI CHO

Bio:

- **Status:** Trainer
- **Alignment:** Good
- **Weight:** 175 lbs.
- **Height:** 5'8"
- **Styles:** Drunken Fist and Mi Zong
- **Weapon:** Jojutsu

DRUNKEN FIST MOVE LIST:

Spinning Backfist: S
Cross Strike: Back - S
Serving Fist: Down - S
Drinking Punch: T
Twisting Flask: Down - T
Battle Punches: Up - T
Lazy Leg: X
Sweep Kick: Back - X
Drinking Wine: Down - X
Drunken Leg: O
Spinning Kick: Back - O
Monkey Kick: Down - O
Taunt: R1
Throw: Toward - R1

Combos:

Kreepy and Jugs: X - T
Twist of Lime: S - S - S
Crushing Grapes: X - X - X
Staggering Steps: T - X - T - T
Zero Tolerance: X - X - T - T
On the Rocks: T - T - S - S - S
Bottoms Up: T - T - S - S – L1 - T – L1
Last Call: T - T - S - S – L1 - T - Back - O
Drunken Fury: T - T - S - S - L1 - T - Up - O

MI ZONG MOVE LIST:

Hook Fist: S
Low Strike: Down - S
Staight Punch: T
Low Knife Hand: Down - T
Roundhouse: X
Sweep Kick: Back - X
Tripping Sweep: Down - X
Side Kick: O
Step Kick: Down - O
Lift Kick: Back - O
Smashing Kick: Up - O
Shove: SM
Throw: Toward - SM

Combos:

Critical Strike: T - T - L1
Lost Track: T - T - Up - O
Iron Broom: T - T - Back - O

JOJUTSU MOVE LIST:

Overhead Strike: S
Strong Overhead Strike: Back - S
Reverse Low Strike: Down - S
Two-Handed Thrust: T
Vertical Smash: Back - T
Leg Sweep: Doon - T
Homerun Swing: X
T-Hit Strike: Toward - X
Low Foot Poke: Down - X
Straight Thrust: Up - X
Mid Reverse Strike: O
Leg Poke: Back - O
High Reverse Strike: Down - O
Sidestep Swing: SM

Combos:

Homerun: T - X
Dancing Stick: T - O - S
Splitting Bamboo: T - O - Back - S
Rolling Wind: T - O - O - Up - X

SPECIAL MOVES LIST:

Puke Puddle: Back - Toward - T
Flip Flop: Down - Back - S
Ground Stomp: Toward - Back - X
Belly Bash: Toward - Toward - O

FATALITY: Back - Back - Back - Down - O

QUAN CHI

Bio:
- **Status:** Sorcerer
- **Alignment:** Evil
- **Weight:** 250 lbs.
- **Height:** 6'7"
- **Styles:** Tang Soo Do and Escrima
- **Weapon:** Broadswords

TANG SOO DO MOVE LIST:
Open Palm: S
Knee Chop: Down - S
Downward Elbow: Back - S
Forward Open Palm: T
Low Spearhead: Down - T
Front Ball Kick: X
Low Parallel Punch: Down - X
Inside Crescent Kick: Toward - X
Spinning Sidekick: Back - X
Sweeping Knife Hook: O
Low Foot Strike: Down - O
One Knuckle Fist Punch: Back - O
Reversal: SM
Throw: Toward - SM

Combos:
Face Breaker: T - T
Path Maker: X - X
Nightfall: Back - S - O
Rushing Palm: S - S - S
Running Stream: T - X - O
Walking Dead: Back -S-X-X
Strong Wind: S - S - T - T
Internal Power: S - S - X - X
Green Mountain: S - S - T - X - O
Pain Killer: S - S - T - X - L1 - O - L1

ESCRIMA MOVE LIST:
Pinasaka: S
Pintok: Down - S
Lightning Strike: Back - S
Backhand Strike: T
Planchada: Down - T
Chest Strike: X
Piercing Elbow: Down - X
Deadly Palm: Back - X
Rising Knee Strike: O
Straight Fist: Toward - O
Cutting Elbow: Down - O
Neijin: SM
Throw: Toward - SM

Combos:
Double Pinasaka: S - S
Hit and Run: X - S - S
Rushing Knee: O - O - L1
Slitting Hand: X - S - Toward - O
Ice Pick: T - O - O - L1
De Cadena: X - S - Back - S

BROADSWORDS MOVE LIST:
Piercing Thrust: S
Double Edged Blow: Down - S
Decieving Strike: T
Dual Blade Swing: Back - T
Winged Strike: Down - T
T-Hit Strike: X
Half Moon Slice: Down - X
Dual Side Slash: O
Circular Slash: Down - O
Strong Slice: SM
Doom Blade: X - O

SPECIAL MOVES LIST:
Skull Fireball: Down - Back - S
Rising Star: Back - Down - O

FATALITY: Back - Back - Toward - Back - X

Bio:

- **Status:** Student
- **Alignment:** Good
- **Weight:** 200 lbs.
- **Height:** 5'8"
- **Styles:** Baji Quan and Lui He Ba Fa
- **Weapon:** Sais

LI MEI

BAJI QUAN MOVE LIST:
Wing Arm: S
Low Scooping Arm: Down - S
Upward Palm Strike: Toward - S
Thrusting Fingers: T
Scooping Arm: Down - T
Circling Hand Strike: Back - T
Scraping Kick: X
Low Kick: Down - X
Lifting Kick: O
Rising Elbow: Down - O
Nailing Kick: Back - O
Taunt: SM
Throw: Toward - SM
Combos:
Setting Sun: O - O - O
All Natural: O - O - O L1 - O
Rising Sun: O - O - L1 - Back - S
Linked Strength: O - O - L1- Back - S - L1

LUI HE BA FA MOVE LIST:
Sideward Palm: S
Hammer Palm: Back - S
Halting Palm: Down - S
Heel Palm Strike: Up - S
Open Fist Strike: T
Low Jab Fist: Down - T
Back Kick: X
Sweeping Kick: Back - X
Back Sweep: Down - X
Spinning Elbow: O
Lifting Knee: Back - O
Low Sideward Palm: Down - O
Shove: SM
Throw: Toward - SM
Combos:
Lost Rose: T - O
Pink Dragon: X - X
Extreme Fists: S - S - S
Unleashed: T - Back - S
Explosive Strength: S - S - Back - O
Rejuvenation: S - S - T - O
Coiled Dragon: S - S - X - X
Golden Path: S - S - T - Back - S
Flower Blossom: S - S - T - Back - S - L1

SAI MOVE LIST:
Forward Thrust: S
Overhead Smash: Back - S
Low Swipe: Down - S
Gut Stab: T
Rising Sai: Up - T
Low Thrust: Down - T
Foot Spike: X
Knee Poke: Down - X
Side Swipe: O
Sweeping Sai: Back - O
Hooking Stab: Down - O
Impale: SM

SPECIAL MOVES LIST:
Flying Fists: Toward - Toward - T
Kartwheel: Down - Back - O
Klock Kick: Toward - Down - X
Sparkler: Down - Back - S

FATALITY: Toward - Toward - Down - Toward - O

SCORPION

HAPKIDO MOVE LIST:
Back Hand Strike: S
Face Strike: Back - S
Twisting Fist: Down - S
Neck Chop: T
Open Palm: Down - T
Axe Kick: X
Knee Knockdown: Toward - X
Hop Sweep: Back - X
Back Sweep: Down - X
Snap Kick: O
Front Sweep: Down - O
Backside Kick: Back - O
Front Thrust Kick: Up - O
Taunt: SM
Throw: Toward - SM
Combos:
Sinking Leaf: Toward - X - Back - X
Flowing Water: T - T - S
Inner Power: T - T - O
Spectre Blast: X - Back - S
Lethal Legs: O - Back - O
Liftoff: O - Up - O
Burning Soul: T - X - Up - O
Doombringer: T - X - Back - S
Painless: T - T - L1 - T - X
Undead Rush: T-T-L1-T-S
Knightmare: T - T - L1 - T - L1 - O
Darkness: T - T - L1 - T - L1 - X
Infernal: T - T - L1 - T - L1 - S - S - X

PI GUA MOVE LIST:
Ridge Hand: S
Knife Hand Chop: Back - S
Low Knife Hand Chop: Down - S
Spear Hand Strike: T
Wing Chop: Toward - T
Spear Hand Sweep: Back - T
Chest Strike: Down - T
Stepping Heel Kick: X
Open Palm Strike: Down - X
Low Heel Kick: O
Low Knife Hand Strike: Down -O
Double Knife Hand Chop: Back - O
Shove: SM
Throw: Toward - SM
Combos:
Stone Breaker: Back - S - X
Falling Tree: T - T - X
Rushing Ridge Hand: T - T - S
Nuisance: T - T - L1 - O
Deranged: T - T - L1 - X
Hell Bound: T - T - L1 - S - S - X

Bio:
- **Status:** Ninja Spectre
- **Alignment:** Neutral
- **Weight:** 250 lbs.
- **Height:** 6'2"
- **Styles:** Hapkido and Pi Gua
- **Weapon:** Ninja Sword

NINJA SWORD MOVE LIST:
Spinning Slash: S
Upward Slash: Down - S
Reverse Stab: T
Edge Slash: Down - T
Rising Slash: X
Charging Slash: Toward - X
Piercing Blade: Down - X
Crescent Blade Strike: O
Sweeping Blade: Down - O
Sidestep Swing: SM
Combos:
Turning Dragon: S - T
Rising Dragon: S - X
Demon Slice: O - X
Moon Strike: O - O
Edge of Pain: O - S - S - X

SPECIAL MOVES LIST:
Spear: Back - Toward - S
Summon Hellfire: Down - Back - T
Backflip Kick: Toward - Back - X

FATALITY: Back - Back - Down - Back - O

Bio:

- **Status:** Special Forces Operative
- **Alignment:** Good
- **Weight:** 190 lbs.
- **Height:** 5'6"
- **Styles:** Kenpo and Tae Kwon Do
- **Weapon:** Kali Sticks

SONYA

KENPO MOVE LIST:
Knife-Hand Strike: S
Double Hammer Fist: Down - S
Spinning Elbow Strike: Back - S
Eye-Gouger: T
Knife-Hand Chop: Back - T
Low Punch: Down - T
Standing Uppercut: Up - T
Back Kick: X
Leg Sweep: Back - X
Low Heel Kick: Down - X
Rising Axe Kick: O
Shovel Kick: Back - O
Low Step Punch: Down - O
Neijin: SM
Throw: Toward - SM
Combos:
Conscious Mind: X - X
Cutting Edge: S - X - X
Big Guns: S - S - O
Warfare: S - S - L1 - O - L1

TAE KWON DO MOVE LIST:
Side Kick: S
Hook Kick: Back - S
Double Hammer Fist: Down - S
Downward Axe Kick: T
Twin Fist Punch: Down - T
Spinning Heel Kick: X
Rolling Strike: Down - X
Ankle Smash: Back - X
T-Hit Axe Kick: O
Nitro Kicks: Back - O
Spinning Back Kick: Down - O
Reversal: SM
Throw: Toward - SM
Combos:
Clearness of Mind: O - O
Take Out: Back - X - X
Blitzkrieg: Back - O - L1
Peaceful World: S - S - Down - X
Special Forces: O - Back - X - X

KALI STICK MOVE LIST:
Straight Snap Strike: S
Low Snap Strike: Down - S
Overhead Strike: Toward - S
Circular Strike: T
Low Scissors Swipe: Down - T
Low Swinging Strike: X
Spinning Strike: Back - X
Low Strike: Down - X
Wrist Snap Strike: O
Chin Jab: Down - O
Circular Power Strike: Back - O
Stick Smash: SM
Combos:
Multi-Level Strikes: T - O - X
Show-Off T - O - Back - X
Furious Blows: O - T - O
Live Hand: O - T - Back - X

SPECIAL MOVES LIST:
Kiss of Death: Down - Back - S
Fly Kick: Toward - Toward - X

FATALITY: Back - Toward - Toward - Down

KENSHI

Bio:

- **Status:** Rogue Swordsman
- **Alignment:** Unknown
- **Weight:** 200 lbs.
- **Height:** 5'9"
- **Styles:** Tai Chi and San Shou
- **Weapon:** Katana

TAI CHI MOVE LIST:
Palm Strike: S
Rising Spade Hand: Back -S
Pushing Hands: Toward - S
Dual Fist Strike: Down - S
Chopping Strike: T
Quick Uppercut: Back - T
Rising Uppercut: Down - T
Straight Kick: X
Low Lean Kick: Down - X
Spinning Roundhouse: O
Low Spin Kick: Down - O
Standing Sweep: Back - O
Taunt: SM
Throw: Toward - SM
Combos:
Empty & Full: S - S
Blind Justice: Back - T - X
Play By Ear: T - T - T - X
Dark Fists: T - T - T - S - S
Fading Light: T - T - T - Back - S
Nightfall: T - T - T - L1 - S - X
Out of Sight: T - T - T - L1 - S - L1
See No Evil: T - T - T - L1 - S - Back - X

SAN SHOU MOVE LIST:
Hook Punch: S
Long Range Fist: Back - S
Low Jab: Down - S
Face Strike: T
Knee Knocker: Toward - T
Rising Elbow: Down - T
Side Kick: X
Low Sweep: Down - X
Propelling Hook Kick: Back - X
Rising Toe Kick: Toward - X
Snapping Roundhouse: O

Spinning Roundhouse: Back - O
Shin Kick: Down - O
Neijin: SM
Throw: Toward - SM
Combos:
Don't Blink: O - O
Natural Way: T - S - X
Near Sight: T - S - L1
All Ears: T - S - Back - X

KATANA MOVE LIST:
Spinning Slash: S
Upward Slash: Down - S
Reverse Stab: T
Edge Slash: Down - T
Rising Slash: X
Charging Slash: Toward - X
Piercing Blade: Down - X
Crescent Blade Strike: O
Sweeping Blade: Down - O
Sidestep Swing: SM
Combos:
Day Break: S - T
Rising Dragon: S - X
Blind Slice: O - X
Moon Strike: O - O
Edge of Pain: O-S-S-X

SPECIAL MOVES LIST:
Telekinetic Slam: Back - Down - Back - S
Telekinetic Toss: Down - Back - O
Telekinetic Push: Toward - Toward - T

FATALITY: Toward - Back - Toward - Down - X

MAVADO

LONG FIST MOVE LIST:
Flat Punch: S
Knee Strike: Back - S
Ducking Claw: Down - S
Long Straight Fist: T
Crane Strike: Back - T
Low Strike: Down - T
Heel Kick: X
Ducking Fist: Down - X
Cutkick: O
Floor Kick: Down - O
Spinning Crane: Back - O
Shove: SM
Throw: Toward - SM
Combos:
Longfist Blast: S - S - T
Forklift: S - S - Back - T

WING CHUN MOVE LIST:
Outside Whip Punch: S
Low Punch: Down - S
Hammerfist: T
Low Whip Jab: Down - T
Sidekick: X
Shin Kick: Down - X
Front Heel Kick: O
Sweep Kick: Down - O
Dragon Tongue: SM
Throw: Toward - SM
Combos:
Mavado Surprise: O - X
Lin Wan Kuen: S - S - S
Determination: T - O - X
Storm Kicks: O - O - X
Rolling Hands: S - T - O - X
Red Dragon: T - O - O - X
Empty Shadow: S - S - Up - S
Control of Power: S - T - O - O - X
Chainsaw: S - T - O - L1 - O - T
Sacred Band: S - T - O - L1 - O - Back - X
Downfall: S - T - O - L1 - O - Back - T

Bio:
- **Status:** Red Dragon
- **Alignment:** Evil
- **Weight:** 575 lbs.
- **Height:** 5'9"
- **Styles:** Long Fist and Wing Chun
- **Weapon:** Hookswords

HOOKSWORD MOVE LIST:
Chest Strike: S
Low Reverse Blow: Down - S
Downward Hook Strike: T
Twin Overhead Strike: Back - T
One Hook Sweep: Down - T
Low High T-Hit: X
Twin Overhead Slam: Back - X
Scissors Swipe: Down - X
Stepping Chest Strike: O
Upward Cross Strike: Down - O
Dual Hook Strike: Toward - O
Sidestep Swing: SM
Combos:
Kabal's Torment: O - O - T
Strength and Balance: O - O - Back - X
Hook N Bash: O - O - Back - T
Blazing Fury: T - O - O - T
Brutal Revenge: T - O - O - Back - X
Kabal's Return: T - O - O - Back - T

SPECIAL MOVES LIST:
Grapple Hook Strike: Toward - Toward - O
Change Sides Hook: Down - Up - T

FATALITY: Back - Back - Up - Up - S

JOHNNY CAGE

Bio:

- **Status:** Movie Star
- **Alignment:** Good
- **Weight:** 590 lbs.
- **Height:** 6'0"
- **Styles:** Karate and Jeet Kune Do
- **Weapon:** Nunchakus

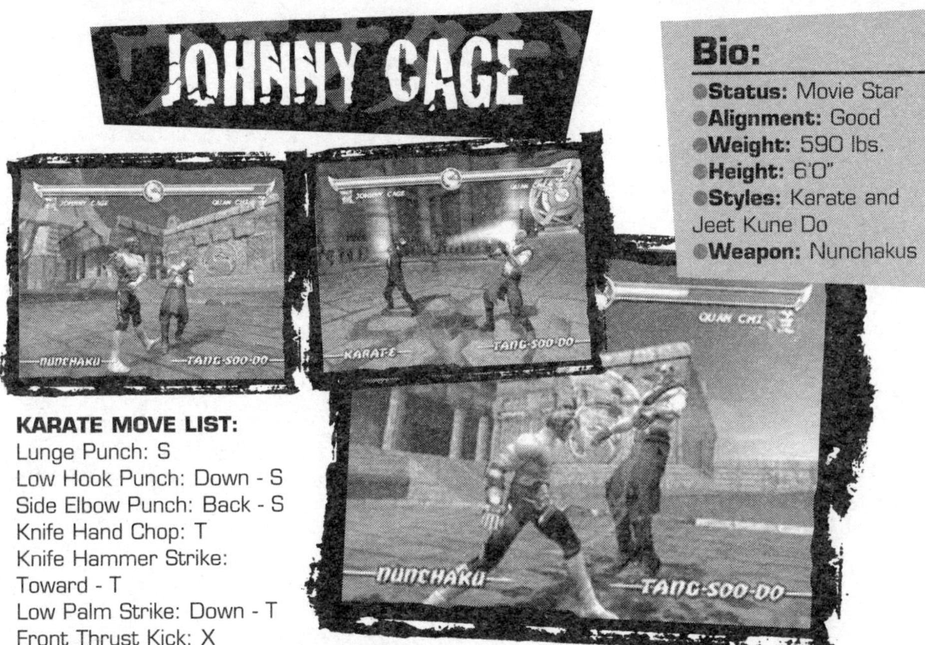

KARATE MOVE LIST:
Lunge Punch: S
Low Hook Punch: Down - S
Side Elbow Punch: Back - S
Knife Hand Chop: T
Knife Hammer Strike: Toward - T
Low Palm Strike: Down - T
Front Thrust Kick: X
Low Jabbing Punch: Down - X
Cutting Kick: Up - X
Side Thrust Kick: O
Low Kick: Down - O
Shin Thrust: Back - O
Flip Kick: Up - O
Double Flip Kick: Up - O - Up - O
Shove: SM
Throw: Toward - SM

Combos:
Smash TV: T - O
Bone Breaker: X - O
Big Blast: S - S - O
Out Take: S - S - L1
The Foot Sword: X - X - X
Cutting Hands: T - X - O
Closing Credits: S - S - Back - S
Chopping Hands: S - T - Toward - T
Cameo: S - T - X - O
Prequel: T - X - X - X
Box Office Smash: S - T - X - X - X
Theatrical Release: S - S - Up O
Directors Cut: S - S - Up - O - Up - O

JEET KUNE DO MOVE LIST:
Leading Straight Punch: S
Hook Fist: Down - S
Knuckle Fist: Back - S
Duck 'n' Jab: T
Low Knuckle Fist: Down - T
Stepping Snap Kick: X
Low Punch: Down - X
Side Kick to Knee: Back - X
Side Kick to Face: O
Sweeping Kick: Back - O
Low Kick: Down - O
High Hooking Kick: Up - O
Taunt: SM
Throw: Toward - SM

Combos:
Straight Blast: S - S
Spotlight: T - T - O
Runner Up: T - T - X - X - L1
Sticky Legs: T - T - X - X - O
Outer Gate: T - T - X - X - Back - O

NUNCHAKU MOVE LIST:
Reverse Shoulder Swing: S
Overhand Strike: Back - S
Bottom Swing: Down - S
Stepping Cross Swing: T
Cross Back Strike: Back - T
Low Knee Strike: Down - T
Underhand Strike: X
Low Circular Swing: Back - X
Double Thrust Strike: Toward - X
Rising Swing: Down - X
Side Kick: O
Roundhouse Kick: Back - O
Low Foot Strike: Down - O
Side Step Swing:SM

Combos:
Gentle Spirit: S - S - X - X
Flowing Strikes: S - S - S - S
Living Legend: S - S - T - Back - T

SPECIAL MOVES LIST:
Forceball: Down - Back - S
Shadow Kick: Back - Toward - O
Johnny Uppercut: Back - SM

FATALITY: Back - Toward - Toward - Down - T

SHOTOKAN MOVE LIST:
Spear Hand Strike: S
Forward Elbow Strike: Back - S
Lower Knee Strike: Down - S
Sword Hand Strike: T
Lower Dual Punch: Down - T
Mountain Punch: Back - T
Rising Thrust Kick: X
Side Snap Kick: Toward - X
Low Sweep Kick: Down - X
Thrust Kick: O
Low Double Side Strike: Down - O
Low Shin Kick: Back - O
Icy Retreat: SM
Throw: Toward - SM

Combos:
T-Hit Trick: X
King's Crown: X - Toward - X
Peaceful Mind: X - Back - T
Icy Pain: S - T - O
Cloud Hands: S - T - Back - S
Iron Horse: S - T - Back - T
Rock Solid: S - T - O - L1 - X
Lin Kuei Storm: S - T - O - L1 - T - X

Zero Below: S - T - O - L1 - T - O
Frozen Frenzy: S - T - O - L1 - Back - S
Frosty: S - T - O - L1 - T - L1
Thin Ice: S - T - O - L1 - T - Back - T
Unthawed: S - T - O - L1 - T - Up - O

DRAGON MOVE LIST:
Back Knuckle Strike: S
Ducking Dual Claws: Down - S
Upper Lunge Punch: Back - S
Sun Fist: T
Dragon Attack: Back - T
Uppercut: Down - T
Roundhouse Kick: X
Low Claw Strike: Down - X
Front Stomp Kick: O
Wheel Turning Kick: Up - O
Mid Claw Strike: Down - O
Neijin: SM
Throw: Toward - SM

Combos:
Tiger in Cave: O - Back - T
Yielding Fire: T - X
Ice Pop: S - S - T
Dragon Dance: S - Back - S
Silent Dragon: S - T - X
Dragon Plays with 7 Stars: S - T - O
Ice Maker: S - T - L1
X-Hit Claws: S - T - Back - T
Twist of the Tiger: S - T - Up - O

KORI BLADE MOVE LIST:
Overhead Swing: S
Ducking Moon: Down - S
Spinning Slash: Back - S
Overhead Smash: Up - S
Blade Lunge: T
Straight Stab: Down - T
Close Swipe: Back - T
Stomp Kick: X
Downwards Stab: Down - X
Back Kick: O
Sweep Kick: Back - O
Twisting Blade: Down - O
Impale: SM
Cut Up: O - O
Bitter Blade: S - Back - S

SPECIAL MOVES LIST:
Freeze: Down - Toward - S
Ice Shaker: Back - Down - T
Cold Shoulder: Back - Toward - O

FATALITY: Back - Toward - Toward - Down - X

SUB-ZERO

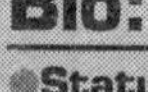

Bio:
- **Status:** Grandmaster
- **Alignment:** Good
- **Weight:** 150 lbs.
- **Height:** 6'2"
- **Styles:** Shotokan and Dragon
- **Weapon:** Kori Blade

KANO

Bio:
- **Status:** Mercenary
- **Alignment:** Evil
- **Weight:** 200 lbs.
- **Height:** 5'8"
- **Styles:** Xing Yi and Aikido
- **Weapon:** Butterfly

XING YI MOVE LIST:
Straight Punch: S
Power Fist: Back - S
Low Palm Strike: Down - S
Axe Strike: T
Eagle Strike: Down - T
Tiger Strike: Toward - T
Front Snap Kick: X
Low Elbow Strike: Down - X
Rising Knee: O
Hopping Back Kick: Back - O
Toe Strike: Dowm - O
Lifting High Kick: Up - O
Reversal: SM
Throw: Toward - SM
Combos:
Sure Fire: O - T
Casualty: O - X
Seek and Destroy: S - S - O - X
Dead Zone: S - S - Up - O
Backlash: S - S - Back - O
Minimum Damage: S - S - T
Maximum Damage: S - S - T - L1
Honor and Disgrace: T - Back - S
Three Powers: S - S - T - Back - S
Assault and Battery: S - S - O - T

AIKIDO MOVE LIST:
Heaven and Earth Throw: S
Low Frontal Punch: Down - S
Breath-Power Throw: T
Low Toe Kick: Down - T
Side Kick: X
Crescent Kick: Back - X
Low Side Kick: Down - X
Frontal Kick: O
Knee Kick: Back - O
Low Step Kick: Down - O
Nejin: SM
Throw: Toward - SM
Combos:
T-Hit Doom: O - Back - X
Underdog: O - O - X
Total Karnage: O - O - Back - X
Destroyer: O - X - L1 - Back - T
Killing Time: O - O - X - L1 - Back - T

BUTTERFLY SWORD MOVE LIST:
Jut Do: S
Piercing Low Strike: Down - S
Downward Circling Sword: Back - S
Twisting Sword: T
Rising Strike: Down - T
Upward Circling Sword: Back - T
Biu Do: X
Push Strike: Toward - X
Cutting Sword: Down - X
Pek Do: O
Rising Chop: Down - O
Combos:
Cutthroat: S - Toward - X
Ear to Ear: Back - S - Back - T
Lost Dragon: O - Toward - X

SPECIAL MOVES LIST:
Cannonball: Back - Toward - S
Eye Laser: Toward - Toward - T

FATALITY: Toward - Up - Up - Down - S

Bio:
- **Status:** Shaolin Monk
- **Alignment:** Good
- **Weight:** 575 lbs.
- **Height:** 5'9"
- **Styles:** Shaolin Fist and Mantis
- **Weapon:** Broadsword

KUNG LAO

PRAYING MANTIS MOVE LIST:
Drilling Punch: S
Low Thrusting Palm: Down - S
Power Forcing Fist: T
Double Mantis Strike: Back - T
Sweeping Punch: Down - T
Leg Sprouting Kick: X
Ward Off Punch: Down - X
Toppling Kick: Back - X
Chest Piercing Kick: O
Seven Star Hit: Down - O
Leg Squatting Kick: Back - O
Single Leg Soaring Kick: Up - O
Taunt: SM
Throw: Toward - SM
Combos:
Lotus Petals: X - X
S8 Elders: S - S - S
Natural Death: S - S - T - O
Cave Mantis: S - S - X - X
Five Blessings: S - S - T - Back - T
Deadly Insect: S - S - S L1 - O - X
White Lotus: S - S - S - L1 - T - O - X
Peaceful Life: S - S - S - L1 - O - O - X
Teachers Pet: S - S - S L1 - O - O - L1
Fallen Hero: S - S - S - L1 - O - O - Toward - T

SHAOLIN FIST MOVE LIST:
Buddha Fist: S
Low Axe Palm: Down - S
Attack the Heart: Back - S
Curved Hook Punch: T
Palm Heel Strike: Down - T
Backfist Strike: Back - T
Fore Knuckle Fist: Toward - T
Roundhouse Strike: X
Low Back Fist: Down - X
Front Kick: O
Low Knuckle Punch: Down - O
Sweeping Blade Kick: Back - O
Neijin: SM
Throw: Toward - SM
Combos:
Double Kicks: O - X
Shaolin Faith: O - Toward - T
Shout of Spirit: S - O - X
Rushing Buddha: T - O - X
Enlightenment: S - O - O - X
Shaolin Beat Down: S - T - O - X
Pins and Needles: S - O - O - L1
Hurricane: S - O - O - Toward - T

BROADSWORD MOVE LIST:
Crosscutting Slash: S
Twisting Body Strike: Toward - S
Piercing Low Lunge: Down - S
Crushing Side Slash: T
Overhead Strike: Down - T
Gut Ripping Stab: X
Rising Slash: Back - X
Low Stab: Down - X
Half Moon Slash: O
Full Moon Strike: Toward - O
Spinning Low Slash: Down - O
Combos:
Sharpen the Mind: T - S
Clouds Over Head: T - T
Tiger Leaps Suddenly: T - Toward - S
Onslaught: O - Down - O
Rise and Shine: O - Toward - S
Dao Strikes: T - O - Down - O
Phoenix Tail: T - O - Toward - S

SPECIAL MOVES LIST:
Hat Throw: Back - Toward - S
Whirlwind Kicks: Down - Back - O

FATALITY: Down - Up - Back - X

NITARA

Bio:

- **Status:** Vampire
- **Alignment:** Neutral
- **Weight:** Unknown
- **Height:** Unknown
- **Styles:** Leopard and Fu Jow Pai
- **Weapon:** Kama

LEOPARD MOVE LIST:

Paw Strike: S
Dual Claw Push: Up - S
Lifting Strike: Down - S
Front Rising Paw: Back - S
Swtiching Paw: T
Soaring Paw: Back - T
Low Jab: Down - T
Spin Kick: X
Step Kick: Down - X
Front Kick: O
Low Kick: Down - O
Wing Flap: SM
Throw: Toward - SM

Combos:

Leopard at Dawn: S - S - Up - S
Leopard at Rest: S - S - Back - S
Snow Leopard: S - S - S - T - O
Golden Leopard: S - S - S - L1 - S - T
Tree Leopard: S - S - S - T - Up - S
Dry Blood: S - S - S - L1 - S - S - X - L1
Blood Thristy: S - S - S - L1 - S - S - X - X

FU JOW PAI MOVE LIST:

Straight Claw: S
Knee Strike: Back - S
Rising Claw: Down - S
Upward Paw: T
Tiger Strike: Back - T
Tiger Scratch: Down - T
Back Kick: X
Spinning Low Kick: Down - X
Roundhouse: O
Lifting Kick: Up - O
Shin Kick: Back - O
Low Toe Kick: Down - O
Nejin: SM
Throw: Toward - SM

Combos:

Bloodshed: X - X
Vampire Bash: S - S - S
Wandering Claws: S - S - T
Black Tiger: S - S - S - X - X
Bloodshot: S - S - S - X - L1

KAMA MOVE LIST:

Dual Overhead Strike: S
Scissor Swipe: Toward - S
Low Rising Swing: Down - S
Rising Swing: T
Upward Swing: Down - T
Low Cross Stike: X
Low Sweeping Slice: Down - X
Overhead Strike: Up - X
Hook Sweep Knockdown: O
Backhand Swipe: Down - O
Charging Overhead: Back - O
Sidestep Swing: SM

Combos:

Bloodbath: S - O
Treacherous Edge: X - O
Kama Fury: Back - O - Back - O
Crucified: Back - O - Back - T
Bloodlust: S - X - O

SPECIAL MOVES LIST:

Unicorn Kick: Back - Down - O
Blood Spit: Toward - Back - T

FATALITY: Up - Up - Toward - S

DRAHMIN

Bio:

- **Status:** Oni Demon
- **Alignment:** Evil
- **Weight:** Unknown
- **Height:** Unknown
- **Styles:** Netherealm and Oni
- **Weapon:** Iron Club

NETHEREALM MOVE LIST:

Big Whack: S
Low Swipe: Down - S
Gut Smash: T
Low Strike: Down - T
Straight Kick: X
Back Kick: Back - X
Rising Blast: Down – X
Hooking Kick: O
Low Kick: Down - O
Taunt: SM
Throw: Toward - SM

ONI MOVE LIST:

Iron Lunge: S
Low Swipe: Down - S
Smashing Iron: Back - S
Crushing Chop: T
Low Strike: Down - T
Frontal Kick: X
Sweep: Back - X
Rising Blast: Down - X
Side Kick: O
Low Kick: Down - O
Shove: SM
Throw: Toward - SM

IRON CLUB MOVE LIST:

Head Smash: S
Leaping Smash: Up - S
Mid Swipe: Down - S
Uppercut: T
Doom Chop: Back - T
Low Strike: Down - T
Iron Strike: X
Iron Sweep: Back - X
Rising Blast: Down - X
Neck Jab: O
Power Swipe: Back - O
Low Kick: Down - O
Nejin: SM
Throw: Toward - SM

SPECIAL MOVES LIST:

Ball-O-Flies: Back - Toward - T
Propeller Clock: Toward - Toward – T
Super Uppercut: Down - Back - S
Ground Smash: Back - Down - O

FATALITY: Back - Toward - Toward - Down - X

HSU HAO

SHUAI CHIAO
MOVE LIST:
Single Hand Strike: S
Lunging Palm: Back - S
Low Wing Strike: Down - S
Uppercut: T
Shoulder Lunge: Toward - T
Crouching Chop: Down - T
Front Snap Kick: X
Crouching Sweep: Down - X
Rising Knee: O
Sweep: Back - O
Low Kick: Down - O
Backflip: SM
Throw: Toward - SM
Combos:
Bottle Opener: T - T
Bone Crusher: S - S - X
Asylum: S - S - Back - S
Chaos: S - S - T - T
Watch This: S - S - T - L1 - Back - T - L1 - Back - T

WRESTLING MOVE LIST:
Back Breaker: S
Shoulder Toss: Back - S
Rising Neck Strike: Down - S
Strong Hook Punch: T
Spinning Backfist: Back - T
Low Jab: Down - T
Straight Kick: X
Low Kick: Down - X
Front Kick: O
Low Shin Kick: Down - O
Reversal: SM
Throw: Toward - SM
Combos:
Insanity: Back - T - Back - T

SUN MOON MOVE LIST:
Quick Chop: S
Piercing Low Strike: Down - S
Downward Circling Strike: Back - S
Twisting Sword: T
Rising Strike: Down - T
Upward Circling Sword: Back - T
Gut Strike: X
Push Strike: Toward - X
Cutting Sword: Down - X
Edge Stab: O
Rising Chop: Down - O
Piercing Strike: SM

Combos:
The Kahn: S - Toward - X
Lost Dragon: O - Toward - X
Settling Sun: Back - S - Back - T

SPECIAL MOVES LIST:
Cyrus Stomp: Back - Toward - X
Kahn Klap: Back - Down - S

FATALITY: Toward - Back - Down - Down - T

Bio:
- **Status:** Red Dragon
- **Alignment:** Evil
- **Weight:** 220 lbs.
- **Height:** 6'2"
- **Styles:** Shuai Chiao and Wrestling
- **Weapon:** Sun-Moon

FROST

Bio:

- **Status:** Lin Kuei
- **Alignment:** Unknown
- **Weight:** 520 lbs.
- **Height:** 5'8"
- **Styles:** Tong Bei and Yuan Yang
- **Weapon:** Daggers

TONG BEI MOVE LIST:
Cold Strike: S
Falling Strike: Down - S
Corkscrew Strike: Back - S
Ice Crusher: Up - S
Slapping Palm: T
Low Rising Strike: Down - T
Icy Maul: Back - T
Northern Lights: Up - T
Cutting Guy Kick: X
Low Roundhouse: Back - X
Power Kick: Up - X
Low Poke: Down - X
Frosty Kick: O
Winter Winds: Up - O
Thrusting Low Kick: Back - O
Frozen Elbow: Down - O
Back Flip: SM
Throw: Toward - SM
Combos:
Shiver: S - T
Spring and Autumn: X - X
Chills: S - S - Back - T
Harmony: T - T - Up - T
Crazy Monkey: S - S - T - Up - O
Tong Bei Fury: S - S - T - T - Up - T
Freezer Burn: S - S - T - T - L1 - O - X
Blizzard: S - S - T - T - L1 - O - S - T
Iceberg: S - S - T - T - L1 - O - Up - X

Icefall: S - S - T - T - L1 - O - Toward - S
Snowball: S - S - T - T - L1 - O - S - S - Up - X
Frostbitten: S - S - T - T - L1 - O - S - S - L1 - S - S - S

YUAN YANG MOVE LIST:
Open Hand Strike: S
Strong Fist: Toward - S
Upward Strike: Down - S
Dual Duck Strike: T
Low Winged Strike: Down - T
Thrusting Roundhouse: X
Grounded Duck: Down - X
Lifting Head Duck: Up - X
Duck Leg Strike: O
Tripping Strike: Back - O
Sweep Kick: Down - O
Neijin: SM
Throw: Toward - SM
Combos:
Mandarin Duck Fists: S - T
Deadly Decoy: O - O - X
Ice Cold: O - O - S - T
Mandarin Duck Legs: O - O - Up - X
Waterfall: O - O - Toward - S
Deceptive Step: S - S - Up - X
Ugly Duckling: O - O - S - S - Up - X
Frigid Frenzy: S - S - L1 - S - S - S
Snowflake: O - O - S - S - L1 - S - S - S

DAGGER MOVE LIST:
Gut Stab: S
Stamping Blade: Up - S
Low Stagger: Back - S
Low Strike: Down - S
Dual Lunge: T
Lifting Dagger: Back - T
Low Stab: Down - T
Side Kick: X
Low Chop: Down - X
Pop Kick: O
Low Moon Strike: Down - O
Impale: SM
Combos:
Frozen Storm: S - S - S - S
Cold Feet: X - X - X

SPECIAL MOVES LIST:
Slide: Down - Toward - O
Ground Ice: Down - Back - X

FATATLITY: Toward - Back - Up - Down - S

MUAY THAI MOVE LIST:
Swing Punch: S
Spinning Strike: Back - S
Cutting Up Elbow: Down - S
Straight Punch: T
Hooking Punch: Back - T
Low Swing Punch: Down - T
Farewell Knee: X
Roundhouse: Up - X
Lower Knee: Down - X
Forward Foot Push: O
Pecking Kick: Down - O
Taunt: SM
Throw: Toward - SM
Combos:
Get Some Sucka: Back - S - T
What You Get: T - T - O
Rush N Hook: T - T - S
Boot Kamp: X - X - O
Im Gonna Get Ya: T - T - Up - X
Jax Special: T - T - Back - S - T
Ballistic Wind: T - T - X - X - O
In Your Face: T - T - L1 - O - X
Insertion: T - T - L1 - O - Back - T
Damage Control: T - T - L1 - O - L1 - O

JUDO MOVE LIST:
Suplex: S
Thrusting Palms: Back - S
Rising Double Fist: Down - S
Leg Trip Throw: T
Standing Uppercut: Back - T
Gut Punch: Down - T
Back Kick: X
Backward Spin Kick: Back - X
Low Sweep: Down - X
Side Snap Kick: O
Wheel Kick: Back - O
Low Kick: Down - O
Reversal: SM
Throw: Toward - SM
Combos:
Groundwork: O - O - X
Metal Fury: O - O - Back - T
No-Mans Land: O - O - L1 - O

TONFA MOVE LIST:
Spear Hand: S
Low Double Strike: Down - S
Double Strike: Toward - S
Downward Strike: T
Scissor Sweep: Down - T
Scissor Strike: X
Uppercut Strike: Down - X
Dashing Strike: Toward - X
Roundhouse Elbow Strike: O
Low Back Hand: Down - O
Tonfa Sweep: Back - O
Sidestep Swing: SM
Kombo Chain:
Stand-Down: O - O

SPECIAL MOVES LIST:
Ground Pound: Toward - Toward - Down - X

Bio:
- **Status:** Special Forces
- **Alignment:** Good
- **Weight:** 350 lbs.
- **Height:** 6'8"
- **Styles:** Muay Thai and Judo
- **Weapon:** Tonfa

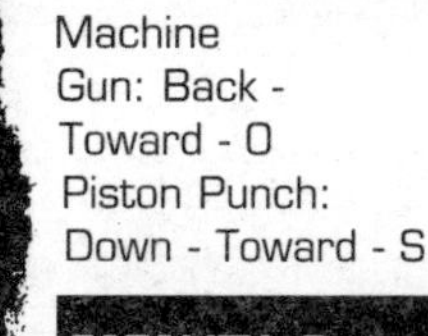

Machine Gun: Back - Toward - O
Piston Punch: Down - Toward - S

FATALITY: Down - Toward - Toward - Down - T

KITANA

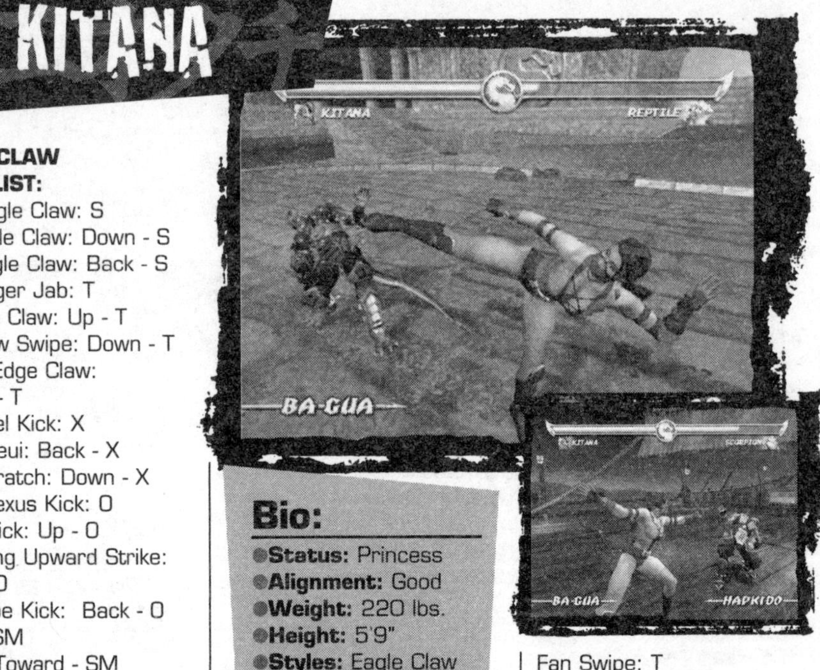

Bio:

- **Status:** Princess
- **Alignment:** Good
- **Weight:** 220 lbs.
- **Height:** 5'9"
- **Styles:** Eagle Claw and Ba Gua
- **Weapon:** Steel Fans

EAGLE CLAW MOVE LIST:

Mide Eagle Claw: S
Low Eagle Claw: Down - S
High Eagle Claw: Back - S
Side Finger Jab: T
Sidestep Claw: Up - T
Low Claw Swipe: Down - T
Double Edge Claw: Toward - T
Side Heel Kick: X
Chyun Teui: Back - X
Claw Scratch: Down - X
Solar Plexus Kick: O
Lifting Kick: Up - O
Crouching Upward Strike: Down - O
Front Toe Kick: Back - O
Shove: SM
Throw: Toward - SM

Combos:

Shooting Star: O - X
Walking Fists: T - S
Grounded: O - Back - O
Lipstick: O - Back - S
Pucker Up: O - Up - O
Broken Talon: S - O - X
Tiny Bubbles: O - O - X
Splitting Bone: O - X - Back - X
Up and Away: S - O - Up - O
Down Boy: S - O - Back - O
Faceplant: S - O - Back - S
Back Off: O - O - Toward - T
Ill Eagle: S - O - O - Toward - T
Lost Love: O - O - L1 - X - Toward - X - L1
Baguash: S - O - O - L1 - X - Toward - X - L1

BA GUA MOVE LIST:

Ox Tongue Palm Strike: S
Dragon Palm Strike: Down - S
Snake's Tail: Back - S
Hooking Strike: T
Spear Hand Thrust: Back - T
Low Snapping Palm: Down - T
Spinning Force Palm: X
Hammer Palm Strike: Toward - X
Low Lifting Palm: Down - X
Stepping Side Kick: O
Swinging Sweep: Back - O
Horse Kick: Up - O
Low Upward Palm: Down - O
Backflip: SM
Throw: Toward - SM

Combos:

Art of Overkill: S - X - Toward - X
Four Dragons: S - X - Toward - X - L1

STEEL FAN MOVE LIST:

Hooking Fan: S
Chest Strike: Toward - S
Low Swipe: Down - S
Fan Swipe: T
Sky Strike: Back - T
Fan Smash: Toward - T
Low Stab: Down - T
Piercing Kick: X
Downward Strike: Down - X
Neck Thrust: O
Low Poke: Back - O
Upward Strike: Down - O
Impale: Back - SM
Sidestep Swing: SM

Combos:

Princess Blast: X - X
Kirin Smash: X - Toward - S
Bootlicker: T - T - T
Forgotten: S - S - Back - T
Royal Pain: T - T - Toward - S
Forever: T - T - T - Toward - T
Edenian Rush: T - T - T - Back - O

SPECIAL MOVES LIST:

Pretty Kick: Up - X
Fan Lift: Back - Toward - S

FATALITY: Down - Up - Toward - Toward - T

RAIDEN

Bio:

- **Status:** Thunder God
- **Alignment:** Good
- **Weight:** 500 lbs.
- **Height:** 7'0"
- **Styles:** Nan Chuan and Jujutsu
- **Weapon:** Staff

NAN CHUAN MOVE LIST:
Lighting Jab: S
Low Double Palm Strike: Down - S
Uppercut: Back - S
Backfist Chop: T
Low Elbow Strike: Down - T
Thunder Chop: Back - T
Dual Thunder Palms: Toward - T
Stepping Snap Kick: X
Shin Strike: Down - X
Hook Leg Knockdown: Back - X
Hop Side Kick: O
Low Chin Strike: Down - O
Reversal: SM
Throw: Toward - SM
Combos:
Thunder Clap: T - X
Electric Strike: T - Back - S
The Middle Way: T - Back - T
Knowledge and Skill: S - S - X
Butterfly Palms: S - S - Back - T
Finishing Touch: S - S - T - X
Natural Way: S - S - T - Back - T
Wake The Dead: S - S - T - Back - S
Power Bolts: S - S - T - L1 - S - Back - S
Out of Order: S - S - T - L1 - S - X - O
Black Thunder: S - S - T - L1 - S - X - L1 - O - O
Sparky: S - S - T - L1 - S - X - L1 - O - Back - T

JUJUTSU MOVE LIST:
Open Hand Strike: S
Bearhand Chop: Back - S
Low Palm Strike: Down - S
Bent Wrist Strike: T
Thunder God Palm: Toward - T
Diagonal Fist: Down - T
Front Snap Kick: X
Sweep: Back - X
Back Sweep: Down - X
Front Thrusting Kick: O
Front Sweep: Down - O
Shove: SM
Throw: Toward - SM
Combos:
Heavenly Strikes: X - O
Essence of Strength: S - S - X - O
Thunder God Fists: S - S - Back - S
Fireworks: S - S - X - L1 - O - O
Chain Lightning: S - S - X - L1 - O - Back - T

STAFF MOVE LIST:
Overhead Strike: S
Reverse Side Strike: Back - S
Low One Handed Poke: Down - S
Upward Strike: T
Low Strike: Down - T
Leaping Strike: X
Sweeping Strike: Down - X
One Handed Poke: Back - X
Reverse Thrust: O
Staff Blast: Up - O
Sweeping Swing: Down - O
T-Hit Swing:SM
Combos:
Catching a Butterfly: O - O - O
Dragon Wild: O - O - Back - T

SPECIAL MOVES LIST:
Shocker: Toward - Toward - S
Lightning Dash: Toward - Toward - O
Lightning Bolt: Down - Back - S

FATALITY: Back - Toward - Toward - Toward - X

HUNG GAR MOVE LIST:
Scratching Claw: S
Low Paw Attack: Down - S
Double Claw Strike: Back - S
Chameleon Palm: T
Low Claw Strike: Down - T
Dual Claw Strike: X
Forward Strike: Down - X
Lizard Smash: Back - X
Low Snap Kick: O
Mid Roundhouse Kick: Down - O
Spinning Roundhouse Kick: Back - O
Hook Sweep Kick: Toward - O
Shove: SM
Throw: Toward - SM
Combos:
Lazy Lizard: S - T
Internal Strikes: X - T
Wise Tiger: S - X - T
Iron Thread: S - X - O - Back - S
Matriach: S - X - O - L1 - S - X
Evolution: S - X - O - L1 - S - S
Zaterrorize: S - X - O - L1 - S - Back - T - L1

CRAB MOVE LIST:
Upward Elbow Strike: S
Spinning Elbow Strike: Back - S
Low Punch: Down - S
Ridge Hand Swipe: T
Dual Uppercut: Back - T
Low Dual Uppercut: Down – T
Spinning Back Kick: X
Hooking Sweep: Back - X
Low Snap Punch: Down - X
Mid Hook Kick: O
Low Hook Kick: Down - O
Reversal: SM
Throw: Toward - SM
Combos:
Boiling Water: Back - S - X
Crab Crawls on Sand: S - S - X
Claws of Fury: S - S - S
Reptilian Rage: S - S - Back - T - L1

KIREHASHI MOVE LIST:
Downward Slash: S
Circular Swing: Back - S
The Cutter: Up - S
Low Lunge: Down - S
Side Slash: T
Spinning Slash: Back - T
Blade Chop: Down - T
Upward Slash: X
Low Swipe: Back - X
Low Poke: Down - X
Mid Lunge: O
Blade Smash: Back - O
Spinning Blade: Down - O
Impale: SM
Combos:
Dead End: T - T
Reptilian Slice: X - X
Shredder: Back - T - Back - T
Rip Torn: S - Back - T - Back - T

SPECIAL MOVES LIST:
Lizard Ball: Toward - Down - O
Acid Spit: Back - Toward - S

FATATLITY: Up - Up - Up - Toward - X

Bio:
- **Status:** Warrior
- **Alignment:** Evil
- **Weight:** 589 lbs.
- **Height:** 6'0"
- **Styles:** Hung Gar and Crab
- **Weapon:** Kirehashi

CYRAX

Bio:

- **Status:** Special Forces
- **Alignment:** Good
- **Weight:** 650 lbs.
- **Height:** 5'8"
- **Styles:** Ninjitsu and Sambo
- **Weapon:** Pulse Blade

NINJITSU MOVE LIST:

Sraight Kick: S
Ninja Strike: Back - S
Low Punch: Down - S
Strong Elbow: T
Double Fist Strike: Up - T
Low Palm Strike: Down - T
Spinning Back Kick: X
Shin Kick: Back - X
Low Kick: Down - X
Front Kick: O
Ducking Mid Kick: Down - O
Back Flip: SM
Throw: Toward - SM

Combos:

Ninja Strikes: S - S - S
Stealth Blast: S - S - T
Cyborg Strikes: S - S - Back - S
Yellow Doom: S - S - X
Full Gore: S - S - Up - T
Pain Killer: S - S - Back - S - L1

SAMBO MOVE LIST:

Quick Jab: S
Hammerfist Strike: Back - S
Low Hook Punch: Down - S
Shoulder Toss: T
Straight Chop: Up - T
Rising Fist: Down - T
Backward Elbow: Back - T
Roundhouse: X
Low Fist Strike: Down - X
Big Leg: O
Low Shin Kick: Down - O
Taunt: SM
Throw: Toward - SM

Combos:

1 Step Rush: S - S - S
Quicksand: S - S - O
Ketchup: S - S - Back - S
Mustard: S - S - Back - T
LK9T9: Back - T - Toward - T - L1
Oil Leak: Back - T - Toward - T - Up - T
LKODO: S - S - Back - T - Toward - T - L1
Self Destruct: S - S - Back - T - Toward - T - Up - T

PULSE BLADE MOVE LIST:

Cutting Blade: S
Sweeping Edge: Back - S
Stomping Blade: Up - S
Downward Blade: Down - S
Circling Swipe: T
Lifting Blade: Back - T
Low T-Hit Strike: Down - T
Back Kick: X
Sweep Kick: Back - X
Twisting Edge: Down - X
Knee Strike: O
Thrusting Sword: Down - O
Impale: SM

SPECIAL MOVES LIST:

Detonator: (Far) Back - Toward - S
Detonator: (Close) Toward - Back - S
Spinkicks: Down - Back - X
Slice and Dice: Back - Toward - O

FATALITY: Toward - Toward - Up - T

Konquest Of The Krypt

There are piles and piles of secrets, extras, hidden characters and bonuses to unlock in this game and they are all here so you don't waste your koins!

KEY:

Koffin Name - Category: Contents

Full List [AA-ZZ]

AA - Alternate Outfit: Quan Chi - 1556 Gold Koins

AB - Artwork: Kung Lao Sketch - 186 Gold Koins

AC - Character: Li Mei - 424 Platinum Koins

AD - Artwork: Moloch Sketches - 96 Sapphire Koins

AE - Extra: MK2 Cabinet Security Panels - 118 Onyx Koins

AF - Hint: RO: Rip Off!!! - 313 Platinum Koins

AG - Artwork: Deadly Alliance is Born - 258 Sapphire Koins

AH - Artwork: Shang Tsung Sketch - 66 Gold Koins

AI - Extra: Quan Chi's Tattoos - 277 Onyx Koins

AJ - Koins: 38 Gold Koins - 26 Jade Koins

AK - Artwork: Moloch Promo Render - 432 Gold Koins

AL - Arena: Shang Tsung's Palace - 287 Ruby Koins

AM - Artwork: Mavado Coat Concepts - 192 Platinum Koins

AN - Hint: PD: Pay Day!!! - 52 Gold Koins

AO - Koins: 57 Sapphire Koins - 105 Onyx Koins

AP - Extra: Quan Chi's Throne - 154 Onyx Koins

AQ - Artwork: Scorpion Concept Sketch - 226 Ruby Koins

AR - Alternate Outfit: Nitara - 2206 Jade Koins

AS - Artwork: Palace Exterior Sketch - 66 Jade Koins

AT - Artwork: Swamplands Sketch - 269 Ruby Koins

AU - Character: Shang Tsung - 463 Gold Koins

AV - Video: Senate of the Elder Gods Test - 497 Ruby Koins

AW - Koins: 88 Ruby Koins - 76 Gold Koins

AX - Extra: Quan Chi's Inner Sanctum - 337 Gold Koins

AY - Artwork: Concept Characters - 258 Platinum Koins

AZ - Artwork: Test Your Sight Concept - 442 Ruby Koins

BA - Artwork: Lin Kuei Temple Concept - 264 Onyx Koins

BB - Extra: Sub-Zero's Medallion - 326 Ruby Koins

BC - Artwork: Giant Drummer Detail - 452 Gold Koins

BD - Alternate Outfit: Kano - 1520 Sapphire Koins

BE - Artwork: Swamplands Sketch - 67 Gold Koins

BF - Koins: 120 Jade Koins - 263 Platinum Koins

BG - Artwork: Baphomet Sketch - 217 Sapphire Koins

BH - Extra: Ultimate MK3 Arcade Marquee - 116 Jade Koins

BI - Artwork: Sonya Concept Sletch - 167 Jade Koins

BJ - Extra: Ghost Ship - 178 Platinum Koins

BK - Artwork: Drum Arena Details - 136 Sapphire Koins

BL - Extra: Portal Sphere - 145 Jade Koins

BM - Artwork: Character Concepts - 207 Onyx Koins

BN - Extra: The Grid: Guest Stars - 720 Onyx Koins

BO - Extra: The Grid: Noob Saibot - 305 Platinum Koins

BP - Extra: The Grid: MK Ninjas - 426 Gold Koins

BQ - Alternate Outfit: Kitana - 1327 Gold Koins

BR - Hint: FK: Fly Killer - 451 Onyx Koins

BS - Artwork: Mavado Sketches - 253 Sapphire Koins

BT - Extra: Blood Energy Drink - 291 Sapphire Koins

BU - Extra: Reptile Skin Lotion - 336 Platinum Koins

BV - Extra: Backstage: MK4 Commercial - 371 Sapphire Koins

BW - Extra: Backstage: MK4 Commercial - 329 Onyx Koins

BX - Extra: Backstage: MK4 Commercial - 212 Platinum Koins

BY - Extra: MK Gold Logo - 183 Gold Koins

BZ - Extra: MK4: Sonya and Tanya - 381 Platinum Koins

CA - Artwork: Shang Tsung's Palace Sketch - 218 Onyx Koins

CB - Artwork: Octo Garden Sketch - 252 Sapphire Koins

CC - Extra: Book of Destiny - 376 Jade Koins

CD - Artwork: Shang Tsungs Soul Concept - 261 Jade Koins

CE - Extra: Great Dragon Egg - 174 Jade Koins

CF - Artwork: Female Character Concepts - 268 Onyx Koins

CG - Hint: JT: Johnny's Tapes - 75 Sapphire Koins

CH - Koins: 92 Sapphire Koins - 48 Jade Koins

CI - Artwork: Test Your Sight Concept - 271 Jade Koins

CJ - Artwork: Quan Chi Sketches - 272 Ruby Koins

CK - Arena: Wu Shi Academy - 556 Jade Koins

CL - Koins: 492 Onyx Koins - 332 Gold Koins

CM - Artwork: House of Pekara Concept - 244 Gold Koins

CN - Secret Character: Cyrax - 3003 Platinum Koins

CO - Extra: Kano's Cereal - 192 Ruby Koins

CP - Extra: Carlos Pesina - 172 Ruby Koins

CQ - Artwork: Senate of Elder Gods Concept - 272 Gold Koins

CR - Artwork: Raiden Sketch - 294 Platinum Koins

CS - Koins: 143 Ruby Koins - 89 Sapphire Koins

CT - Extra: Dragonfly Story - 588 Ruby Koins

CU - Artwork: Swamplands Sketch - 257 Sapphire Koins

CV - Koins: 71 Jade Koins - 121 Sapphire Koins

CW - Artwork: Academy Promo Render - 226 Ruby Koins

CX - Video: Scorpion Goes Back to Hell - 203 Gold Koins

CY - Artwork: Soul Cage Concept - 116 Ruby Koins

CZ - Artwork: Hsu Hao Concepts - 362 Onyx Koins

DA - Koins: 18 Sapphire Koins - 72 Ruby Koins

DB - Artwork: Soul Chamber Concept - 257 Sapphire Koins

DC - Extra: MK3: Kung Lao vs Jax - 838 Onyx Koins

DD - Extra: Lifeguard Sonya - 355 Gold Koins

DE - Artwork: Character Concepts - 126 Gold Koins

DF - Extra: Dan 'Toasty' Forden - 286 Platinum Koins

DG - Character: Sonya Blade - 57 Jade Koins

DH - Artwork: Shokan Warriors - 199 Gold Koins

DI - Extra: Quan Chi on the Sax - 254 Sapphire Koins

DJ - Koins: 98 Ruby Koins - 186 Platinum Koins

DK - Alternate Outfit: Johhny Cage - 1460 Ruby Koins

DL - Video: Scorpion Cloth Test - 230 Platinum Koins

DM - Arena: Acid Bath - 428 Onyx Koins

DN - Extra: 18 Jade Koins - 234 Sapphire Koins

DO - Koins: 221 Onyx Koins - 39 Gold Koins

DP - Extra: Mortal Kombat 2 Print Ad - 224 Jade Koins

DQ - Hint: SF: Smelly Feet - 656 Platinum Koins

DR - Artwork: Mavado Sketches - 273 Sapphire Koins

DS - Secret Arena: Nethership - 1472 Ruby Koins

DT - Artwork: Li Mei Sketch - 332 Ruby Koins

DU - Extra: MK3 Behind the Scenes - 368 Onyx Koins

DV - Empty - 257 Ruby Koins

DW - Video: Cave Arena Concept - 157 Ruby Koins

DX - Koins: 579 Ruby Koins - 292 Jade Koins

DY - Hint: SS: Sword Sale - 94 Gold Koins

DZ - Empty - 258 Onyx Koins

EA - Arena: The Lost Tomb - 258 Sapphire Koins

EB - Extra: Ed Boon - 237 Ruby Koins

EC - Artwork: Swamplands Sketch - 248 Sapphire Koins

ED - Koins: 949 Platinum Koins - 633 Platinum Koins

EE - Extra: Mythologies Home Verion - 1200 Platinum Koins

EF - Extra: Quality Assurance: Chicago - 267 Gold Koins

EG - Extra: MK3 Arcade Marquee - 74 Platinum Koins

EH - Artwork: Reptile Sketch - 253 Onyx Koins

EI - Extra: Action Figures - 512 Sapphire Koins

EJ - Extra: Action Figures - 547 Jade Koins

EK - Extra: Action Figures - 424 Ruby Koins

EL - Extra: Action Figures - 434 Platinum Koins

EM - Extra: Action Figures - 405 Gold Koins

EN - Extra: Action Figures - 246 Onyx Koins

EO - Extra: Action Figures - 289 Sapphire Koins

EP - Extra: Action Figures - 166 Jade Koins

EQ - Extra: Action Figure Vehicles - 256 Sapphire Koins

ER - Character: Bo' Rai Cho - 527 Platinum Koins

ES - Extra: Mortal Kombat 3 Ultimate Print Ad - 167 Platinum Koins

ET - Artwork: Quan Chi's Face Texture - 86 Onyx Koins

EU - Artwork: Dairou Drawings - 262 Ruby Koins

EV - Arena: Drum Arena - 356 Ruby Koins

EW - Extra: Quan Chi's Chest Armor - 286 Platinum Koins

EX - Hint: ST: Sarna Test - 243 Onyx Koins

EY - Artwork: Cyrax Sketch - 254 Platinum

EZ - Artwork: Blood Stone Mine Concept - 412 Platinum

FA - Artwork: Cyrax Test Render - 263 Gold Koins

FB - Extra: A Long Time Ago (Smash TV) - 248 Ruby Koins

FC - Extra: A Softer Side to Cyrax - 310 Sapphire Koins

FD - Extra: Portal Story - 156 Onyx Koins

FE - Artwork: Li Mei Sketch - 242 Gold Koins

FF - Extra: MK1: Sub-Zero vs. Scorpion - 1199 Gold Koins

FG - Artwork: Dragonfly Concept Render - 291 Gold Koins

FH - Artwork: House of Pekara Concept - 215 Ruby Koins

FI - Extra: Deadly Alliance Koins - 262 Platinum Koins

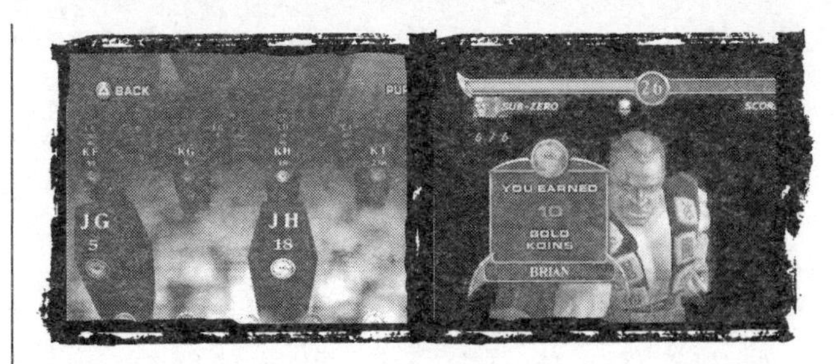

FJ - Extra: MK3 Arcade Cabinet - 179 Ruby Koins

FK - Extra: Bug Blaster - 520 Platinum

FL - Video: Early MKDA Promo - 264 Sapphire Koins

FM - Artwork: Palace Exterior Sketch - 76 Sapphire Koins

FN - Koins: 1800 Jade Koins - 93 Jade Koins

FO - Extra: MK2 Characters - 76 Ruby Koins

FP - Artwork: Palace Exterior Sketch - 46 Gold Koins

FQ - Extra: MK T-shirts - 283 Platinum

FR - Extra: MK Youth Clothing - 401 Gold Koins

FS - Extra: MK Sweatshirts - 389 Onyx Koins

FT - Extra: MK T-shirts - 126 Sapphire Koins

FU - Empty - 20 Onyx Koins

FV - Koins: 243 Platinum Koins - 83 Platinum Koins

FW - Hint: Unleash Hell (UH) - 666 Ruby Koins

FX - Extra: Comic Book Art, 1 of 41 - 492 Sapphire Koins

FY - Extra: Comic Book Art, 2 of 41 - 27 Ruby Koins

FZ - Extra: Comic Book Art, 3 of 41 - 136 Onyx Koins

GA - Extra: Comic Book Art, 4 of 41 - 572 Gold Koins

GB - Extra: Comic Book Art, 5 of 41 - 458 Jade Koins

GC - Extra: Comic Book Art, 6 of 41 - 412 Gold Koins

GD - Extra: Comic Book Art, 7 of 41 - 74 Sapphire Koins

GE - Extra: Comic Book Art, 8 of 41 - 277 Ruby Koins

GF - Extra: Comic Book Art, 9 of 41 - 124 Platinum Koins

GG - Extra: Comic Book Art, 10 of 41 - 63 Jade Koins

GH - Extra: Comic Book Art, 11 of 41 - 418 Platinum Koins

GI - Extra: Comic Book Art, 12 of 41 - 100 Sapphire Koins

GJ - Extra: Comic Book Art, 13 of 41 - 326 Platinum Koins

GK - Extra: Comic Book Art, 14 of 41 - 379 Platinum Koins

GL - Extra: Comic Book Art, 15 of 41 - 128 Ruby Koins

GM - Extra: Comic Book Art, 16 of 41 - 555 Onyx Koins

GN - Extra: Comic Book Art, 17 of 41 - 91 Gold Koins

GO - Extra: Comic Book Art, 18 of 41 - 422 Sapphire Koins

GP - Extra: Comic Book Art, 19 of 41 - 58 Jade Koins

GQ - Extra: Comic Book Art, 20 of 41 - 532 Jade Koins

GR - Extra: Comic Book Art, 21 of 41 - 599 Onyx Koins

GS - Extra: Comic Book Art, 22 of 41 - 185 Gold Koins

GT - Extra: Comic Book Art, 23 of 41 - 307 Ruby Koins

GU - Extra: Comic Book Art, 24 of 41 - 134 Sapphire Koins

GV - Extra: Comic Book Art, 25 of 41 - 507 Platinum Koins

GW - Extra: Comic Book Art, 26 of 41 - 264 Ruby Koins

GX - Extra: Comic Book Art, 27 of 41 - 88 Onyx Koins

GY - Extra: Comic Book Art, 28 of 41 - 351 Platinum Koins

GZ - Extra: Comic Book Art, 29 of 41 - 575 Ruby Koins

HA - Extra: Comic Book Art, 30 of 41 - 62 Gold Koins

HB - Extra: Comic Book Art, 31 of 41 - 626 Ruby Koins

HC - Extra: Comic Book Art, 32 of 41 - 215 Onyx Koins

HD - Extra: Comic Book Art, 33 of 41 - 176 Sapphire Koins

HE - Extra: Comic Book Art, 34 of 41 - 478 Jade Koins

HF - Extra: Comic Book Art, 35 of 41 - 203 Onyx Koins

HG - Extra: Comic Book Art, 36 of 41 - 555 Gold Koins

HH - Extra: Comic Book Art, 37 of 41 - 222 Platinum Koins

HI - Extra: Comic Book Art, 38 of 41 - 225 Jade Koins

HJ - Extra: Comic Book Art, 39 of 41 - 637 Onyx Koins

HK - Extra: Comic Book Art, 40 of 41 - 138 Gold Koins

HL - Extra: Comic Book Art, 41 of 41 - 145 Sapphire Koins

HM - Artwork: Bank Interior Sketch - 217 Onyx Koins

HN - Artwork: Lung Hai Temple Sketch - 382 Jade Koins

HO - Artwork: Scorpion Preliminary Model - 402 Jade Koins

HP - Secret Arena: House of Pekara - 2093 Onyx Koins

HQ - Extra: Sektor's Helmet - 192 Onyx Koins

HR - Artwork: Konquest Mode Concepts - 187 Jade Koins

HS - Extra: Herman Sanchez - 272 Jade Koins

HT - Video: Ice Palace Test - 462 Jade Koins

HU - Extra: MK Pinball - 435 Ruby Koins

HV - Extra: MK Gold Print Ad - 306 Jade Koins

HW - Artwork: Fire Well Concept - 56 Ruby Koins

HX - Koins: 38 Jade Koins - 238 Onyx Koins

HY - Extra: Kenshi's Sword - 408 Sapphire Koins

HZ - Extra: Shang Tsung's Soulnado - 526 Onyx Koins

IA - Extra: MK4 Logo - 37 Ruby Koins

IB - Artwork: Forest Sketch - 275 Platinum Koins

IC - Extra: MK Rock 'Em Sock 'Em - 326 Platinum Koins

ID - Extra: Sub-Zero's Coffee Mug - 340 Jade Koins

IE - Extra: 32 Pack of Adult Diapers - 653 Sapphire Koins

IF - Artwork: River Front Concept - 195 Ruby Koins

IG - Artwork: Lava Shrine Exterior Concept - 208 Gold Koins

IH - Hint: IV: Icy Vixen - 567 Jade Koins

II - Secret Arena: Lava Shrine - 1843 Gold Koins

IJ - Extra: Quan Chi's Amulet - 314 Ruby Koins

IK - Artwork: Lava Shrine Priests - 503 Platinum Koins

IL - Hint: DK: Dressed to Kill - 207 Gold Koins

IM - Artwork: Church Concept - 227 Gold Koins

IN - Koins: 57 Gold Koins - 37 Sapphire Koins

IO - Hint: PH: Phat! - 244 Onyx Koins

IP - Extra: Halloween Masks - 257 Onyx Koins

IQ - Artwork: Fortress Exterior Sketches - 257 Gold Koins

IR - Koins: 91 Sapphire Koins - 55 Jade Koins

IS - Extra: Sub-Zero's Blade - 244 Ruby Koins

IT - Artwork: Character Concepts - 269 Ruby Koins

IU - Artwork: Dairou Sketch - 342 Jade Koins

IV - Secret Character: Frost - 208 Ruby Koins

IW - Hint: CN: Cyber Ninja - 198 Platinum Koins

IX - Extra: MKDA Merchandise - 265 Sapphire Koins

IY - Video: MK Gold Endings - 281 Onyx Koins

IZ - Artwork: Jax Renderings - 201 Onyx Koins

JA - Stage: Kuatan Palace - 105 Gold Koins

JB - Extra: Programmers - 392 Sapphire Koins

JC - Artwork: Frost Sketches - 287 Gold Koins

JD - Artwork: Swamplands Test Render - 305 Jade Koins

JE - Koins: 59 Ruby Koins - 82 Platinum Koins

JF - Artwork: Drum Arena Sketch - 332 Ruby Koins

JN - Extra: John Nocher - 252 Jade Koins

JO - Extra: MK2 Arcade Board - 161 Onyx Koins

JP - Extra: John Podlasek - 169 Gold Koins

JQ - Artwork: Kitana Sketches - 237 Ruby Koins

JR - Alternate Outfit: Raiden - 1685 Ruby Koins

JS - Artwork: Dragonfly Render - 294 Ruby Koins

JT - Extra: Johnny Cage Videos - 259 Platinum Koins

JG - Extra: Jon Greenberg - 272 Jade Koins

JH - Artwork: Hsu Hao Sketches - 271 Gold Koins

JI - Extra: MK4 Print Ad - 266 Jade Koins

JJ - Koins: 772 Sapphire Koins - 402 Gold Koins

JK - Artwork: Li Mei Sketch - 291 Jade Koins

JL - Koins: 92 Gold Koins - 168 Onyx Koins

JM - Artwork: Shang Tsung Drawings - 218 Sapphire Koins

JU - Artwork: Palace Interior Sketch - 266 Platinum Koins

JV - Extra: John Vogel - 334 Ruby Koins

JW - Extra: Kano's Reminder - 164 Sapphire Koins

JX - Artwork: Raiden Test Render - 167 Gold Koins

JY - Extra: MK4 Home Version - 183 Sapphire Koins

JZ - Empty - 25 Jade Koins

KA - Artwork: Swamplands Sketch - 412 Onyx Koins

KB - Artwork: Elder God Hall Sketch - 247 Jade Koins

KC - Video: Dragonfly Test - 292 Gold Koins

KD - Extra: Artists - 342 Jade Koins

KE - Artwork: Nitara Sketch - 402 Gold Koins

KF - Character: Mavado - 128 Jade Koins

KG - Extra: Edenia Golf Outfitters - 608 Jade Koins

KH - Extra: Can of Squid - 382 Platinum Koins

KI - Secret Character: Kitana - 2931 Sapphire Koins

KJ - Extra: MK Baseball Caps - 248 Platinum Koins

KK - Extra: MK4 Characters - 694 Sapphire Koins

KL - Artwork: Cyrax Sketches - 202 Platinum Koins

KM - Extra: MK Strategy Guides - 350 Jade Koins

KN - Koins: 15 Gold Koins - 7 Sapphire Koins

KO - Artwork: Konquest Mode Concepts - 197 Sapphire Koins

KP - Hint: MW: Mongol Warrior - 276 Ruby Koins

KQ - Extra: Alexander Barrentine - 282 Onyx Koins

KR - Secret Arena: Palace Grounds - 4222 Sapphire Koins

KS - Koins: 216 Jade Koins - 503 Platinum Koins

KT - Artwork: Moloch Test Render - 275 Onyx Koins

KU - Koins: 322 Platinum Koins - 219 Jade Koins

KV - Artwork: Arena Concepts - 256 Sapphire Koins

KW - Empty - 257 Sapphire Koins

KX - Alternate Outfit: Li Mei - 1406 Sapphire Koins

KY - Extra: MK1: Cage vs. Kano - 843 Platinum Koins

KZ - Artwork: Character Concepts - 263 Jade Koins

LA - Artwork: Blood Particle Details - 56 Ruby Koins

LB - Artwork: Game Play Wall Trick Ideas - 258 Jade Koins

LC - Artwork: Game Play Kicks and Dodges - 462 Sapphire Koins

LD - Artwork: Game Play Fatalities - 302 Onyx Koins

LE - Artwork: Game Play Face Strikes - 312 Platinum Koins

LF - Artwork: Game Play Special Moves - 305 Gold Koins

LG - Artwork: Game Play Throws - 195 Ruby Koins

LH - Artwork: Game Play Fatalities - 165 Jade Koins

LI - Artwork: Game Play Throws - 135 Sapphire Koins

LJ - Extra: Nitara's Crystal - 134 Gold Koins

LK - Video: Wu Shi Academy Test - 268 Onyx Koins

LL - Secret Character: Reptile - 3822 Gold Koins

LM - Extra: Luis Mangubat - 165 Onyx Koins

LN - Extra: Chrome Bling - 306 Onyx Koins

LO - Extra: Deadly Alliance Website - 329 Onyx Koins

LP - Artwork: Sub-Zero Sketch - 442 Ruby Koins

LQ - Extra: MK1 Arcade Goro - 477 Sapphire Koins

LR - Extra: MKDA Box Art Concepts - 176 Gold Koins

LS - Extra: MKDA Box Art Concepts - 157 Sapphire Koins

LT - Extra: MKDA Logo Concepts - 105 Onyx Koins

LU - Extra: MKDA Box Art Concepts - 170 Jade Koins

LV - Extra: MKDA Box Art Concepts - 140 Ruby Koins

LW - Extra: Midway Creative Media - 332 Gold Koins

LX - Empty - 147 Platinum Koins

LY - Extra: Mk4: Scorpion vs. Raiden - 160 Sapphire Koins

LZ - Hint: FL: First Look - 511 Onyx Koins

MA - Character: Johnny Cage - 471 Ruby Koins

MB - Extra: Mike Boon - 188 Gold Koins

MC - Artwork: Wu Shi Academy Sketches - 262 Platinum Koins

MD - Extra: Tools and Technology - 80 Onyx Koins

ME - Extra: MKDA Print Ad - 237 Jade Koins

MF - Koins: 102 Onyx Koins - 58 Jade Koins

MG - Extra: MK4 Road Tour - 134 Platinum Koins

MH - Extra: MK4 Road Tour - 83 Gold Koins

MI - Extra: MK4 Arcade Debut - 96 Gold Koins

MJ - Empty - 268 Onyx Koins

MK - Extra: MK1 Arcade - 188 Platinum Koins

ML - Alternate Outfit: Shang Tsung - 1170 Gold Koins

MM - Artwork: Bridge Arena Concept - 215 Ruby Koins

MN - Arena: Portal - 176 Onyx Koins

MO - Artwork: Drahmin Sketches - 177 Jade Koins

MP - Extra: MK Basketball Concept - 314 Gold Koins

MQ - Koins: 412 Jade Koins - 278 Gold Koins

MR - Arena: Lung Hai Temple - 412 Ruby Koins

MS - Artwork: Outworld Concept Sketch - 253 Platinum Koins

MT - Extra: Mike Taran - 227 Gold Koins

MU - Artwork: Sarna Ruins Concept - 218 Sapphire Koins

MV - Artwork: Hsu Hao Sketches - 372 Platinum Koins

MW - Secret Character: Hsu Hao - 3317 Jade Koins

MX - Artwork: Palace Exterior Sketch - 302 Platinum

MY - Artwork: Moloch's Ball Sketches - 167 Jade Koins

MZ - Extra: Assassin for Hire - 383 Sapphire Koins

NA - Artwork: Sonya Sketch - 177 Ruby Koins

NB - Artwork: House of Pekara Render - 287 Jade Koins

NC - Extra: Nigel Casey - 275 Platinum Koins

ND - Empty - 212 Sapphire Koins

NE - Artwork: Jax Concept Sketch - 270 Ruby Koins

NF - Artwork: Scorpion Promo Render - 392 Ruby Koins

NG - Koins: 252 Platinum Koins - 63 Sapphire Koins

NH - Artwork: Hachiman Sketch - 147 Onyx Koins

NI - Artwork: Kitana Sketches - 422 Gold Koins

NJ - Extra: MK Lunch Time - 326 Gold Koins

NK - Koins: 116 Onyx Koins - 77 Jade Koins

NL - Artwork: Wu Shi Academy Monk - 252 Gold Koins

NM - Artwork: Scorpion Online Promo Image - 182 Sapphire Koins

NN - Artwork: Blaze Sketches - 452 Jade Koins

NO - Extra: Kabal's Helmet - 426 Jade Koins

NP - Artwork: Kitana Sketches - 422 Gold Koins

NQ - Artwork: Quan Chi Promo Render - 157 Sapphire Koins

NR - Hint: BT: Blood Thirsty? - 425 Sapphire Koins

NS - Extra: Nick Shin - 270 Ruby Koins

NT - Extra: Artic Hold - 275 Gold Koins

NU - Artwork: Quan Chi's Fortress Sketches - 254 Onyx Koins

NV - Extra: Kenshi's Glass Eyes - 290 Gold Koins

NW - Artwork: Lost Tomb Sketch - 875 Gold Koins

NX - Extra: Damnation Charcoal - 365 Sapphire Koins

NY - Extra: Brian Lebaron - 281 Sapphire Koins

NZ - Artwork: The Mine Arena Concept - 446 Gold Koins

OA - Artwork: Movie Storyboards 1 of 8 - 105 Onyx Koins

OB - Artwork: Movie Storyboards 2 of 8 - 248 Platinum Koins

OC - Artwork: Movie Storyboards 3 of 8 - 322 Gold Koins

OD - Artwork: Movie Storyboards 4 of 8 - 288 Ruby Koins

OE - Artwork: Movie Storyboards 5 of 8 - 326 Jade Koins

OF - Artwork: Movie Storyboards 6 of 8 - 412 Sapphire Koins

OG - Artwork: Movie Storyboards 7 of 8 - 266 Onyx Koins

OH - Artwork: Movie Storyboards 8 of 8 - 224 Platinum Koins

OI - Extra: Midway Movie Group - 263 Jade Koins

OJ - Artwork: Interactive Arena Concept - 462 Onyx Koins

OK - Empty - 326 Jade Koins

OL - Artwork: Evil Masters Sketch - 136 Platinum Koins

OM - Koins: 177 Jade Koins - 88 Ruby Koins

ON - Artwork: Quan Chi Sketches - 227 Jade Koins

OO - Extra: Mortal Kandies - 274 Onyx Koins

OP - Koins: 125 Gold Koins - 24 Jade Koins

OQ - Extra: MK4 Logo Treatment - 95 Sapphire Koins

OR - Extra: Alan Villani - 450 Platinum Koins

OS - Empty - 166 Onyx Koins

OT - Koins: 222 Onyx Koins - 47 Onyx Koins

OU - Extra: Back to School with MK - 338 Ruby Koins

OV - Artwork: Reptile's Lair Concept - 96 Onyx Koins

OW - Artwork: Fallen Giants Arena Sketch - 422 Sapphire Koins

OX - Koins: 352 Gold Koins - 352 Ruby Koins

OY - Video: Blade Arena Test - 218 Sapphire Koins

OZ - Hint: IS: Ice Sword: 243 Platinum Koins

PA - Artwork: Lung Hai Temple Concept - 272 Ruby Koins

PB - Koins: 6 Platinum Koins - 12 Gold Koins

PC - Extra: Football Raiden - 20 Sapphire Koins

PD - Koins: 1056 Platinum Koins - 461 Ruby Koins

PE - Artwork: Kung Lao Render Test - 392 Ruby Koins

PF - Extra: Reptile's De-Evolution - 343 Ruby Koins

PG - Extra: Paulo Garcia - 442 Ruby Koins

PH - Alternate Outfit: Bo' Rai Cho - 1200 Onyx Koins

PI - Hint: HP: Haunted Place - 638 Jade Koins

PJ - Artwork: Drum Arena Details - 292 Onyx Koins

PK - Koins: 475 Platinum Koins - 157 Platinum Koins

PL - Artwork: Dojo Concept Sketch - 382 Gold Koins

PM - Artwork: Kenshi Sketch - 253 Platinum Koins

PN - Secret Character: Blaze - 684 Onyx Koins

PO - Koins: 108 Gold Koins - 71 Ruby Koins

PP - Extra: MK Gear - 516 Sapphire Koins

PQ - Artwork: Lava Shrine Sketch - 283 Sapphire Koins

PR - Koins: 25 Sapphire Koins - 11 Platinum Koins

PS - Extra: Moloch the Hobbyist - 294 Jade Koins

PT - Artwork: Slaughter Yard Concept - 207 Ruby Koins

PU - Koins: 267 Onyx Koins - 175 Ruby Koins

PV - Empty - 206 Sapphire Koins

PW - Secret Arena: Sarna Ruins - 2006 Sapphire Koins

PX - Extra: Goro Statuette - 493 Onyx Koins

PY - Extra: Backstage: MK Mythologies - 316 Ruby Koins

PZ - Artwork: Lava Shrine Sketch - 186 Jade Koins

QA - Extra: Quality Assurance: Chicago - 142 Sapphire Koins

QB - Artwork: Mavado Sketches - 272 Jade Koins

QC - Arena: Lin Kuei Temple - 216 Platinum Koins

QD - Video: MK4 Arena Concept - 268 Sapphire Koins

QE - Empty - 346 Gold Koins

QF - Extra: MKDA Hats and Shirts - 311 Ruby Koins

QG - Hint: LL: Lurking Lizard - 251 Ruby Koins

QH - Koins: 638 Onyx Koins - 342 Jade Koins

QI - Artwork: Lung Hai Temple Sketch - 192 Sapphire Koins

QJ - Empty - 49 Ruby Koins

QS - Artwork: Fan Art, 5 of 5 - 825 Onyx Koins

QT - Extra: MK1 Get Overe Here! - 58 Onyx Koins

QU - Extra: MK4 Logo Designs - 346 Gold Koins

QV - Extra: Reptile's Past - 318 Gold Koins

QW - Extra: MK2 Arcade - 233 Ruby Koins

QX - Alternate Outfit: Hsu Hao - 1518 Jade Koins

QK - Character: Kenshi - 244 Ruby Koins

QL - Extra: MK3 Promo Art - 488 Sapphire Koins

QM - Extra: MK1 Characters - 644 Jade Koins

QN - Koins: 147 Gold Koins - 96 Gold Koins

QO - Artwork: Fan Art, 1 of 5 - 1616 Gold Koins

QP - Artwork: Fan Art, 2 of 5 - 1214 Jade Koins

QQ - Artwork: Fan Art, 3 of 5 - 950 Ruby Koins

QR - Artwork: Fan Art, 4 of 5 - 512 Sapphire Koins

QY - Extra: MKDA at E3 Expo - 238 Gold Koins

QZ - Arena: Quan Chi's Fortress - 501 Jade Koins

RA - Hint: XG: Ex-God - 268 Gold Koins

RB - Extra: Robert Blum - 253 Platinum Koins

RC - Extra: Midway Creative Media - 272 Ruby Koins

RD - Alternative Costume: Mavado - 1455 Jade Koins

RE - Extra: MK3 Print Ad - 107 Sapphire Koins

RF - Video: Swamp Bird Test Video - 135 Jade Koins

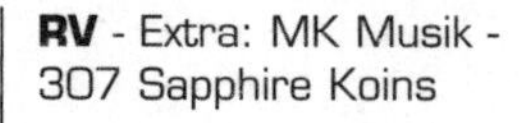

RG - Artwork: Sub-Zero Sketch - 187 Gold Koins

RH - Artwork: Bridge Arena Concept - 208 Jade Koins

RI - Koins: 28 Jade Koins - 61 Onyx Koins

RJ - Extra: MKDA Print Ads - 189 Gold Koins

RK - Extra: Evolution of Kombat - 1000 Jade Koins

RL - Koins: 159 Onyx Koins - 5 Ruby Koins

RM - Artwork: Kautan Palace Sketch - 182 Onyx Koins

RN - Koins: 208 Gold Koins - 203 Platinum Koins

RO - Koins: 1 Ruby - 27 Gold Koins

RP - Extra: MK1 Test Your Might - 31 Sapphire Koins

RQ - Artwork: Shang Tsung Sketches - 225 Onyx Koins

RR - Artwork: Shang Tsung's Palace Sketch - 224 Sapphire Koins

RS - Extra: Randy Severin - 267 Platinum Koins

RT - Koins: 258 Platinum Koins - 374 Gold Koins

RU - Artwork: Lava Shrine Sketch - 176 Onyx Koins

RV - Extra: MK Musik - 307 Sapphire Koins

RW - Artwork: Shang Tsung's Palace Sketch - 262 Ruby Koins

RX - Empty - 105 Sapphire Koins

RY - Artwork: Mavado Sketch - 274 Onyx Koins

RZ - Koins: 437 Gold Koins - 317 Sapphire Koins

SA - Secret Character: Jax Briggs - 3780 Ruby Koins

SB - Extra: Steve Beran - 291 Jade Koins

SC - Extra: Shawn Cooper - 226 Sapphire Koins

SD - Extra: Quality Assurance: San Diego - 326 Onyx Koins

SE - Extra: Reptile's Sword - 308 Platinum Koins

SF - Extra: Shang Tsung's Insouls - 138 Jade Koins

SG - Koins: 97 Platinum Koins - 94 Ruby Koins

SH - Alternate Outfit: Sonya Blade - 1834 Ruby Koins

SI - Artwork: Tiamat Sketch - 292 Sapphire Koins

SJ - Extra: MK4 Scorpion - 353 Onyx Koins

SK - Artwork: Jax Preliminary Model - 176 Sapphire Koins

SL - Extra: Tools and Technology - 117 Sapphire Koins

SM - Extra: MKDA Print Ad - 56 Jade Koins

SN - Character: Quan Chi - 175 Gold Koins

SO - Extra: MKDA Promo Pieces - 2 Sapphire Koins

SP - Empty - 63 Gold Koins

SQ - Extra: Peptic Thunder - 167 Platinum Koins

SR - Extra: MK4 Goro vs. Cage - 342 Ruby Koins

SS - Extra: Kung Lao Dragon Sword - 214 Platinum Koins

ST - Video: Sarna Ruins Test - 153 Jade Koins

SU - Artwork: Kenshi's Story Sketch - 106 Sapphire Koins

SV - Koins: 36 Sapphire Koins - 145 Ruby Koins

SW - Alternate Outfit: Drahmin - 1152 Jade Koins

SX - Extra: MK4 Arcade Marquee - 215 Onyx Koins

SY - Extra: Cyrax's Arm - 486 Onyx Koins

SZ - Character: Kung Lao - 322 Sapphire Koins

TA - Extra: Todd Allen - 177 Ruby Koins

TB - Artwork: Quan Chi's Fortress Sketches - 259 Platinum Koins

TC - Artwork: Palace Exterior SKetch: 135 Onyx Koins

TD - Koins: 172 Platinum Koins - 118 Ruby Koins

TE - Artwork: Character Concepts - 261 Gold Koins

TF - Extra: MK4 Characters - 470 Jade Koins

TG - Extra: Tony Goskie - 262 Gold Koins

TH - Artwork: Konquest Mode Concepts - 282 Gold Koins

TI - Secret Character: Nitara - 4022 Gold Koins

TJ - Artwork: Koin Sketches - 259 Sapphire Koins

TK - Hint: RD: Red Dragon - 94 Sapphire Koins

TL - Artwork: Acid Bath Sketch - 360 Jade Koins

TM - Artwork: Hsu Hao Sketches - 251 Ruby Koins

TN - Artwork: Early MKDA - 211 Ruby Koins

TO - Artwork: Early MKDA - 316 Jade Koins

TP - Artwork: Early MKDA Jax - 294 Onyx Koins

TQ - Artwork: Early MKDA Scorpion - 616 Platinum Koins

TR - Artwork: MKDA Promo Image - 392 Jade Koins

TS - Extra: Artists - 352 Onyx Koins

TT - Artwork: Test Your Might Sketch - 147 Platinum Koins

TU - Koins: 98 Onyx Koins - 197 Gold Koins

TV - Artwork: Wu Shi Academy Sketches - 273 Onyx Koins

TW - Koins: 180 Gold Koins - 129 Ruby Koins

TX - Artwork: Goro's Throne Sketch - 167 Gold Koins

TY - Extra: Baraka - 390 Gold Koins

TZ - Extra: Animators - 195 Gold Koins

UA - Extra: MK4 PC Version - 205 Jade Koins

UB - Alternate Outfit: Frost - 1261 Gold Koins

UC - Koins: 320 Onyx Koins - 3 Sapphire Koins

UD - Artwork: Drahmin Sketch - 252 Gold Koins

UE - Hint: WT: Winged Transport - 210 Gold Koins

UF - Extra: MK4 Liu Kang Fatality - 371 Gold Koins

UG - Koins: 67 Platinum Koins - 245 Onyx Koins

UH - Alternate Costume - Scorpion - 1660 Jade Coins

UI - Extra: Cooking with Scorpion - 270 Platinum Koins

UJ - Extra: Goro on the Kit - 225 Sapphire Koins

UK - Koins: 45 Platinum Koins - 35 Onyx Koins

UL - Artwork: Kai Sketch - 252 Jade Koins

UM - Koins: 50 Gold Koins - 33 Platinum Koins

UN - Extra: MK4 Print Ad - 152 Sapphire Koins

UO - Extra: MK Trading Cards - 243 Jade Koins

UP - Extra: MK Trading Cards - 406 Ruby Koins

UQ - Extra: Undefeatable Army - 185 Ruby Koins

UR - Secret Character: Drahmin - 6500 Sapphire Koins

US - Koins: 32 Sapphire Koins - 72 Platinum Koins

UT - Artwork: Bridge Arena Concept - 157 Onyx Koins

UU - Empty - 1214 Jade Koins

UV - Koins: 520 Sapphire Koins - 256 Jade Koins

UW - Extra: MKDA at E3 Expo - 255 Gold Koins

UX - Character: Scorpion - 509 Onyx Koins

UY - Extra: MK Hits the Big Screen - 359 Jade Koins

UZ - Koins: 107 Ruby Koins - 78 Onyx Koins

VA - Extra: Shao Kahn's Armor - 299 Platinum Koins

VB - Artwork: Blaze Sketch - 116 Ruby Koins

VC - Extra: 3 PT Staff, Butterfly Knives - 209 Jade Koins

VD - Extra: Aikido - 152 Ruby Koins

VE - Extra: Baji Quan and Crab - 173 Gold Koins

VF - Extra: Basic Fighting Strikes - 212 Sapphire Koins

VG - Extra: Basic Fighting Strikes - 362 Onyx Koins

VH - Extra: Broadswords - 72 Platinum Koins

VI - Extra: Cudgel - 184 Jade Koins

VJ - Extra: Drunken Master - 58 Ruby Koins

VK - Extra: Dragon and Eagle Claw - 268 Gold Koins

VL - Extra: Escrima and Crane - 180 Sapphire Koins

VM - Extra: Shuai Chiao and Shaolin Fist - 198 Onyx Koins

VN - Extra: Hapkido and Nan Chuan - 86 Platinum Koins

VO - Extra: Hookswords and Sai - 247 Jade Koins

VP - Extra: Hung Gar and Jujutsu - 356 Ruby Koins

VQ - Extra: Jojutsu - 241 Gold Koins

VR - Extra: Judo - 174 Sapphire Koins

VS - Extra: Kali Sticks and Nanchaku - 21 Onyx Koins

VT - Extra: Kama and Katara - 405 Platinum Koins

VU - Extra: Karate - 180 Jade Koins

VV - Extra: Long Fist and Muay Thai - 192 Ruby Koins

VW - Extra: Motion Capture Markers - 162 Gold Koins

VX - Extra: Pi Gua and Jeet Kune Do - 248 Sapphire Koins

VY - Extra: Praying Mantis, Lui He Ba Fa - 35 Onyx Koins

VZ - Extra: Sambo - 223 Platinum Koins

WA - Extra: Straight Sword - 194 Jade Koins

WB - Extra: Tai Chi - 242 Ruby Koins

WC - Extra: Tae Kwon Do - 156 Gold Koins

WD - Extra: Tonfa - 186 Sapphire Koins

WE - Extra: Tong Bei and Yuan Yang - 186 Onyx Koins

WF - Extra: Wing Chun and Snake - 214 Platinum Koins

WG - Extra: Xing Yi and Tang Soo Do - 186 Jade Koins

WH - Koins: 18 Ruby Koins - 24 Platinum Koins

WI - Extra: Konquest Concept Sketch - 242 Jade Koins

WJ - Koins: 248 Sapphire Koins - 165 Gold Koins

WK - Artwork: Frost Sketches - 76 Platinum Koins

WL - Koins: 44 Jade Koins - 22 Gold Koins

WM - Empty - 36 Ruby Koins

WN - Character: Sub-Zero - 143 Sapphire Koins

WO - Artwork: Acid Buddha Detail - 270 Ruby Koins

WP - Artwork: Drahmin Sketches - 247 Ruby Koins

WQ - Koins: 78 Onyx Koins - 151 Sapphire Koins

WR - Extra: MK3 Home Version - 125 Ruby Koins

WS - Koins: 165 Platinum Koins - 44 Onyx Koins

WT - Secret Arena: Dragonfly - 1400 Jade Koins

WU - Artwork: Lung Hai Temple Sketches - 256 Onyx Koins

WV - Extra: 97 Jade Koins - 424 Jade Koins

WW - Artwork: Dragon Arena Concept - 262 Jade Koins

WX - Extra: Hsu Hao Implant - 315 Gold Koins

WY - Artwork: Bo' Rai Cho Sketches - 264 Sapphire Koins

WZ - Character: Kano - 145 Onyx Koins

XA - Extra: The Grid - 172 Gold Koins

XB - Artwork: Cage Sketch - 272 Platinum Koins

XC - Artwork: Quan Chi's Sanctum Sketch - 352 Sapphire Koins

XD - Artwork: Acid Buddha Detail - 326 Gold Koins

XE - Koins: 294 Onyx Koins - 147 Onyx Koins

XF - Extra: Mortal Kombat Gold Characters - 265 Gold Koins

XG - Secret Character: Raiden - 3116 Jade Koins

XH - Artwork: Cyrax Sketches - 352 Onyx Koins

XI - Extra: MK 3 Behind the Scenes - 457 Platinum Koins

XJ - Artwork: Quan Chi Render - 197 Platinum Koins

XK - Hint: DS: Death Ship - 37 Jade Koins

XL - Koins: 3 Ruby Koins - 843 Onyx Koins

XM - Hint: SA: Steel Arms - 254 Sapphire Koins

XN - Empty - 27 Gold Koins

XO - Alternate Costume: Reptile - 1736 Sapphire Koins

XP - Extra: MK4 Gift Cards - 436 Gold Koins

XQ - Extra: Raiden Performance Audio - 199 Jade Koins

XR - Artwork: Konquest Mode Concepts - 288 Ruby Koins

XS - Artwork: Kung Lao Sketch - 283 Platinum Koins

XT - Extra: MK3 Characters - 65 Jade Koins

XU - Extra: Mortal Friday - 194 Onyx Koins

XV - Artwork: Organic Arena Concept - 503 Onyx Koins

XW - Video: Baraka's Demise - 96 Ruby Koins

XX - Extra: Shao Kahn's Medal - 365 Onyx Koins

XY - Extra: Shang Tsung's Palace Story - 55 Platinum Koins

XZ - Artwork: Marsh Concept - 255 Onyx Koins

YA - Alternate Outfit: Sub-Zero - 1999 Sapphire Koins

YB - Extra: Ketchup and Mustard - 358 Jade Koins

YC - Artwork: Moloch Promo Render - 257 Platinum Koins

YD - Extra: MK Stickers and Tattoos - 412 Gold Koins

YE - Artwork: Temple Oarsman - 274 Platinum Koins

YF - Koins: 64 Platinum Koins - 16 Platinum Koins

YG - Artwork: Swamplands Test Render - 312 Sapphire Koins

YH - Koins: 82 Sapphire Koins - 78 Jade Koins

YI - Extra: MK2 Arcade Marquee - 197 Gold Koins

YJ - Alternate Outfit: Kung Lao - 1208 Ruby Koins

YK - Artwork: Dragon Fly Concept - 225 Platinum Koins

YL - Artwork: Jax Concept Sketch - 199 Jade Koins

YM - Alternate Outfit: Kenshi - 1435 Platinum Koins

YN - Koins: 26 Gold Koins - 61 Ruby Koins

YO - Artwork: Sonya Sketch - 294 Sapphire Koins

YP - Secret Character: Mokap - 511 Gold Koins

YQ - Extra: Tools and Technology - 146 Gold Koins

YR - Extra: MK3 Home Version - 143 Gold Koins

YS - Extra: 10 Worst MKDA Subtitles - 151 Platinum Koins

YT - Koins: 227 Sapphire Koins - 384 Sapphire Koins

YU - Extra: MK4 Comic Book - 374 Platinum Koins

YV - Artwork: Graveyard Concept - 86 Platinum Koins

YW - Extra: Fashion Model Li Mei - 376 Gold Koins

YX - Koins: 242 Ruby Koins - 83 Gold Koins

YY - Empty - 85 Ruby Koins

YZ - Artwork: Kenshi Test Render - 255 Onyx Koins

ZA - Empty - 63 Onyx Koins

ZB - Artwork: Spider Arena Concept - 106 Gold Koins

ZC - Artwork: Frost Color Sketches - 218 Platinum Koins

ZD - Secret Arena: Moloch's Lair - 98 Ruby Koins

ZE - Artwork: Zebron - 257 Jade Koins

ZF - Artwork: Lava Shrine Sketch - 237 Ruby Koins

ZG - Video: Facial Animation Test - 201 Onyx Koins

ZH - Artwork: The Krypt Concept - 372 Sapphire Koins

ZI - Artwork: Hell Concept - 432 Jade Koins

ZJ - Artwork: Water Temple Concept - 272 Onyx Koins

ZK - Koins: 164 Sapphire Koins - 216 Ruby Koins

ZL - Artwork: Drum Arena Sketch - 126 Jade Koins

ZM - Alternate Outfit: Jax - 1410 Ruby Koins

ZN - Empty - 145 Sapphire Koins

ZO - Hint: LO: Log On - 466 Jade Koins

ZP - Extra: MK1 Print Ad - 129 Jade Koins

ZQ - Artwork: Sub-Zero Promo Render - 282 Jade Koins

ZR - Koins: 600 Gold Koins - 244 Sapphire Koins

ZS - Extra: MK Home Graphics - 381 Sapphire Koins

ZT - Extra: Animators - 215 Sapphire Koins

ZU - Artwork: Kuatan Palace Sketch - 201 Platinum Koins

ZV - Koins: 116 Ruby Koins - 182 Onyx Koins

ZW - Alternate Outfit: Cyrax - 1485 Sapphire Koins

ZX - Hint: BD: Black Dragon - 718 Ruby Koins

ZY - Extra: The Fans Speak - 186 Platinum Koins

ZZ - Koins: 355 Ruby Koins - 254 Gold Koins

NBA HOOPZ

Taunt opponent:
Hit ■, ▲, ●, or ✖.

Score An Easy basket:
Run up to the basket while hiting Turbo, at the basket, hit ▲, then ✖.

NBA STREET

Unlock Cheat mode:
After entering one of the following icon codes:
Unlimited turbo:
Enter Shoe, Basketball, Backboard, Basketball.
No turbo:
Enter Turntable, Microphone, Microphone, Backboard.
Authentic uniforms:
Enter Basketball, Basketball, Turntable, Turntable.
Casual uniforms:
Enter Turntable, Turntable, Basketball, Basketball.
ABA socks:
Enter Microphone, Microphone, Microphone, Microphone.
Tiny players:
Enter Microphone, Basketball, Microphone, Basketball.
Big heads:
Enter Microphone, Turntable, Shoe, Turntable.
Tiny heads:
Enter Microphone, Shoe, Basketball, Shoe.
Less blocks:
Enter Backboard, Turntable, Shoe, Backboard.
Less steals:
Enter Backboard, Turntable, Microphone, Basketball.
No player indicators:
Enter Microphone, Basketball, Basketball, Microphone.
No shot Indicator:
Enter Microphone, Backboard, Shoe, Microphone.
No shot clock:
Enter Microphone, Microphone, Basketball, Backboard.
No alley-oops:
Enter Backboard, Microphone, Turntable, Shoe.
No 2-pointers:
Enter Backboard, Backboard, Basketball, Backboard.
No auto replays:
Enter Turntable, Shoe, Turntable, Turntable.
WNBA ball:
Enter Basketball, Turntable, Shoe, Basketball.
EA Big ball:
Enter Basketball, Turntable, Microphone, Basketball.
Beach ball:
Enter Basketball, Turntable, Turntable, Shoe.
Soccer ball:
Enter Basketball, Shoe, Turntable, Basketball.
ABA ball:
Enter Basketball, Turntable, Turntable, Basketball.
Beach ball:
Enter Basketball, Turntable, Turntable, Shoe.
Medicine ball:
Enter Basketball, Turntable, Turntable, Backboard.
NuFX ball:
Enter Basketball, Turntable, Backboard, Basketball.
Volley ball:
Enter Basketball, Turntable, Turntable, Microphone.
Mega dunking:
Enter Backboard, Basketball, Turntable, Basketball.
No dunks:
Enter Backboard, Basketball, Turntable, Shoe.
More gamebreakers:
Enter Turntable, Microphone, Backboard, Shoe.
Less gamebreakers:
Enter Turntable, Backboard, Microphone, Shoe.
No gamebreakers:
Enter Turntable, Microphone, Microphone, Shoe.
Springtime Joe "The Show":
Enter Turntable, Turntable, Basketball, Turntable.
Summertime Joe "The Show":
Enter Turntable, Basketball, Basketball, Turntable.
Athletic Joe "The Show":
Enter Turntable, Shoe, Basketball, Turntable.
Captain Quicks:
Enter Backboard, Basketball, Shoe, Turntable.
Explosive rims:
Enter Turntable, Shoe, Microphone, Basketball.

Harder distance shots:
Enter Shoe, Shoe, Backboard, Basketball.
Easy distance shots:
Enter Shoe, Turntable, Backboard, Basketball.
Ultimate power:
Enter Backboard, Turntable, Turntable, Basketball.
Mad handles:
Enter Backboard, Shoe, Turntable, Basketball.
Super swats:
Enter Backboard, Backboard, Turntable, Basketball.
Sticky fingers:
Enter Backboard, Microphone, Turntable, Basketball.
Player names:
Enter Basketball, Turntable, Shoe, Backboard.
No HUD display:
Enter Turntable, Microphone, Turntable, Shoe.
Disable all CHEAT:
Enter Turntable, Turntable, Turntable, Turntable.

NEED FOR SPEED: HOT PURSUIT 2

Unlock Car codes:
If you try to save a car you that was unlocked by a code, the car will not save. You will have to enter the code each time you play.

Unlock Aston Martin V12 Vanquish:
Press R2, ⇨, R2, ⇨, ▲, ⇦, ▲, ⇦ at the main menu.
Unlock BMW Z8:
Press ■, ⇨, ■, ⇨, R2, ▲, R2, ▲ at the main menu.
Unlock Chevrolet Corvette Z06:
Press ⇦, R2, ⇦, R2, L1, R1, L1, R1 at the main menu.
Unlock Ferrari 360 Spider:
Press R2, ■, R2, ■, ▲, L2, ▲, L2 at the main menu.
Unlock Ferrari F50:
Press L1, ▲, L1, ▲, ⇨, L2, ⇨, L2 at the main menu.
Unlock Ferrari F550:
Press L1, ■, L1, ■, ⇨, R1, ⇨, R1 at the main menu. A
Unlock Ford Pursuit Mustang Cobra R:
Press ⇦, ■, ⇦, ■, R2, R1, R2, R1 at the main menu.
Unlock Ford TS50:
Press ⇨, ⇦, ⇨, ⇦, R2, ■, R2, ■ at the main menu.
Unlock HSV Coupe GTS:
Press L1, L2, L1, L2, R1, ▲, R1, ▲ at the main menu.
Unlock Lamborgini Diablo 6.0 VT:
Press ⇨, R2, ⇨, R2, R1, L1, R1, L1 at the main menu.
Unlock Lotus Elise:
Press ▲, R2, ▲, R2, ⇦, ■, ⇦, ■ at the main menu.
Unlock McLaren F1:
Press ▲, L1, ▲, L1, R1, ⇦, R1, ⇦ at the main menu.
Unlock McLaren F1 LM:
Press ■, L1, ■, L1, ▲, ⇨, ▲, ⇨ at the main menu.
Unlock Mercedes CLK GTR:
Press R2, R1, R2, R1, ⇦, ▲, ⇦, ▲ at the main menu.
Unlock Porsche Carrera GT:
Press ⇦, ⇨, ⇦, ⇨, R1, R2, R1, R2 at the main menu.

NFL 2K2

Unlimited cap limit in franchise mode:
Pause in game in franchise mode then hold L1 + R1 and hit ⇦ x2, ⇨ x2, ▲, ■, ⇧ x4, ⇩, ● x2.

NFL 2K3

Faster drafts:
Select franchise mode. Hold ▲ while other teams are making their choices to speed up the draft process.

NFL BLITZ 2002

Cheat mode:
Hit L2, R2, and ✖ (Juke, Turbo, and Hurdle) to change the icons below the helmets on the versus screen. To enter the following code: 1-2-3 ⇦, hit L2, R2 x2, ✖ x3 and then finally ⇦.

EFFECT	CODE
Extra time after plays	0-0-1 ⇨
No CPU assistance	0-1-2 ⇩
See more field1	0-2-1 ⇨
Big feet	0-2-5 ⇦
Big shoulders	0-2-5 ⇨
Chimp mode	0-2-5 ⇧
Classic NFL Blitz ball	0-3-0 ⇦
Chrome ball	0-3-0 ⇦
Fast running speed	0-3-2 ⇦
Indians team	0-4-5 ⇦
Super blitzing	0-5-4 ⇧
Tourney mode in two team game	1-1-1 ⇩
Super field goals	1-2-3 ⇦
Clear weather	1-2-3 ⇨
Cowboys team	1-3-5 ⇦
No punting	1-4-1 ⇧
Huge head for ball carrier	1-4-5 ⇦
Big head for ball carrier	2-0-0 ⇨
Big head for team	2-0-3 ⇨

No first downs	2-1-0 ⇧
Allow stepping out of bounds	2-1-1 ⇦
More code entry time	2-1-2 ⇨
Always QB	2-2-2 ⇦
Always receiver	2-2-2 ⇨
Ground fog	2-3-2 ⇩
Fast passes	2-4-0 ⇦
Midway team	2-5-3 ⇨
Rollos team	2-5-4 ⇧
Bilders team	3-1-0 ⇧
Smart CPU teammates	3-1-4 ⇩
No target receiver highlight	3-2-1 ⇩
Noftle mode	3-2-5 ⇧
Extra offense plays	3-3-3 ⇩
Neo Tokyo team	3-4-4 ⇩
More fumbles	3-4-5 ⇧
Showtime mode	3-5-1 ⇨
No interceptions	3-5-5 ⇧
Crunch Mode team	4-0-3 ⇨
Power-up offense	4-1-2 ⇧
Unlimited turbo	4-1-5 ⇧
Power-up defense	4-2-1 ⇧
Brew Dawgs team	4-3-2 ⇩
Gsmers team	5-0-1 ⇧
Power-up linemen	5-2-1 ⇧
No random fumbles1	5-2-3 ⇩
Armageddon team	5-4-3 ⇨
No replays	5-5-4 ⇨
Snowy weather	5-5-5 ⇦
Rainy weather	5-5-5 ⇨

NFL BLITZ 2003

Cheat mode:
Hit L2, R2, and ✖ to change the icons below the helmets on the versus screen. For Example, to enter 1-2-3 ⇩, hit L2, R2 x2, ✖ x3 and ⇩.

EFFECT	CODE
Extra time	0-0-1 ⇨
Disable Auto-Passing icon	0-0-3 ⇩
Auto-Passing icon	0-0-3 ⇧
No CPU assist	0-1-2 ⇩
Show more field	0-2-1 ⇨
Big feet	0-2-5 ⇦
Power loader	0-2-5 ⇨
Chimp mode	0-2-5 ⇧
Chrome ball	0-3-0 ⇩
Classic ball	0-3-0 ⇦
Faster running	0-3-2 ⇦
Central Park	0-3-3 ⇨
Arctic Station	0-3-4 ⇩
Training Grounds	0-3-5 ⇧
Super Blitzing	0-5-4 ⇧
Tournament mode	1-1-1 ⇩
Super field goals	1-2-3 ⇦
Clear weather	1-2-3 ⇨
No punting	1-4-1 ⇧
Huge heads	1-4-5 ⇦
Big heads	2-0-0 ⇨
Big head teams	2-0-3 ⇨
No first downs	2-1-0 ⇧
Allow out of bounds	2-1-1 ⇦
More code entry time	2-1-2 ⇨
Always QB	2-2-2 ⇦
Always receiver	2-2-2 ⇨
Ground fog	2-3-2 ⇩
Fast passes	2-4-0 ⇦
Midway team	2-5-3 ⇨
Rollos team	2-5-4 ⇧
Bilders team	3-1-0 ⇧
Smart CPU teammates	3-1-4 ⇩
No highlighting receivers	3-2-1 ⇩
Noftle mode	3-2-5 ⇧
Extra play for offense	3-3-3 ⇩
Neo Tokyo team	3-4-4 ⇩
More fumbles	3-4-5 ⇧
Showtime mode	3-5-1 ⇨
No interceptions	3-5-5 ⇧
Crunch Mode team	4-0-3 ⇨
Power-up offense	4-1-2 ⇧
Unlimited turbo	4-1-5 ⇧
Power-up defense	4-2-1 ⇧
Brew Dawgs team	4-3-2 ⇩
Gsmers team	5-0-1 ⇧
Power-up Linemen	5-2-1 ⇧
No random fumbles	5-2-3 ⇩
Armageddon team	5-4-3 ⇨
No replays	5-5-4 ⇨
Weather: Snow	5-5-5 ⇦
Weather: Rain	5-5-5 ⇨

NHL 2002

All-Star teams:
Play through a season and finish the All-Star game. Save the game and now you will find that two All-Star teams are available to select.

NHL HITZ 2002

Cheat mode:
Hit ■, ▲, and ● to change the icons in the first, second, and third onscreen boxes. For example, to enter 1-2-3 ⇩, hit ■, ▲ x2, ● x3 and ⇩.

EFFECT	CODE
Big head player	2-0-0 ⇨
Huge head player	3-0-0 ⇨
Big head team	2-2-0 ⇦
Huge head team	3-3-0 ⇦
Big hits	2-3-4 ⇩
Late hits	3-2-1 ⇩
Hitz time	1-0-4 ⇨
No crowd	2-1-0 ⇨
Pinball boards	4-2-3 ⇨
Show shot speed	1-0-1 ⇧
Show the team's hot spot	2-0-1 ⇧
No fake shots	4-2-4 ⇩
No puck out	1-1-1 ⇩
No one-timers	2-1-3 ⇦
Big puck	1-2-1 ⇧
Huge puck	3-2-1 ⇧
Bulldozer puck	2-1-2 ⇦
Tennis ball	1-3-2 ⇩
Snow mode	1-2-1 ⇦
Rain mode	1-4-1 ⇦
Domino effect	0-1-2 ⇨
Turbo boost	0-0-2 ⇧
Unlimited turbo	4-1-3 ⇨

Win fights for goals 2-0-2 ⇦
Skills versus 2-2-2 ⇩
First to 7 wins 3-2-3 ⇦
More time to enter codes 3-3-3 ⇨
Hockey Ball 1-3-3 ⇦
Disable previous code 0-1-0 ⇩

ONI

Master code:
Hit Select during the game. Highlight "Help", and then hit L2, L1, L2, ■, ●, and ■. The following sub codes may now be enabled. The master code must be entered before each sub code.

Unlimited health:
Enable the "Master code", and then hit R3, L3, R3, and ●. Enter the code again to disable its effects.

Unlimited ammunition:
Enable the "Master code", and then hit L2 x2, L1, and L3. Enter the code again to disable its effects.

Ballistic ammunition clips filled:
Enable the "Master code", and then hit ● x3, and R3. Enter the code again to disable its effects.

Enable One hit kills:
Enable the "Master code", and then hit L3, R3, ●, and ■. Konoko can now kill enemies with one hit. Enter the code again to disable its effects.

Enable Level skip:
Enable the "Master code", and then hit L3, R3, L2, and L1.

Enable Character select:
Enable the "Master code", and then hit L2 x4. Keep hiting L2 to cycle through the characters available on the current level. Each has special moves different from Konoko.

Tiny characters:
Enable the "Master code", and then hit L3, R3, ■, and ●. Enter the code again to disable its effects.

Big characters:
Enable the "Master code", and then hit R3, ■, ●, and L3. Enter the code again to disable its effects.

Big head:
Enable the "Master code", and then hit START, ■, ●, and START. Enter the code again to disable its effects.

Unlock Fists Of Legend mode:
Enable the "Master code", and then hit R3, L3, ●, and ■. Enter the code again to disable its effects. When activated, this code makes your enemies fly further when punched.

Enable Gatling Guns mode:
Enable the "Master code", and then hit L2, L2, L1, and L3. Most weapons can fire without pausing, and all weapons will have unlimited ammunition. Enter the code again to disable its effects.

Enable Unlimited Phase Cloak:
Enable the "Master code", and then hit L1, R3, L2, and L3. Enter the code again to disable its effects.

ONIMUSHA: WARLORDS

Unlock Alternate costumes:
Panda
Successfully complete the game with at least ten Fluorites found and save. Choose to start a new game and a "Shinnosuke Normal/Special" option will be available. The special version will show Shinnosuke in a panda costume with a baby panda in a front pocket clapping his hands. The panda suit will be shown in most short clips but not all FMV sequences. Hit L2 to wear or remove the panda head.

Princess Dragon
Successfully complete the game with an S rank by getting most of the Fluorites. Choose to start a new game and an option for Kaede's new princess dragon design costume will be unlocked. She wears a red skirt with little wings on the back and a small tail.

Watch Onimusha 2 FMV sequence:

Successfully complete the game and save. Choose to start a new game and a "Special Report" option will be available. This allows a small sequence from the game's sequel to be viewed.

Unlock Speed trial mini-game:
Collect all 20 Fluorites (blue rocks) during the game. Complete and save the game. The Onimusha Spirits speed trial mini-game will be unlocked. Successfully complete the mini-game to unlock an option to play the regular game with the Bishamon Sword, unlimited ammunition, 99 Soul Absorbers, and automatic magic regeneration.

Unlock Easy mode:
Start a game and die ten to fifteen times. After enough deaths, a message will appear, stating that a new easy mode is open. You cannot Beat an S rank when playing in easy mode.

Bishamon O Flute
There are two places in there game where a very strange man hanging from the ceiling by his feet stares at you and ignores you. Later in the game, after you use the Evil Plate and open the door, he will talk to you. The man will now take you to the Dark Realm. In the Dark Realm, kill monsters until two portals open, one to go up and one to go down. Keep going down to the last level (9th or 10th) collecting all the items en route. Open the box on the deepest level to get the Bishamon O flute. Keep the flute just before the last fight with the Demon King, where it can be used to get the Bishamon Sword.

Bishamon Sword
In the Demon Realm (just after you destroy the Ultimate Creation) is a save mirror and three doors. Go to the door that looks like an iron gate. Use the Bishimon O flute on it and enter. Go to the Bishimon Sword jutting out of the Skull Demon wall object and take it. It is more powerful and faster than all three of your weapons put together.

Fire Orb and Bow
After defeating Reynaldo, go to the fire to the left to get a Fire Orb. Before leaving to the castle, enhance the Fire Orb to level 2. To get a Bow in the castle, go to the place where the bucket is and cut it. Go upstairs and there will be a trick crate. To open it, hit ⇨ once and ✖ twice. Then hit ⇦ and hit ✖ once. Next, hit ⇨ and hit ✖ once. Finally, hit ⇦ once and hit ✖. You now should have the Bow. Make sure you have normal arrows before using the Bow. You can find 10 normal arrows when you first enter the castle and see the samurai.

Better gauntlet
Reach 20,000 souls and when you go to enhance you will have a better gauntlet. Go when you have 50 to get the Golden Ogre Gauntlet. Capture 50,000 souls to get an even better gauntlet.

Enhancing
When enhancing, collect about 25,000 souls. The number next to the soul meter should say 25. Enhance all of your weapons and Orbs to level two. After collecting the Wind Orb, use the remaining souls to bring that to level three, since it is weak.

Save your green and red mana for the fourth sword. It can be found just beyond the destroyed master's house (level four or five). By saving points, you can build the weapon up to full immediately.

Great armour
There is a chest behind the waterfall containing the great armour.

Flourite locations
Collect each of the following 20 Flourites to unlock the Oni Spirits mini-game.

A Flourite can be found in one of the small alcoves with brown doors near the Seiryu in the Under Temple area.

Just after the Boss fight in the South area, break some urns and search the floor under them to find a Flourite.

In the Keep after running into Kaede with Yumemaru, you will find the Flourite in a small cupboard over the treasure box near the stairs.

Head off to the upstairs level of the Keep, and pass through the room just past the red magic door on the catwalk. Step through the next room to find the

Flourite under the stairs, near the treasure box containing the Arrows.

Head off to the upper reaches of the Keep. You will find a Flourite across from Volume Two of the Seiryu, just after the intermission sequence where Tokichiru takes off into the night.

Head off to the Keep Underground. Head down the second hall of glass-encased red samurai. There is a Flourite in the left corner, near the last samurai.

Head off to the Keep Underground. A Flourite is hidden inside the iron maiden in the same room where you get the Blue Key.

Head off to the West Area when playing as Kaede. Find the secret room and use the Gear to enter. There is a Flourite in front of the Buddha statue.

Playing as Kaede in the West Area. Step into the burning room just past the gate that required the Gold and Silver Plates. Through the door left of this entrance is a narrow staircase. Next to the staircase in a heap of barrels, which contains a Flourite.

Head off to the West

ONIMUSHA 2: SAMURAI'S DESTINY

Unlock Easy mode:
Start a game and die three times. A message will appear to indicate that a new easy difficulty setting is available. You cannot Beat an Onimusha rank when playing in easy mode.

Unlock Hard mode:
Successfully complete the game under the normal difficulty setting.

Unlock Critical mode:
Successfully complete the game under the hard difficulty setting.

Unlock Ending bonuses:
Successfully complete the game to unlock the Scenario Route option, Man In Black mode, and Team Onimusha mode, as well as a FMV preview of Onimusha 3.

Unlock Team Oni one hit kills:
Successfully complete the Team Oni mode to unlock an option to replay Team Oni with one hit kills.

Unlock Ultimate mode:
Successfully complete the game under the hard difficulty setting. Enter the "Special Features" menu and enable the "Ultimate Mode" option to begin a new game with the Rekka-Ken Sword, 20,000 in money, 30 Perfect Medicines, 10 Talismans, all level 3 armours, unlimited ammunition, unlimited magic, and skill always full.

Unlock Critical mode:
Successfully complete the Team Oni mini-game. You must hit with a One Flash attack in order to do damage to opponents.

Unlock Puzzle Quest mode:
Successfully complete the game with all Paintings.

Unlock Jubei's alternate costume:
Collect the Fashionable Goods item and successfully complete the game with an "S" rank. Enter the "Special Features" menu and enable the "Extra Jubei" option to dress hin in leather and sunglasses (hit L2 to toggle).

Unlock Oyu's alternate costume:
Get a 100% scenario completion by playing the game multiple times to make good alliances with all NPCs. After all scenarios are unlocked in the "Scenario Route" viewer, enter the "Special Features" menu and enable the "Extra Oyu" option to dress her in a 1970's style costume.

area. You can find a Flourite just outside the door after obtaining the Vision Staff with Samanosuke.

Head off to the West area. There is a Flourite on the hill with the sled just outside the castle.

Head off to the West Area. This is a Flourite blinking in the path on your way to the room with the statue where you got the Matchlock.

Head off to the East Area with Samanosuke. There is a bell on top the roof. There is a Flourite In the walkway around the bell.

Play as Samanosuke and find the Flourite on the pier just past the Magic Mirror room in the East Area. Head off to the East Area. Just when you begin playing as Kaede you will enter a shrine just past the locked door you need to pick. A Flourite can be found on the floor just to the right of the door.

When playing as Kaede in the East Area, climb a ladder in the bridge house Magic Mirror room. Destroy the crates here to find another Flourite.

Head off to the East Area while playing as Kaede. You can find another Flourite on a chest in the room where you get the final book of the Suzaku.

A Flourite is in the sixth level of the Dark Realm.

A Flourite is in eleventh level of the Dark Realm.

A Flourite is in the seventeenth level of the Dark Realm.

ORPHEN

Restart battle:
Pause the game if your defeat cannot be avoided during a battle. Select "Equip" and resume the game at the start of the battle, with all energy restored.

Regain health
If you are running low on health, just shoot or attack the Electric elementals (small wavy line of electricity). They will go away and refill your health. They will reappear soon after that, allowing you to refill your health as many times needed

PAC-MAN WORLD 2

Unlock Pac-Man mini-game:
Collect 10 tokens during the game to unlock the classic Pac-Man arcade game.

Unlock Pac-Attack mini-game:
Collect 30 tokens during the game to unlock the classic Pac-Attack arcade game.

Unlock Pac-Mania mini-game:
Collect 100 tokens during the game to unlock the classic Pac-Mania arcade game.

Unlock Ms. Pac-Man mini-game:
Collect 180 tokens during the game to unlock the classic Ms. Pac-Man arcade game.

Unlock Music test:
Collect 60 tokens during the game to unlock the "Jukebox" option.

Unlock Pre-production art and programmers:
Collect 150 tokens during the game to unlock the "Museum" option.

PARAPPA THE RAPPER 2

Unlock Shuriken mode:
Hold R1 + R2 then choose a stage at the selection screen. Shurikens will replace the buttons during a song.

Enable Fast start:
Hold L1 + L2 then choose a stage at the selection screen.

Unlock Blue hat:
Successfully complete the game to unlock a blue hat for Parappa. Hit the Right Analog-stick at the "Hit Start" screen to select the new color.

Unlock Pink hat:
Successfully complete the game with the blue hat to unlock a pink hat for Parappa. Hit the Right Analog-stick at the "Hit Start" screen to select the new color.

Unlock Yellow hat:
Successfully complete the game with the pink hat to unlock a yellow hat for Parappa. Hit the Right Analog-stick at the "Hit Start" screen to select the new color.

Unlock Song test:
Successfully complete the game with the yellow hat to unlock a new dog house that allows you to listen to any song in levels that you finished with a cool rating.

Unlock Bonus stage:
To unlock a bonus stage after any regular stage, finish the stage with a good score (near 1,000 points). You will be brought to Chop Chop Master Onion Head who gives you a fun, yet somewhat repetitious bonus game between the end of the stage you just finished and returning to the stage selection map.

Secret song:
Go though the opening FMV sequence to the part where PaRappa is writing his name and all the characters appear. Wait until a demo of the game appears. Go though the demo and the opening FMV sequence will appear again. Go though that and go though the part where PaRappa writes his name and wait again. Instead instead of them showing a demo, the colorful noodles will appear on the sides of the screen and the song will start playing.

View Sunny's music video:
Successfully complete the game with the yellow hat, then do the "Secret song" trick. Go though the whole song, then a music video with Sunny singing her intro music on stage will begin.

PARIS-DAKAR RALLY

Unlock All cars:
Enter ILUMBERJACK as a driver name.

PIRATES: THE LEGEND OF BLACK KAT

Invincibility for Katarina:
Hold R1 + R2 and hit ✖, ●, L3, ▲,R3, SELECT, R3, L1, L2, ■.

Invincibility for the Wind Dancer:
Hold R1 + R2 and hit SELECT, ▲, L1, ✖, R3, L2, ■, R3, ●, L3.

Reveal buried treasure chests:
Hold R1 + R2 and hit ●, ✖, ■, ▲, L1, SELECT, L3, L2, L3, R3. Green Xs will appear on the captain's log maps to indicate the location of buried treasure chests.

Reveal all treasure chests:
Hold R1 + R2 and hit R3, ✖, ▲, L3, ●, L1, SELECT, L3, ■, L2.

All treasure chest keys:
Hold R1 + R2 and hit ●, SELECT, ✖, ■, R3, L1, L3, L2, ▲, L3.

Wind Dancer:
Hold R1 + R2 and hit L2, ▲, R3, L3, ✖, ■, R3, SELECT, L1, ●.

Unlimited items:
Hold R1 + R2 and hit ▲, L1, SELECT, L2, R3, L3, ■, ✖, R3, ●. Once found, an item will be available in unlimited amounts.

Extra gold:
Hold R1 + R2 and hit ▲, R3, L3, ✖, ■, R3, SELECT, L1, ●. Sail to another map to get the Galleon.

Unlimited wind boost:
Hold R1 + R2 and hit SELECT, L1, R3, ●, L2, ▲, ✖, L3.

Advance to Katarina's next sword:
Hold R1 + R2 and hit R3, SELECT, L2, L3, ■, ✖, L1, ●, L3, ▲.

Alternate Glacial Gulf music:
Hold R1 + R2 and hit L1, ✖, ▲, L2, ■, ●, L3, SELECT, R3, L3 to hear music from SSX when sliding down in Glacial Gulf.

High pitched voices:
Hold R1 + R2 and hit R3, ●, SELECT, ✖, R3, ▲, L1, ■, L2, L3.

Kane poison head:
Hold R1 + R2 and hit ▲, L2, L1, ■, L3, ✖, L3, ●, R3, SELECT.

POLICE 911

Extra lives:
Beat the "Commissioner" rank without losing any lives or getting suspended to get 100 lives.

PORTAL RUNNER

Level skip:
Hit START to pause the game, then hold L1 and Hit ●, ⇦, ●, ⇨, ●, ■, ⇦ x2, ⇨, R2.

Full health:
Hit START to pause the game, then hold L2 and hit ● x3, ■ x2, R2, R1, ⇧, ●, ■

All FMV sequences:
Hold L1 and hit ⇦, ⇨, ⇦, ⇩, ⇧, ⇩, R1, ●, R2, ■ at the main menu. The "Movies" selection will be unlocked at the options screen. This also unlocks the "Extras" option.

THE POWERPUFF GIRLS: RELISH RAMPAGE

30% health boost:
Press L1, L2, L1, ■, R2, R1, R2.

100% health boost:
Press L2, R1, R2, L1, ✖, ▲, ●, ■, R2, L1, L2, R1.

Extra Chemical X Bottle:
Press ✖ x2 , ●, ✖, ●, L1x2 , ✖ x2 , ●, ✖, ●, L1x2 .

PRISONER OF WAR

All levels unlocked:
Enter ger1eng5 as a case-sensitive password.

No levels unlocked:
Enter defaultm as a case-sensitive password.

All daily events:
Enter alltimes as a case-sensitive password.

All core events:
Enter coretimes as a case-sensitive password.

No core events except current:
Enter farleymydog as a case-sensitive password.

First person view:
Enter Boston as a case-sensitive password to unlock the "First Person View" option. Alternately, get an "A" rank in Camp 5 (Colditz).

Overhead view:
Enter Foxy as a case-sensitive password to unlock the "Top Down View" option. Alternately, get an "A" rank in Camp 4 (Stalag Luft).

Unlimited money or rocks:
Enter Dino as a case-sensitive password to unlock the "Infinite Goodies" option. Alternately, get an "A" rank in Camp 4 (Stalag Luft).

Change guard size:
Enter Muffin as a case-sensitive password to unlock "Size" option. Alternately, get an "A" rank in Camp 2 (Stalag Luft).

Change guard awareness:
Enter Quincy as a case-sensitive password to unlock the "Awareness" option. Alternately, get an "A" rank in Camp 1 (Holding Camp).

Cannot be shot:
Enter Fatty as a case-sensitive password to unlock the "Defiance" option. Alternately, get an "A" rank in Camp 3 (Colditz).

View game creation date and time:
Enter Dt as a case-sensitive password.

Toggle in-game saves:
Enter Togsavecan as a case-sensitive password

PRO RALLY 2002

Unlock All cars, tracks and modes:
Enter PEROPAVO as a name.

Unlock All cars:
Enter MACHOMAN as a name.

Unlock All tracks:
Enter MORATA as a name.

Unlock All arcade mode bonuses:
Enter THEMASTER as a name.

Unlock All game modes:
Enter PACMAN as a name.

Unlock Challenge mode:
Enter CUAQUEZ as a name.

Unlock Trophy mode:
Enter MADDUCK as a name.

Unlock Championship in professional mode:
Enter OOOH SI as a name.

PRO EVOLUTION SOCCER

Unlock European Classic team:
Win the European Cup as England.

Unlock Holland Classic team:
Win the European Cup as Holland.

Unlock Italy Classic team:
Win the European Cup as Italy.

Unlock Germany Classic team:
Win the European Cup as Germany.

Unlock Brazil Classic team:
Win the American Cup as Brazil.

Unlock Argentina Classic team:
Win the American Cup as Argentina.

Unlock World All-Star team:
Win the International Cup as any team.

Unlock European All-Star team:
Win the International Cup as France.

Unlock Chicken team:
Win the International Cup

PRO EVOLUTION SOCCER 2

Unlock Classic Argentina team:
Win the South American Cup as Argentina.
Unlock Classic Brazil team:
Win the South American Cup as Brazil.
Unlock Classic England team:
Win the European Cup as England.
Unlock Classic France team:
Win the European Cup as France.
Unlock Classic Germany team:
Win the European Cup as Germany.
Unlock Classic Holland team:
Win the European Cup as Holland.
Unlock Classic Italy team:
Win the European Cup as Italy.
Unlock European All-Stars team:
Win the International Cup with any team.
Unlock World All-Stars team:
Win the International League as any team.
Unlock Bonus players:
Win the Master League Division 1 to unlock a new set of players.
Unlock Realistic faces:
Win the Asian Cup as Japan to unlock more realistic faces for that team in edit mode.

and Master League Division 1 under the hard difficulty setting as Korea and Manchester.
Unlock Bonus players:
Win the Division 1 Master League to unlock 11 bonus players in freeloan mode. Repeat this two more times to unlock all 33 bonus players.
Winners cup:
Win all cups, leagues, and Division 1 Master League.

PROJECT EDEN

Unlock Cheat mode:
Hit ✖ during the game to display the team menu. Next, hold Select, hit Left Analog-stick ⇧ and rotate it clockwise three times then immediately rotate it anti-clockwise three times, while continuing to hold Select. Your selected character will run around when this is done. While in the same menu, you should notice that a new icon has appeared under the log icon in the lower right hand corner of the screen. Highlight it and hit ✖ to display the cheat menu. The cheat menu allows all weapons, invincibility, unlimited weapon energy, level skip, and level selection.

PROJECT ZERO

Ending bonuses:
Successfully complete the game to unlock the "Battle Mode", "Ghost List", "Sound Test", and "Special Function" options as well as alternate costumes.
Unlock Alternate ending:
Successfully complete the game under the nightmare difficulty setting. You must play from beginning to end.
Unlock Chapter select:
Successfully complete the game under the nightmare difficulty setting. A "Chapter" option will be unlocked in story mode.
Unlock Nightmare mode:
Successfully complete the game in battle mode.

QUAKE 3: REVOLUTION

Level skip:
Hold R1 + R2 + L1 +

SELECT, and hit ✖, ●, ■, ▲, ✖, ●, ■, ▲ during the game. If done correctly, you will automatically win the match.

Pause in multi-player mode:
Since the game does not have a pause option in the multi-player mode, simply hit Start, highlight "Quit" and hit ✖. Your game will be paused, but it will not quit unless you select "Yes". To resume the game, select "No".

Rocket jump:
Pick up a Rocket Launcher and switch to it, then point your gun straight down. Jump, and when you are at your highest point, quickly fire the Rocket Launcher. If done correctly, your character will go high in the air. You will most likely lose a little bit of health while doing this, so be careful.
BFG jump:
This works similarly to the rocket jumpm except it sends you higher. Aim the BFG at the ground, jump, and at the highest point of the jump, shoot down. You will rocket into the air. If done on a spring pad, you will jump higher.

Special item:
If you hear a sound similar to the wind during the game, this is a sign that one or more special items have just appeared. Special items include Quad Damage, Double Damage, Haste, Double Haste, Invincibility, Mega Health, etc.

Bonus characters and level:
Successfully complete the game in campaign mode under the "I Can Win" difficulty setting. A bonus level and two more characters will appear after the credits. Successfully complete the bonus level to unlock it and the new characters in multi-player mode.

RAYMAN 2: REVOLUTION

Unlock Cheat mode:
Go to any map except the first and enter the options screen. Select "Sound",

RATCHET AND CLANK

Cheat mode:
You must complete the game, then enter one of the following codes as Ratchet in game to unlock the corresponding cheat option at the "Goodies" menu when the game is paused.
Big head mode for Clank:
Quickly press Flip Back, Hyper-Strike, Comet-Strike, Double Jump, Hyper-Strike, Flip Left, Flip Right, Full Second Crouch.
Big head mode for enemies:
Quickly press Stretch Jump, Flip Back x3, Stretch Jump, Flip Back x3, Stretch Jump, Flip Back x3, Full Second Crouch.
Big head mode for NPCs:
Quickly press Flip Left, Flip Right, Flip Back x3, Comet-Strike, Double Jump, Comet-Strike, Hyper-Strike.
Big head mode for Ratchet:
Quickly press Flip Back x3, Full Second Crouch, Stretch Jump, Full Second Glide.
Temporary invincibility whenever health is full:
Quickly press Comet-Strike x4 , Flip Back, Full Second Crouch, Flip Back, Full Second Crouch, Comet-Strikex4
Mirrored levels:
Quickly press Flip Left x4, Multi-Strike, Hyper-Strike, Flip Right x4, Double Jump, Crouch.
Trippy contrails:
Quickly press Wall Jump(10), Double Jump, Hyper-Strike. You will see an effect behind you during rail slides.

highlight the "Mute" option, then hold L1 + R1 and hit L2, R2, L2, R2, L2, R2. A cheat menu will appear.

Unlock Secret multi-player maps:
Go to the first map, then enter the options screen. Select "Language", then select "Voices". Highlight the "Raymanian" option, then hold L1 + R1 and hit L2, R2, L2, R2, L2, R2. Three additional multi-player maps will be unlocked.

Baby Soccer secret map names:
Hold L1 + R1 and hit L2, R2, L2, R2, L2, R2 during the game in Baby Soccer.

RAYMAN ARENA

Unlock All characters:
Enter PUPPETS as a name, then hit L2 + ● + ■ to enter it.

Unlock All levels:
Enter ALLRAYMANM as a name, then hit L2 + ● + ■ to enter it.

Unlock All battle levels:
Enter ALLFISH as a name, then hit L2 + ● + ■ to enter it.

Unlock All race levels:
Enter ALLTRIBES as a name, then hit L2 + ● + ■ to enter it.

Unlock All skins:
Enter CARNIVAL as a name, then hit L2 + ● + ■ to enter it.

Old movie-style screen:
Enter OLDTV as a name, then hit L2 + ● + ■ to enter it.

RC REVENGE PRO

Unlock All cars:
Hit L1, L2, R1, R2, ●, ■ at the main menu.

Unlock All tracks:
Hit L1, R1, R2, ■, ● at the main menu.

Unlock Unlock next cup:
Hit L1, R1, R2, L2 at the main menu. Enter this code repeatedly to unlock all seven championships.

READY 2 RUMBLE BOXING: ROUND 2

Master code:
Hit ⇦, ⇨, ⇦ x2, ⇨, ⇧, ⇩, R1 x5, R2 at the character selection screen to unlock all CHEAT in the game.

Unlock All characters:
Hit ⇦ x2, ⇨, R2, ⇦, ⇨ x2, R1 x2, R2 at the character selection screen.

Unlock Champion costumes:
Hit ⇦, ⇩, ⇨ x2, ⇧, R1, R2, R1 x20, R2 at the character selection screen. Hit ■ to cycle through the costumes.

Unlock Holiday costumes:
Hit ⇦ x2, ⇩, ⇨, ⇧, R1 x8, R2, R1 x4, R2 at the character selection screen. Hit ■ to cycle through the costumes.

Unlock All training:
Hit ⇦, ⇩, ⇧, ⇩, ⇧, R1 x20, R2 at the character selection screen.

Unlock New Year's Day secrets:
Hit ⇨, ⇧, ⇩ x3, R1, R2 at the character selection screen.

Unlock Valentine's Day secrets:
Hit ⇨, ⇧, ⇩ x3, R1 x2, R2 at the character selection screen.

Unlock St. Patrick's Day secrets:
Hit ⇨, ⇧, ⇩ x3, R1 x3, R2 at the character selection screen.

Unlock Easter secrets:
Hit ⇨, ⇧, ⇩ x3, R1 x4, R2 at the character selection screen.

Unlock Independence Day secrets:
Hit ⇨, ⇧, ⇩ x3, R1 x5, R2 at the character selection screen.

Unlock Halloween secrets:
Hit ⇨, ⇧, ⇩ x3, R1 x6, R2 at the character selection screen.

Unlock Thanksgiving secrets:
Hit ⇨, ⇧, ⇩ x3, R1 x7, R2 at the character selection screen.

Unlock Christmas secrets:
Hit ⇨, ⇧, ⇩ x3, R1 x8, R2 at the character selection screen.

Unlock Thin boxer:
Hit ⇨ x2, ⇧, ⇩, ⇨, R1, R2 at the character selection screen.

Unlock Fat boxer:
Hit ⇨ x2, ⇧, ⇩, ⇨, R1 x2, R2 at the character selection screen.

Unlock Undead boxer:
Hit ⇦, ⇧, ⇨, ⇩, R1 x2, R2 at the character selection screen.

Unlock Big head:
Hit ⇨ x2, ⇧, ⇩, ⇨, R1 x3 at the character selection screen to unlock all CHEAT in the game.

Unlock Big gloves:
Hit ⇦, ⇨, ⇧, ⇩, R1, R2 at the character selection screen to unlock all CHEAT in the game.

Rumble level 1:
Pause the game, then hit R1, R2, ⇩, ⇧ x2, ⇦, R1 x3, R2.

Rumble level 2:
Pause the game, then hit R1 x2, R2, ⇩, ⇧ x2, ⇦, R1 x4, R2.

Rumble level 3:
Pause the game, then hit R2, R1 x2, R2, R1, R2, R1 x4, R2, ⇦, ⇨, ⇧, ⇩.

Faster speed:
Hit ⇨ x2, ⇧, ⇩, ⇨, R1 x4, R2 at the character selection screen to unlock all CHEAT in the game.

Extra camera angles:
Hit R1 x20, R2, R1, R2, R1 x21, R2, R1 x18, R2, R1 x9, R2, R1 x14, R2, R1 x5, R2, ⇦, ⇨, ⇧, ⇩, R2 at the character selection screen to unlock all CHEAT in the game. Pause the game to access.

Final match:
Hit R2, ⇩, ⇨, ⇧, ⇦, R1 x6, R2, R1 x2, R2 at the character selection screen to unlock all CHEAT in the game.

Freak E. Deke and Michael Jackson:
Hit R1 x13, R2, R1 x10, R2 at the character selection screen in arcade mode.

REDCARD SOCCER 2003

Cheat mode:
Enter BIGTANK as your player nameto unlock all teams, stadiums, and finals mode.

Unlock Apes team and Victoria Falls stadium:
Defeat the Apes team in World Conquest mode.

Unlock Dolphins team and Nautilus stadium:
Defeat the Dolphins team in World Conquest mode.

RED FACTION 2

Unlock Master cheat code:
Enter ■, ●, ▲, ●, ■, ✖, ▲, ✖ at the cheats screen under the options menu.

Unlock Master code:
Enter ▲, ▲, ✖, ✖, ■, ●, ■, ● at the cheats screen under the options menu.

Unlock Level select:
Enter ●, ■, ✖, ▲, ■, ●, ✖, ✖ at the cheats screen under the options menu.

Unlock Super health:
Enter ✖, ✖, ■, ▲, ■, ▲, ● at the cheats screen under the options menu.

Unlock Unlimited ammunition:
Enter ■, ▲, ✖, ●, ■, ●, ✖, ▲ at the cheats screen under the options menu.

Unlock Unlimited grenades:
Enter ●, ✖, ●, ■, ✖, ●, ✖, ● at the cheats screen under the options menu.

Unlock Rapid rails:
Enter ●, ■, ●, ■, ✖, ✖, ▲, ▲ at the cheats screen under the options menu.

Unlock Bouncy grenades:
Enter ●, ●, ●, ●, ●, ●, ●, ● at the cheats screen under the options menu.

Unlock Gibby explosions:
Enter ▲, ●, ✖, ■, ▲, ●, ✖, ■ at the cheats screen under the options menu.

Unlock Gibby bullets:
Enter ●, ●, ●, ●, ▲, ✖, ●, ● at the cheats screen under the options menu.

Unlock Instagib ammunition:
Enter ✖, ✖, ✖, ✖, ■, ●, ✖, ✖ at the cheats screen under the options menu.

Unlock Directors cut:
Enter ■, ✖, ●, ▲, ●, ✖, ■, ▲ at the cheats screen under the options menu.

Unlock Walking dead:
Enter ✖, ✖, ✖, ✖, ✖, ✖, ✖, ✖ at the cheats screen under the options menu.

Unlock Kraken team and Nagai stadium:
Conquer Finals mode, and defeat the Martian team and Kraken team.

Unlock Martians team and USAFB001 stadium:
Defeat the Martians team in World Conquest mode.
Unlock Matadors team and Coliseum stadium:
Defeat the Matadors team in World Conquest mode.

Unlock Ninjas team and Youhi Gardens stadium:
Defeat the Samurai team in World Conquest mode.

Unlock Penguins team and South Pole stadium:
Defeat the Penguins team in World Conquest mode.

Unlock Seals team and Aircraft Carrier stadium:
Defeat the Seals team in World Conquest mode.

Unlock SWAT team and Nova City stadium:
Defeat the SWAT team in World Conquest mode.

Unlock Tonatiuh, Xochicalco teams and Tepoztlan stadium:
Defeat the Tonatiuh, Xochicalco team in World Conquest mode.

Unlock Zombies team and Haunted Mansion stadium:
Defeat the Zombies team in World Conquest mode.

Unlock Finals mode:
Win all matches in World Conquest mode.

RESIDENT EVIL: SURVIVOR 2

View Secret Report:
Collect all the messages in each level to unlock the Secret Report.

Unlock Vs. Roach mode:
Successfully complete the first mission in dungeon mode.

Unlock Panzerfaust EX:
Successfully complete the game in Vs. Roach mode to unlock the Panzerfaust EX in Vs. Roach Mode with unlimited ammunition.

Unlock Chris Redfield:
Successfully complete Inferno mission 6 to unlock Chris Redfield with a Linear Launcher with unlimited ammunition in dungeon mode.

Unlock Rodrigo:
Successfully complete all the dungeon missions, including Inferno mission 7, to unlock Rodrigo with only a combat knife in dungeon mode.

REIGN OF FIRE

Level select:
Press ⇧, ⇦, ● x2 , ⇦ x2 , ■, ⇩, ⇧, ● at the main menu.

Level skip:
Press ■, ▲, ⇦, ⇩, ⇨, ▲, ⇨, ⇧, ✖ in game.

Invincibility:
Press ✖, ▲, ⇨, ⇦, ●, ⇧, ⇩ x2, ⇨, ● x2 in game.

Extra damage:
Press ✖, ▲, ⇨, ⇧, ⇨, ▲, ●, ⇨ in game.

Burn everything:
Press ■, ▲, ⇦, ⇩, ■, ● in game.

Goat mode:
Press ▲, ⇨, ⇦ x2 , ●, ▲, ■, ⇨, ⇧ in game.

RESIDENT EVIL CODE: VERONICA X

Unlock Battle mode:
Successfully complete the game under any difficulty setting. The game will automatically save after the credits have completed. A battle mode option will be unlocked at the main menu.

Unlock first person view:
Successfully complete the game under the easy or normal difficulty setting.

Unlock Linear launcher:
Get an A ranking with Steve Burnside, Chris and Albert Wesker and both versions of Claire in battle mode to unlock the linear launcher. It will appear in your inventory during the next battle mode game.

Play as Steve Burnside in battle mode:
Get the gold Luger replica from the basement office in Disc 2. The correct drawer sequence is red, green, blue, and bottom. You can also unlock Steve Burnside by performing well in battle mode as Chris.

Steve Burnside cross-fire with sub machine guns:
While playing in battle mode, kill all but one zombie in any room. While equipped with sub machine guns, walk up to the zombie and hit ✖, and Steve will cross his sub machine guns. For best results, play in third person so you can see the cross-fire. If there is more than one zombie, Steve might aim at two zombies rather than cross-firing at one.

Play as alternate Claire in battle mode:
Perform well with the original Claire in battle mode.

Play as alternate Chris in battle mode:
Complete battle mode as Wesker. He is armed only with a knife.

Play as Albert Wesker in battle mode:
Take Albert Wesker's sunglasses from the floor in the Incubation Lab after the intermission sequence when playing as Chris. Alternately, perform well in battle mode with Steve Burnside.

Self-destruct code
Enter "Veronica" as the code when playing as Chris on Disc 2 when you have to open all doors and elevators to save Claire with 5:00 minutes to evacuate.

Find a magnum for Wesker
Locate the casino room where everyone got a first aid from the slot machine. Wesker will hit it and the bottom will open and reveal a magnum instead of a first aid spray. Although it only has six shots, it will only take five to kill Alexia type 1.

Unlock Grenade launcher
Before you go up to the Residential House on the Hill, take the ladder in the area outside in the "Training Facility" where Alfred ambushed you with the sniper rifle. It will lead you back to where you played as Steve. You can get a grenade launcher and ammo, but you need the Blue Card Key.

Portrait puzzle solution
This is the sequence to solve the puzzle in the room with the portraits. The number in brackets is their position clockwise when facing the door.
Beautiful woman holding tea set x4.
Middle aged man with red-haired twins x7.
Red-haired man holding a teaset x2.
Red-haired man with earthenware plate x6.
Man with earthenware vase x1.
Man with candlestick x5.
Young man from projector.

REZ

Unlock Area 2:
Successfully complete Area 1.

Unlock Area 3:
Successfully complete Area 2.

Unlock Area 4:
Successfully complete Area 3.

Unlock Area 5:
Get a 100% ranking in Area 1 through Area 4.

RIDGE RACER 5

Unlock Third person view onscreen display:
Hold Select while racing in the third person perspective to display onscreen info that includes the amount of hiture being used on various controller buttons.

Unlock Control introduction sequence:
Hit L1 and R1 during the introduction sequence with the girl walking down the street to cycle through three different effects for the portion that uses the in-game graphics. Hit R1 for black and white graphics. Hit R1 a second time and the graphics will have a yellow tint. Hit R1 a third time to add blur effect, which will eliminate jagged graphics. Hit L1 to cycle back through the various effects.

Quick start:
When in time attack mode, hold R2 + L2 at the start to get a speed boost from the instant light turns green.

Unlock Duel mode:
Finish in first place in lap and overall time in the Standard Time Attack GP.

Unlock Bonus cars:
Successfully complete each of the Grand Prix circuits to unlock new cars. Breaking the Time Attack high scores also unlocks additional cars.

Unlock 50's Super Drift Caddy:
Finish in first place in the Danver Spectra race in duel mode to unlock the 50's Super Drift Caddy car in free run, time attack, and duel mode.

Unlock Devil Drift:
Finish in first place in the Rivelta Crinale race in duel mode to unlock the Devil Drift car in free run, time attack, and duel mode.

Unlock VW Beetle:
Finish in first place in the Solort Rumeur race in duel mode to unlock the new style

ROCKY

Unlock The Gold Class Tournament
Beat the Silver version of the Knockout Tournament.
Unlock The Mickey Goldmill
Beat Movie Mode while playing through on the Champ setting.
Unlock The Rocky Statue
Beat Movie Mode while playing through on the Contender setting.
Unlock The Silver Class Tournament
Beat the Bronze version of the Knockout Tournament.

VW Beetle car (with super grip handling) in free run, time attack, and duel mode.

Unlock McLaren F1 clone:
Finish in first place in the Kamata Angelus race in duel mode to unlock the McLaren F1 clone in free run, time attack, and duel mode.

Unlock 99 lap mode:
Set the top score in each race of the Time Attack GP in Extra Mode, finishing in first place.

Unlock Pac-Man mode:
Exceed 3,000 kilometers in total distance raced to unlock the Pac-Man Race. Win the Pac-Man race to unlock a red roadster with a Pac-Man driver and the Ghosts on scooters as opponents.

RUMBLE RACING

The following codes can be entered when the load/save screen under options is toggled. If the code does not work, replace the letter "I" with the number "1", "B" for "8", or the letter "O" for the number "0" (or vice versa).

Unlock Buckshot:
Enter UBTCKSTOH as a password.

Unlock Cobalt:
Enter TLACOBTLA as a password.

Unlock Gamecus:
Unlock Enter BSUIGASUM as a password.

Unlock High Roller:
Enter HGIROLREL as a password.

Unlock Interceptor:
Enter CDAAPTN1A as a password.

Unlock Redneck Rocket:
Enter KCEROCTEK as a password.

Unlock Revolution:
Enter PTOATRTO1 as a password.

Unlock Road Trip:
Enter ABOGOBOGA as a password.

Unlock Sporticus:
Enter OPSRTISUC as a password.

Unlock Stinger:
Enter AMHBRAAMH as a password.

Unlock Thor:
Enter THTORHROT as a password.

Unlock Van Itty:
Enter VTYANIYTT as a password.

Unlock Vortex:
1AREXT1AR as a password.

Unlock XXS Tomcat:
Enter NALDSHHSD as a password.

Unlock Pro Cup 2, Falls Down track, and Cataclysm car:
Enter P1PROC1PU as a password.

Unlock Pro Cup 3, The Gauntlet track, EsCargot car:
Enter Q2PROC2YT as a password.

Unlock Elite cup series, Surf and Turf track, Elite Class cars, Road Kill car:
Enter AEPPROPUC as a password.

Unlock Elite cup 2, Coal Cuts track, Jolly Roger car:
Enter ILETEC1MB as a password.

Unlock Elite Cup 3, Malice car, Wild Kingdom track:
Enter ILCTEC2VB as a password.

Unlock Elite Cup 4, Over Easy track, Direwolf car:
Enter ILQTEC3PU as a password.

Unlock EA Elite Cup, Outer Limits track, Blue Devil car:

Enter LEAITEPUC as a password.

Unlock Grand Champion video, EA Stunt Cup:
Enter YEAMPLOWW as a password.

Unlock Circus Minimus track:
Enter ZEAGTLUKE as the code.

RUN LIKE HELL

Unlock Getting past the first Brute:
Press ▲, ■, ●, ■ to get past the first Brute that blocks you.

Unlock Entering Storage Room B:
Enter ■, ●, ●, ■, ✖ as the combination.

Unlock Opening the guard room door:
After going through Storage Room B and getting on the deck, enter ▲, ■, ✖, ▲, ✖ at the guard room door.

RUNE: VIKING WARLORD

God mode:
Pause the game and hit ■, ●, ⇦, ⇨, ●, ■.

Maximum Rune power:
Pause the game and hit ⇧, ⇩, ⇦, ⇨, ■, ●.

RYGAR: THE LEGENDARY ADVENTURE

In-game restart:
Press and hold Start + Select in game.
Unlock Easy mode:
Die three times under the normal difficulty setting to unlock easy mode.
Unlock Hard mode:
You must complete the game under the normal difficulty setting to unlock hard mode.
Unlock Legendary mode:
You must complete the game under the hard difficulty setting to unlock hard mode.
Unlock Guitarmor:
You must complete the game under the normal difficulty setting.
Unlock Hamburgarmor:
You must complete the game under the hard difficulty setting with an "A" rank.
Unlock Rollerarmor:
You must complete the game under the hard difficulty setting.

SAVAGE SKIES

Unlock All creatures:
Hit ⇦, ⇨, ⇦ x2, ⇨, ✖ at the main menu.
Unlock All multi-player levels:
Hit ⇦, ⇨, ⇦, ⇨, ⇧, ⇦, ⇨, ✖ at the main menu.
Invincibility:
Hit Start to pause the game, then hit ⇦ x2, ⇨ x2, ⇧ x2, ✖.
Mark all objectives complete:
Hit Start to pause the game, then hit ⇦, ⇨ x2, ⇩, ⇧, ⇩, ⇩, ✖.
Crystal:
Hit Start to pause the game, then hit ⇦, ⇨, ⇦, ⇧, ⇨, ⇩, ⇦, ✖ x2.

SCOOBY DOO: NIGHT OF 100 FRIGHTS

All power-ups:
Pause the game then hold L1 + L2 + R1 + R2 and quickly hit ●, ■, ●, ■, ●, ■ x3, ● x2, ■, ● x3.

All FMV sequences:
Pause the game then hold L1 + L2 + R1 + R2 and quickly hit ■ x3, ● x3, ■, ●, ■.

View credits:
Pause the game then hold L1 + L2 + R1 + R2 and quickly hit ■, ● x2, ■, ●, ■.

SHADOW OF MEMORIES

Replay mode:
When you complete the game, one of five endings will appear. An extra menu will now be available at the title screen, which allows you to view the percentage completed for every chapter. You can also start the completed game over again at the beginning to try to do better.

Restore energy units:
When you find yourself running out of energy units, allow yourself to die. The moment you are brought back to life, you will get an energy unit for free. For example, if you let yourself die five times in a row you will get five energy units for free. Do this trick each time you begin a new chapter.

Extra ending:
Unlock all five normal endings. A special prologue will appear, allowing you to play again and unlock the "Extra" ending. In EX Mode, you must find the elixir of life for Mrs. Wagner.

SHAUN PALMER'S PRO SNOWBOARDER

Master code:
Highlight the "Options" selection at the main menu. Then, hold L2 + ⇦ and hit ▲, ■, ▲, ●, ▲. All CHEAT will be unlocked.

Unlock All character goals and boards:
Highlight the "Options" selection at the main menu. Then, hold R2 + ⇨ and hit ▲, ■, ▲, ●, ▲. This also unlocks the two secret characters.

Unlock Bonus characters:
Highlight the "Options" selection at the main menu. Then, hold L1 + ⇦ and hit ▲ x2, ●, ▲.

Level select:
Highlight the "Options" selection at the main menu. Then, hold R1 + ⇨ and hit ▲, ■, ▲, ●, ▲.

Maximum stats:
Highlight the "Options" selection at the main menu. Then, hold L1 + ⇨ and hit ▲ x2, ●, ▲.

SHINOBI

Bonuses:
Collect the gold Oboro Clan Coins in game to unlock bonus options in the extras menu.
Play as Moritsune:
Collect 30 Oboro Clan Coins in game.
Play as Joe Musashi:
Collect 40 Oboro Clan Coins in game.
VR stage:
Collect 50 Oboro Clan Coins in game.
Hard difficulty setting:
You must complete the game under the normal difficulty setting.
Insane difficulty setting:
You must complete the game under the hard difficulty setting.

SILENT HILL 2

Extra options menu:
Hit L1 or R1 at the options screen to display an extra options menu with blood colour, map zoom, and other selections.

In-game reset:
Hit L1 + L2 + R1 + R2 + SELECT + START during the game.

Completion bonuses:
Successfully complete the game. Start another game and enter the extra options menu to access new features. A "Bullet Adjust" option can be set, allowing the normal amount of ammunition found at a location to be doubled or tripled. A "Noise Effect" option can be toggled. Another new option can be toggled, allowing scenes to be viewed without distortion.

Additional riddle difficulty:
Successfully complete the game under the easy, normal, and hard riddle difficulty settings. Select the hard riddle difficulty again and begin a new game with a new combination of riddles.

Reveal signs:
Unlock all five endings, then start a new game. All signs will now be revealed.

Book Of Lost Memories:
Successfully complete the game. Start a new game and look for the newspaper stand near the Texxon Gas Station. The Book Of Lost Memories can be found inside.

Unlock The Book Of The Crimson Ceremony:
This book can be found in the reading room on the second floor of the "Nightmare" hotel.

Unlock The Chain Saw:
Successfully complete the game under the normal difficulty and normal riddle difficulty settings. Start a new game to find the Chain Saw among logs before the cemetery.

Unlock Dog Key:
Successfully complete the game with the "Rebirth" ending. Start a new game and a doghouse will now appear near Jack's Inn and the gas station. Look inside the doghouse to find the Dog Key. It is used to open the observation room in the "nightmare" hotel.

Unlock Hyper Spray:
Successfully complete the game two times. Start a new game to find the Hyper Spray on the south side of the motor home.

Unlock Obsidian Goblet:
Successfully complete the game. Start a new game and enter the Historical Society building. The Obsidian Goblet can be found on a shelf.

Unlock White Chrism:
Successfully complete the game. Start a new game to find White Chrism vial in the kitchen of apartment 105 in Blue Creek Apartments.

Introduction FMV sequence audio:
If you wait at the title screen for a while, the introduction FMV sequence will begin. In some scenes, there will be no audio. Successfully complete the game one time and the audio will be restored to those scenes.

SILENT SCOPE

Professional Challenge mode:
Hold Trigger at the mode selection screen and highlight "Training" or "Arcade". Keep Trigger held and hit START x4. The aiming ring and enemy markers will be disabled in this mode.

Night Vision Challenge mode:
Hold Trigger at the mode selection screen and highlight "Training" or "Arcade". Keep Trigger held and hit START x5. The game will begin at night and require the Night Vision scope. Alternately, hit ⇧, ⇦, ⇩, ⇨, ⇧, ■, ▲ at the mode selection screen.

Professional Night Vision Challenge mode:
Hold Trigger at the mode selection screen and highlight "Training" or "Arcade". Keep Trigger held and hit START x6. The game will begin at night, with no aiming ring or enemy markers.

Convert health to time:
Hit START to pause the game in arcade mode, then hit ⇧ x2, ⇩ x2, ⇦, ⇨, ⇦, ⇨, ✖, ●. One half of a life will be converted into five extra seconds. This code can be repeated.

Convert time to health:
Hit START to pause the game in arcade mode, then hit ▲, ✖, ⇨, ⇦, ⇨, ⇦, ●, ✖, ⇨, ⇦, ⇨, ⇦, ⇩ x2, ⇧ x2. Five seconds from the timer will be converted to one half of a life. This code can be repeated.

Mirrored levels:
Hit ⇦ x2, ⇨, ■, ⇩ x2, ⇧, ▲, ⇧, ⇨, ⇩, ⇧, ⇦, ⇩, Square at the mode selection screen.

Unlock First person view:
Hit ⇧ x4, ⇩ x4 at the mode selection screen.

Disable aiming ring:
Hit ⇨ x3, ■ at the mode selection screen.

Disable enemy markers:
Hit ⇨ x4, ⇦, ⇩, ⇧, ⇨ at the mode selection screen.

Disable scope:
Hit ⇨, ⇩, ⇨, ■, ⇨, ⇩, ⇨, ■ at the mode selection screen.

Unlock Love mode:
Hit ⇦, ⇨, ⇨, ■, ▲ at the mode selection screen.

Unlock Turbo mode:
Hit ⇩, ▲, ⇧, ■, ▲, ⇩, ⇨, ⇩, ⇨, ■, ▲ at the mode selection screen.

Unlock Hidden mode:
Hit ⇨, ⇩, ⇨, ■, ⇧, ■ x2, ▲, ⇩, ⇨, ⇩, ⇨, ■, ▲ at the mode selection screen.

100 Challenge mode:
Successfully complete all nine Outdoor Shooting Range challenges to unlock 100 Challenge Mode.

SILENT SCOPE 2: DARK SILHOUETTE

Convert health to time:
Hit START to pause the game in arcade mode, then hit ⇧ x2, ⇩ x2, ⇦, ⇨, ⇦, ⇨, ✖, ●. One half of a life will be converted into five extra seconds. This code can be repeated.

Convert time to health:
Hit START to pause the game in arcade mode, then hit ●, ✖, ⇨, ⇦, ⇨, ⇦, ⇩ x2, ⇧ x2. Five seconds from the timer will be converted to one half of a life. This code can be repeated.

Disable enemy markers:
Hit ⇨ x4, ⇦, ⇩, ⇧, ⇨ at the mode selection screen.

Get Three credits:
After continuing the game 16 times, you will be able to increase the credits to three on the options screen.

Get Four credits:
After continuing the game 31 times, you will be able to increase the credits to four on the options screen.

Get Unlimited credits:
After continuing the game 101 times, you will be able to increase the credits to infinite on the options screen.

Get Additional lives:
Intentionally lose the game by dying repeatedly to increase the number of lives per credit between four to six.

Get Additional time:
Intentionally lose the game by allowing the timer to run out repeatedly to increase the time limit between seventy and eighty.

Unlock Time attack boss mode:
After you defeat the big Boss by shooting him three times, he will hang from the tower. Shoot the chain and complete the game that way to unlock time attack boss mode.

Unlock Survival boss mode:
After you defeat the big Boss by shooting him three times, he will hang from the tower. If you shoot him or the girl, they will both fall. You will complete the game and unlock survival boss mode.

SILPHEED: THE LOST PLANET

Unlock All weapons:
Enter GLOIRE as a name.

THE SIMPSONS: ROAD RAGE

Horizontal split screen:
Hold L1 + R1 and hit ■ x4 at the options menu. The screen will be split horizontally instead of vertically in two-player mode.

Alternate views:
Hold L1 + R1 and hit ▲ x4 at the options menu. Additional views will be unlocked at the pause screen. To unlock another set of views, hold L1 + R1 and hit ▲, ✖ x3 at the options menu.

Night-time:
Hold L1 + R1 and hit ✖ x4 at the options menu.

Flat characters:
Hold L1 + R1 and hit ● x4 at the options menu. All the people (except the character you selected) will be flat.

Show collision lines:
Hold L1 + R1 and hit ▲ x2, ✖ x2 at the options menu.

No map display:
Hold L1 + R1 and hit ■, ▲ x2, ● at the options menu.

Drive red brick car:
Hold L1 + R1 and hit ▲ x2, ■, ● at the options menu. This car is controlled by Homer and is small, fast and heavy.

Drive as Smithers in Mr. Burn's limousine:
Hold L1 + R1 and hit ▲ x2, ■ x2 at the options menu.

Drive Nuclear Bus:
Hold L1 + R1 and hit ▲ x2, ■, ✖ at the options menu.

Special car moves:
Hold L1 + R1 and hit ✖, ▲ x2, ✖ at the options menu. Hold Gas + Brake + Handbrake while steering left or right while in mid-air to execute the Road Rage Roll. Hold Gas + Handbrake while stationary, then release Handbrake to execute the Speed Boost.

Time trial mode:
Hold L1 + R1 and hit ●, ▲, ■, ✖ at the options menu. There are no passengers, pedestrians or traffic in this mode. Hit the Horn to start, stop, and reset the timer.

Slow motion:
Hold L1 + R1 and hit ✖, ●, ▲, ■ at the options menu.

Halloween mode:
Hold L1 + R1 and hit ▲ x2, ●, ✖ at the options menu. Select any character to play as Bart in a Frankenstein costume. Alternatively, set the system date to October 31.

New Year's Day mode:
Hold L1 + R1 and hit ▲ x2, ●, ■ at the options menu. Select any character to play as Krusty in a tuxedo, Alternatively, set the system date to January 1.

Thanksgiving mode:
Hold L1 + R1 and hit ▲ x2, ● x2 at the options menu. Select any character to play as Marge in a pilgrim dress. Alternatively, set the system date to the third Thursday in November.

Christmas mode:
Hold L1 + R1 and hit ▲ x2, ●, ▲ at the options menu. Select any character to play as Apu in a Santa costume. Alternatively, set the system date to December 25.

Disable all active codes:
Hold L1 + R1 and hit START x4 at the options menu.

Unlock Car built for Homer:
Complete all ten levels in mission mode to unlock the car built for Homer.

SIMPSONS: SKATEBOARDING

Unlocking cheats:
You must complete the game as any character or collecting all items in Skatefest with Chief Wiggum to unlock a cheat.

Bonus skaters:
Finish in first place on two different Timed Trick Contest stages to unlock an additional skater.

SKY ODYSSEY

Unlock Auto Gyro:
Successfully complete all levels in sky canvas mode with more than 90 points.

Unlock Corsair:
Accumulate enough acrobatic points in adventure Mode to have ten of your mission grades marked with circles.

Unlock Gold UFO:
Successfully complete all levels in target mode with a gold rank.
Unlock Me-262:
Successfully complete adventure mode.

Unlock Silver UFO:
Successfully complete all levels in the adventure mode with an A rank.

Unlock Stealth fighter:
Successfully complete target mode with a total time of 10 minutes. You do not have to get them in any order or colour, simply get the targets and land in less than 10 minutes.

SKY SURFER

Cool Moves:
Scorpion: Hit ●, ▲, ✖
Menhouse Surprise:
Hit ■, ▲, ✖
Opening Touring CA:
Hit ■ x3, ●
The Plate: Hit ▲, ✖, ▲, ✖
Tidy Bowel In The Hole:
Hit ■, ✖, ●, ✖
Bending Reed: Hit ▲, ■, ✖, ●
Propeller: Hit ■, ▲, ✖, ●
Free Fall: Hit ▲, ✖ x2, ▲
Burner Speed: Hit ● x3, ■
Snow Ball: Hit ▲, ■ x2, ●
Avalanche: Hit ▲, ● x2, ■
Rolling Barrel Left:
Hit ✖, ● x2, ✖
Rolling Barrel Right:
Hit ✖, ■ x2, ✖

SLED STORM

Master code:
Hold L1 + R1 and hit ●, ■, ⇧, ●, ▲, ⇩ at the "Hit Start" screen.

Unlock All characters:
Hold L1 + R1 and hit ●, ▲, ●, ▲, ●, ⇩ at the "Hit Start" screen.

Unlock All sleds:
Hold L1 + R1 and hit ●, ■, ●, ■, ●, ⇦ at the "Hit Start" screen.

Unlock Hover sled:
Hold L1 + R1 and hit ●, ▲, ■, ●, ▲, ⇨ at the "Hit Start" screen.

Unlock All tracks:
Hold L1 + R1 and hit ●, ⇦, ●, ⇨, ●, ⇧ at the "Hit Start" screen.

Unlock Rival challenge mode:
Complete the game in championship mode as any character to unlock rival challenge mode.

Unlock Black Diamond track:
Win championship mode as any character to unlock the Black Diamond track.

SLY COOPER AND THE THIEVIUS RACCOONUS

Ending bonuses:
Get all the bottles hidden within a level. A FMV sequence, special move, or background information will be unlocked.
You must complete the game to unlock the introduction sequence from the Japanese version of the game.
Find all Thievius Raccoonus pages to unlock the Thievius Raccoonus ending sequence.
You must complete all Master Thief Runs to unlock a background FMV sequence.

SMASH COURT PRO TOURNAMENT

Unlock Red Ace:
Win the game in arcade mode under the hard difficulty setting as a male character with no losses. Select exhibition mode and move past Rafter on the character selection screen to access Red Ace.

Unlock Hitomi Yoshino:
Win the game in arcade mode under the hard difficulty setting as a female character with no losses. Select exhibition mode and move past Rafter on the character selection screen to access Red Ace.

Unlock Ultimate difficulty:
Successfully complete time attack mode on the hard difficulty setting.

SMUGGLER'S RUN

Unlock Invisibility:
Pause the game, then hit R1, L1 x2, R2, L1 x2, L2. Repeat this code to disable its effect.

Lighter cars:
Pause the game, then hit

L1, R1 x2, L2, R2 x2. Repeat this code to disable its effect.

Unlock No gravity:
Pause the game, then hit R1, R2, R1, R2, ⇧ x3. Repeat this code to disable its effect.

Increase time warp:
Pause the game, then hit R1, L1, L2, R2, ⇨ x3. This can be repeated up to three times to increase the effect.

Decrease time warp:
Pause the game, then hit R2, L2, L1, R1, ⇦ x3. This can be repeated up to three times to increase the effect.

Unlock Lowrider:
Pause the game then quickly enter the "Increase time warp" code three times. Note: This only works on joyride mode and only on certain cars of a certain team and on certain levels for each car.

Make traffic fly
Enable the "No gravity" and "Lighter cars" code. Tap or slam into a car. Depending on how hard it was hit, the car will slowly or very quickly begin to "fly" into the air.

SMUGGLER'S RUN 2: HOSTILE TERRITORY

Drive a limousine:
Pause the game, then hold R1 and hit ■, ✖ x3, ▲, L1, R1. Quit the game, go to main menu, then hit R1 + L1 + L2 + R2 + ■. Choose Joy Ridin' mode and you will be able to select a limousine.

Unlock Transparent car:
Pause the game, then hit ⇦, ⇧, ⇨, ⇩, ⇨, ⇧, ⇦, L2.

Unlock Invisible car:
Pause the game, then hit R1, L1 x2, R2, L1 x2, L2.

Unlock Lighter cars:
Pause the game, then hit L1, R1 x2, L2, R2 x2.

No gravity:
Pause the game, then hit R1, R2, R1, R2, ⇧ x3.

Increase time warp:
Pause the game, then hit R1, L1, L2, R2, ⇨ x3.

Decrease time warp:
Pause the game, then hit R2, L2, L1, R1, ⇦ x3.

Increase frame rate:
Pause the game, then hit R3, L3 x2, R3, ⇦, ●, ⇦, ●.

Unlimited countermeasures:
Pause the game, then hit R3 x3, R1 x2, R2 x2.

Unlock ATV Boost:
Successfully complete Smuggler's Mission 14.

Unlock ATV Monster:
Successfully complete Smuggler's Mission 10.

Unlock Baja Truck Bombs:
Successfully complete Smuggler's Mission 7.

Unlock Baja Truck:
Successfully complete Smuggler's Mission 4.

Unlock D-5 Hondo:
Successfully complete Smuggler's Mission 11.

Unlock Du Monde Oil Slick:
Successfully complete Smuggler's Mission 5.

Unlock Dual Career Countermeasures:
Successfully complete Smuggler's Mission 36.

Unlock Grenadier Bombs:
Successfully complete Smuggler's Mission 25.

Unlock Grenadier:
Successfully complete Smuggler's Mission 24.

Unlock Hondo Oil Slick:
Successfully complete Smuggler's Mission 15.

Unlock Hoverbike:
Beat a "Great" rank on all Smuggler's missions.

Unlock Kavostov Halftrack:
Successfully complete Smuggler's Mission 27.

Unlock Kavostov Smoke Screen:
Successfully complete Smuggler's Mission 29.

SOLDIER OF FORTUNE

Invincibility:
Hit SELECT during the game, then hold R1 + L1 + R2 + L2 + ■ and hit ⇦. Repeat the code to disable its effect.

Full ammunition:
Hit SELECT during the game, then hold R1 + ■ and hit ⇦. Note: This code will reset your current weapons to only those available during level 1. Repeat the code to disable its effect.

Heavy weapons:
Hit SELECT during the game, then hold L2 + R2 + ■ and hit ⇦.

Hand to hand weapons and explosives:
Hit SELECT during the

game, then hold L1 + R1 + ■ and hit ⇦.

No clipping:
Hit Select during the game, then hold L1 + L2 + R1 + ■ and hit ⇦. You may now walk through walls.

No target:
Hit SELECT during the game, then hold L1 + L2 + ■ and hit ⇦. Repeat the code to disable its effect.

No gravity:
Hit SELECT during the game, then hold L1 + L2 + R2 + ⇦ + ■ and hit START.

SOCOM: US NAVY SEALS

Unlock More weapons:
Successfully complete the game under the "Ensign" difficulty setting to unlock terrorist weapons in the armoury during single player mode. Successfully complete the game under the "Lieutenant" difficulty setting to unlock the MGL (Multiple Grenade Launcher).

Unlock Level select:
Successfully complete the game under the "Lieutenant JG" difficulty setting.

Unlock Lieutenant JG difficulty:
Successfully complete the game under the "Ensign" difficulty setting.

Unlock Lieutenant difficulty:
Successfully complete the game under the "Lieutenant JG" difficulty setting.

Unlock Lieutenant Commander difficulty:
Successfully complete the game under the "Lieutenant" difficulty setting.

Unlock Commander difficulty:
Successfully complete the game under the "Lieutenant Commander" difficulty setting.

Unlock Captain difficulty:
Successfully complete the game under the "Commander" difficulty setting.

Unlock Rear Admiral difficulty:
Successfully complete the game under the "Captain" difficulty setting.

Unlock Admiral difficulty:
Successfully complete the game under the "Rear Admiral" difficulty setting.

SPIDER-MAN: THE MOVIE

Master code:
Enter the "Specials" menu and enter ARACHNID as the code. All levels in the level warp option, all gallery options (movie viewer/ production art), and combo moves will be unlocked.

Unlimited webbing:
Enter the "Specials" menu and enter ORGANICWEBBING as the code. Alternatively, accumulate 50,000 points during the game

All fighting controls:
Enter the "Specials" menu and enter KOALA as the code.

Level select:
Enter the "Specials" menu and enter IMIARMAS as the code.

Level skip:
Enter the "Specials" menu and enter ROMITAS as the code. Pause the game and select the "Next Level" option to advance to the next level.

Bonus training levels:
Enter the "Specials" menu and enter HEADEXPLODY as the code.

Play as Mary Jane:
Enter the "Specials" menu and enter GIRLNEXTDOOR as the code.

Play as The Shocker:
Enter the "Specials" menu and enter HERMANSCHULTZ as the code.

Play as a scientist:
Enter the "Specials" menu and enter SERUM as the code.

Play as a police officer:
Enter the "Specials" menu and enter REALHERO as the code.

Play as Captain Stacey (helicopter pilot):
Enter the "Specials" menu and enter CAPTAINSTACEY as the code.

Play as Skulls Gang Thug:
Enter the "Specials" menu and enter KNUCKLES as the code.

Play as Uncle Ben's Killer:
Enter the "Specials" menu and enter STICKYRICE as the code.

Play as Shocker's Thug:
Enter the "Specials" menu and enter THUGSRUS as the code.

Matrix-style attacks:
Enter the "Specials" menu and enter DODGETHIS as the code.

Goblin-style costume:
Enter the "Specials" menu and enter FREAKOUT as the code.

Small Spider-Man:
Enter the "Specials" menu and enter SPIDERBYTE as the code. When this code is enabled, your shadow will remain normal-sized.

Big head and feet for Spider-Man:
Enter the "Specials" menu and enter GOESTOYOURHEAD as the code.

Enemies have big heads:
Enter the "Specials" menu and enter JOELSPEANUTS as the code.

First person view:
Enter the "Specials" menu and enter UNDERTHEMASK as the code.

Unlimited Green Goblin glider power:
Enter the "Specials" menu and enter CHILLOUT as the code.

Pinhead Bowling mini-game:
Accumulate 10,000 points during the game to unlock the Pinhead bowling mini-game in the training menu.

Vulture FMV sequence:
Accumulate 20,000 points during the game to unlock a Vulture FMV sequence in the CG menu.

Shocker FMV sequence:
Accumulate 30,000 points during the game to unlock a Vulture FMV sequence in the CG menu.

Green Goblin FMV sequence:
Successfully complete the game on the hero or greater difficulty setting.

Play as Alex Ross:
Successfully complete the game on the normal or higher difficulty setting to unlock the Alex Ross costume in the specials menu.

Play as the Green Goblin:
Successfully complete the game on the hero or super hero difficulty setting to unlock the Green Goblin costume option at the specials menu. Select that option to play as Harry Osborn in the Green Goblin costume with his weapons in an alternate storyline where he tries to correct the Osborn family's reputation.

Alternate Green Goblin costume:
If you are using the Alex Ross Spider-Man, play any level with the Green Goblin in it and he will have an alternate costume that resembles his classic costume more. Note: This will only work when you are in the Alex Ross costume and the Green Goblin alternate costume will not be in the very last in-game scene.

Play as Peter Parker:
Successfully complete the game on the easy or higher difficulty setting to unlock the Peter Parker costume in the specials menu.

Play as wrestler:
Successfully complete the game on the easy or higher difficulty setting to unlock the wrestler costume in the specials menu. To unlock this easily, first unlock the "Unlimited webbing" cheat. When you get to the ring, zip to the top and keep on shooting Spidey Bombs.

SPLASHDOWN

Cheat mode:
Select "Options" at the main menu. Hold R2 and quickly hit ⇧ x2, ⇩ x2, ⇦, ⇨, ⇦, ⇨, ■, ●, ■, ● at the options menu. The Cheat Name screen will appear to confirm correct code entry. Enter one of the following case-sensitive codes then hit ✖ to exit back to the options screen. You can now continue your game and see the effects of the cheat.

Cannot be knocked off:
Enter TopBird as a case-sensitive code. The CPU can no longer knock you off your SeaDoo, but you can still knock them off.

Hard tracks with normal AI settings:
Enter Hobble as a case-sensitive code.

Maximum performance meter:
Enter PMeterGo as a case-sensitive code. If you miss a buoy, you will stall with this code on.

Unlock All courses:
Enter Passport as a case-sensitive code. This also unlocks Steve and the Bermuda Triangle.

Unlock All characters:
Enter All Char as a case-sensitive code. This also unlocks Steve.

Unlock All wetsuits:
Enter LaPinata as a case-sensitive code.

Expert AI:
Enter AllOutAI as a case-sensitive code. The AI will run the best race possible on all courses. This is already active by default under the hard difficulty setting.

All ending FMV sequences:
Enter Festival as a case-sensitive code.

Play Time Trials against a UFO:
Enter IBelieve as a case-sensitive code.

Play Time Trials against a miniature F-18 jet:
Enter F18 as a case-sensitive code.

Play Time Trials against ghost of currently selected player:
Enter SEADOO as a case-sensitive code.

Unlock Ending bonus:
Successfully complete the game under the hard difficulty setting to unlock Steve as a playable character and the Bermuda Triangle level.

Unlock Hidden track:
Collect 100 balloons in countdown mode.

SPY HUNTER

Cheat mode:
CHEAT are unlocked by completing all mission objectives (not just the primary objectives) within a set amount of time. To activate the CHEAT, enter "System Options", and then choose "Extras", and "Cheat Grid". To play the FMV sequences unlocked in the cheat menu, choose the "Movie Player" option that is above "Cheat Grid".

Saliva Spy Hunter Video:
Complete level 1 in 3:40.
Green HUD (Heads Up Display): Complete level 2 in 3:35.
Saliva Your Disease Video:
Complete level three in 2:40.
Night Vision: Complete level four in 3:15.
Early Test Anamatic Video:
Complete level 5 in 3:25.
Extra Cameras: Complete level 6 in 3:45.
Rainbow HUD (Heads Up Display): Complete level 7 in 3:10.
Inversion Camera:
Complete level 8 in 3:05.
Concept Art Video:
Complete level 9 in 3:45.
Fisheye View: Complete level 10 in 3:15.
Camera Flip: Complete level 11 in 3:10.
Puke Camera: Complete level 12 in 3:30.
Making Of Video: Complete level 13 in 2:15.
Tiny Spy: Complete level 14 in 5:10.
Hover Spy: Complete the entire game.
Super Spy: Complete all 65 objectives in the game for unlimited ammunition and invincibility for your car.

Unlock The Making Of Spy Hunter FMV sequence:
Choose an agent at the start of the game and select an empty slot. Enter MAKING or MODEL as a name. Your player namewill disappear and a clucking sound will confirm correct code entry. After this is done, enter your own name and start the game. Select "System Options", then "Extras", then "Movie Player" to access the FMV sequence.

Unlock Saliva: Spy Hunter Theme FMV sequence:
Choose an agent at the start of the game and select an empty slot. Enter GUNN as a name. Your player namewill disappear and a clucking sound will confirm correct code entry. After this is done, enter your own name and start the game. Select "System Options", then "Extras", then "Movie Player" to access the FMV sequence.

Unlock Saliva: Your Disease FMV sequence:
Choose an agent at the start of the game and select an empty slot. Enter SALIVA as a name. Your player namewill disappear and a clucking sound will confirm correct code entry. After this is done, enter your own name and start the game.Select "System Options", then "Extras", then "Movie Player" to access the FMV sequence.

Unlock Spy Hunter Concept Art FMV sequence:
Choose an agent at the start of the game and select an empty slot. Enter SCW823 as a name. Your player namewill disappear and a clucking sound will confirm correct code entry. After this is done, enter your own name and start the game. Select "System Options", then "Extras", then "Movie Player" to access the FMV sequence.

Unlock Early Test Animatic

FMV sequence:
Choose an agent at the start of the game and select an empty slot. Enter WWS413 as a name. Your player namewill disappear and a clucking sound will confirm correct code entry. After this is done, enter your own name and start the game. Select "System Options", then "Extras", then "Movie Player" to access the FMV sequence.

Double turbo:
Quickly hit ✖ x2 and your car, boat, or motorcycle will get turbo. Slow down and use normal fuel for the turbo to recharge.

SSX

Master code:
Hit ■ at the character selection screen to enter the options menu. Then, hold L1 + L2 + R1 + R2 and hit ⇩, ⇦, ⇧, ⇨, ✖, ●, ▲, ■. All courses, players, boards, and costumes will be unlocked. Repeat the code to disable its effects.

Unlock All players and courses:
Hit ■ at the character selection screen to enter the options menu. Then, hold L1 + L2 + R1 + R2 and hit ⇩, ⇦, ⇧, ⇨, ✖, ■, ▲, ●. Repeat the code to disable its effects.

Unlock Running man mode:
Hit ■ at the character selection screen to enter the options menu. Then, hold L1 + L2 + R1 + R2 and hit ■, ▲, ●, ✖, ■, ▲, ●, ✖ at the options screen. Your boarder will run down the course with his or her board on their back. Repeat this code to disable its effects.

Unlock All course hints:
Hit ■ at the character selection screen to enter the options menu. Then, hold L1 + L2 + R1 + R2 and hit ●, ✖, ●, ✖, ●, ✖, ●, ✖ at the options screen. Repeat this code to disable its effects.

Full attributes:
Hit ■ at the character selection screen to enter the options menu. Then, hold L1 + L2 + R1 + R2 and hit ✖ x7, ■. This cheat will give you only one board to ride with, no matter which one you select — it may be better to build up your rider without using this code.

No outfits:
Hit ■ at the character selection screen to enter the options menu. Then, hold L1 + L2 + R1 + R2 and hit ● x7, ✖.

Unlock Mallorca board:
Hit ■ at the character selection screen to enter the options menu. Then, hold L1 + L2 + R1 + R2 and hit ✖ x4, ▲ x4 at the options screen. You cannot change boards unless you enter the code a second time to disable it.

Faster speed:
Hit ■ at the character selection screen to enter the options menu. Then, hold L1 + L2 + R1 + R2 and hit X x8. The speed of your rider will be increased, but it will not be reflected on the character info screen.

.

Unlock Merqury City Meltdown course:
Win a medal on the Elysium Alps course.

Unlock Mesablanca course:
Win a medal on the Merqury City Meltdown course.

Unlock Tokyo Megaplex course:
Win a medal on the Mesablanca course.

Unlock Aloha Ice Jam course:
Win a medal on the Tokyo Megaplex course.

Unlock Pipedream course:
Win a medal on the Tokyo Megaplex course.

Unlock Untracked course:
Win a medal on the Aloha Ice Jam course.

Play as Jurgen:
Win a gold medal in any mode. Alternately, win a gold medal as Mac.

Play as JP:
Win two gold medals in any mode. Alternately, win a gold medal as Moby.

Play as Zoe:
Win three gold medals in any mode. Alternately, win a gold medal as Elise.

Play as Hiro:
Win four gold medals in any mode. Alternately, win a gold medal as Kaori.

Unlock Alternate cosutmes:
Successfully complete all green circle or blue square tricks to unlock two additional sets of costumes.

Unlock More boards:
An additional snowboard is unlocked each time your snowboarder earns a new rank.

SSX TRICKY

Master code:
Hold L1 + R1 and hit ✖, ▲, ⇨, ●, ■, ⇩, ▲, ■, ⇦, ●, ✖, ⇧ at the title screen. Release L1 + R1.

Full stat points:
Hold L1 + R1 and hit ▲ x2, ⇨, ▲ x2, ⇩, X x2, ⇦, ✖ x2, ⇧ at the title screen. Release L1 + R1. All the boarders will have full stat points.

Mallora board:
Hold L1 + R1 and hit ✖ x2, ⇨, ● x2, ⇩, ▲ x2, ⇦, ■ x2, ⇧ at the title screen. Release L1 + R1. Choose Elise and start a track. Elise will have the Mallora Board and a blue outfit. This code only works for Elise.

Sticky boards:
Hold L1 + R1 and hit ■ x2, ⇨, ▲ x2, ⇩, ● x2, ⇦, ✖ x2, ⇧ at the title screen. Release L1 + R1.

Running man mode:
Hold L1 + R1 + R2 + L2 hit ■, ▲, ●, ✖, ■, ▲, ●, ✖ at the options screen.

Mix Master Mike:
Hold L1 + R1 and hit X x2, ⇨, ✖ x2, ⇩, ✖ x2, ⇦, ✖ x2, ⇧ at the title screen. Release L1 + R1. Choose any boarder at the character selection screen and he or she will be replaced by Mix Master Mike on the course.

Unlock Pipedream course:
Win a medal on all Showoff courses.

Unlock Untracked course:
Win a medal on all Race courses.

Unlock Uberboards:
Unlock all of the tricks for a character to get their uberboard, which is their best board.

Unlock Fugi board:
Get a gold medal on every course with all boarders with their uberboard to unlock a Fugi board. It is the ultimate board and allows you to do a "???" every time.

Unlock Alternate costumes:
To earn more costumes, complete all chapters in your trick book. To unlock the final chrome costume, complete world circuit mode with a "Master" rank.

Play as Brodi:
Win a gold medal in world circuit mode.

Play as Zoe:
Win two gold medals in world circuit mode.

Play as JP:
Win three gold medals in world circuit mode.

Play as Kaori:
Win four gold medals in world circuit mode.

Play as Marisol:
Win five gold medals in world circuit mode.

Play as Psymon:
Win six gold medals in world circuit mode.

Play as Seeiah:
Win seven gold medals in world circuit mode.

Play as Luther:
Win eight gold medals in world circuit mode.

STAR TREK VOYAGER: ELITE FORCE

Full ammunition:
Hit START to pause the game, then hold R1 + R2 and hit SELECT to restore the ammunition of the currently selected weapon. The code must be re-enabled after loading or upon entering new areas.

Unlimited ammunition:
Hit START to pause the game, then hold L1 + L2 + R1 + R2 + ■ and hit SELECT. Resume the game and your ammunition will read 999.

All weapons:
Hit START to pause the game, then hold L1 + L2 + L3+ R1 + R2 and hit SELECT. Hit ⇦ or ⇨ to cycle through the weapons. The code must be re-enabled after loading or upon entering new areas.

Autotarget mode:
Hit START to pause the game, then hold L1 + L2 and hit SELECT. A small text message will appear in the upper left corner of the screen the game is resumed that displays the status of this cheat. The code must be re-enabled after loading or upon entering new areas.

Refill armor to 100:
Hit START to pause the game, then hold L1 + R1 and hit SELECT. The code must be re-enabled after loading or upon entering new areas.

Undying mode (999 health):
Hit START to pause the game, then hold L1 + L2 + R1 + R2 and hit SELECT. A small text message will appear in the upper left

corner of the screen the game is resumed that displays the status of this cheat. You can still take damage with this code. The code must be re-enabled after loading or upon entering new areas.

God mode:
Hit START to pause the game, then hold L1 + L2 + R3 + R1 + R2 and hit SELECT. The code must be re-enabled after loading or upon entering new areas.

Undead mode:
Hit START to pause the game, then hold R1 + R2 + R3 + L1 + L2 + L3 + SELECT. The code must be re-enabled after loading or upon entering new areas.

STAR WARS: JEDI STARFIGHTER

Master code:
Enter PNYRCADE as the code.

Invincibility:
Enter QUENTIN as the code.

Mara Jade's Z-95 Headhunter ship:
Enter HEADHUNT as the code. The Z-95 has homing missiles and a strong dual laser.

Disable cockpit displays:
Enter NOHUD as the code.

Alternate camera angles:
Enter DIRECTOR as the code. Hit Select to cycle camera views or R1 to zoom in.

Reversed controls:
Enter JARJAR as the code. The message "Jar Jar Mode" will appear to confirm correct code entry.

Programmer message:
Enter MAGGIE as the code.

Unlock Advanced Freefall ship:
Beat the bonus objective in Act 3 Mission 1.

Unlock Advanced Havoc ship:
Beat the bonus objective in Act 3 Mission 3.

Unlock Advanced Jedi Starfighter:
Beat the bonus objective in Act 2 Mission 4.

Unlock Advanced Zoomer ship:
Beat the bonus objective in Act 2 Mission 3.

Unlock Republic Gunship:
Beat the bonus objective in Act 3 Mission 5.

Unlock Sabaoth Fighter:
Beat the bonus objective in Act 2 Mission 5.

STAR WARS BOUNTY HUNTER

Get Concept Art
To get concept art from the game, earn Credits as secondary bounty pay. The more Credits you earn, the more art you unlock.
1 Page: 3000 Credits
10 Pages: 30,000 Credits
20 Pages: 60,000 Credits
30 Pages: 90,000 Credits
40 Pages: 120,000 Credits
50 Pages: 150,000 Credits
60 Pages: 180,000 Credits
70 Pages: 210,000 Credits
80 Pages: 240,000 Credits
90 Pages: 270,000 Credits
110 Pages: 330,000 Credits or more

Unlock All Concept Art
To unlock all concept art, go to the Cheat code screen and enter this

cheat code: R ARTISTS ROCK.
Unlock All TGC Cards
Unlock all TGC Cards by going to the Cheat code screen and entering this cheat code: GO FISH.

Unlock Chapters
To unlock whole chapters, enter these cheat codes at the Cheat code Setup screen:
Chapter 1: SEEHOWTHEYRUN
Chapter 2: CITYPLANET
Chapter 3: LOCKDOWN
Chapter 4: DUGSOPLENTY
Chapter 5: BANTHAPOODOO
Chapter 6: MANDALORIANWAY
Unlock Comic Pages
To unlock pages of the Dark Horse comic, just you must complete missions! You'll unlock three pages per mission, until the final stage.

Unlock Missions
Enter these cheat codes at the Cheat code screen to unlock missions:

1: BEAST PIT
2: GIMMEMYJETPACK
3: CONVEYORAMA
4: BIGCITYNIGHTS
5: IEATNERFMEAT
6: VOTE4TRELL
7: LOCKUP
8: WHAT A RIOT
9: SHAFTED
10: BIGMOSQUITOS
11: ONEDEADDUG
12: WISHIHADMYSHIP
13: MOSGAMOS
14: TUSKENS R US
15: BIG BAD DRAGON
16: MONTROSSISBAD
17: VOSAISBADDER
18: JANGOISBADDEST

Unlock TIE Fighter:
Beat the bonus objective in Act 1 Mission 4.

Unlock X-Wing:
Beat the bonus objective in Act 1 Mission 3.

Unlock Slave 1 ship:
Beat the hidden objective in all missions.

STAR WARS: RACER REVENGE - RACER 2

Unlock Cheat mode:
To enable cheat mode, set a record (Best Lap, Best 3 Lap, Most KO's) and enter NO TIME on your player nameentry screen. The following codes may now be activated.

Unlock All tracks:
Enable cheat mode. Then, hold L1 + L2 + R1 + R2 and hit quickly hit ⇨, ⇦, ⇨, ⇦, ●, ■, ●, ■ at the main menu.

Unlock Hard mode:
Enable cheat mode. Then, hold L1 + L2 + R1 + R2 and hit quickly hit ▲ at the main menu.

All art galleries:
Enable cheat mode. Then, hold L1 + L2 + R1 + R2 and hit quickly hit ⇨, ■, ⇦, ●, ⇩, ✖, ⇧, ▲ at the main menu.

Bonus racers
Select tournament mode. Win the first four tracks in first place to unlock a new racer.

Unlock Anakin (Episode 1):
Get the fastest lap time for every track.

Unlock Clegg Fasthold:
Rank higher than the track favourite on the Watchtower Run course.

Unlock Darth Maul:
Get the top KO score for every track.

Unlock Darth Vader:
Unlock Anikin (Episode 1), Watto, and Darth Maul, then win tournament mode as one of those racers.

Unlock Gasgano:
Rank higher than the track favourite on the Badlands course.

Unlock Knire Dark:
Rank higher than the track favourite on the Ballest Complex course.

Unlock Kraid Nemmeso:
Rank higher than the track favourite on the Ruins Of Carnuss Gorgull course.

Unlock Mars Guo:
Rank higher than the track favourite on the Grand Reefs course.

Unlock Mawhonic:
Win the last of the first four circuits in tournament mode.

Unlock Scorch Zanales:
Rank higher than the track favourite on the Citadel course.

Unlock Sebulba (Episode 1):
Win first place in all three tournaments as Sebulba.

Unlock Tzidik Wrantojo:
Rank higher than the track favourite on the Nightlands course.

Unlock Wan Sandage:
Rank higher than the track favourite on the Serres Sarrano course.

Unlock Watto:
Get in the fastest three lap times for every track.

Unlock All tracks:
Complete the tracks in tournament mode to unlock the corresponding track in the other game modes.

Repair without losing speed:
When you are racing and have damage, hold L2 + R2 to get repaired without losing speed.

STAR WARS: STARFIGHTER

Master code:
Enter OVERSEER as the code. Everything except the multi-player levels will be unlocked.

Invincibility:
Enter MINIME as the code. The message "Invincibility" will appear to confirm correct code entry.

Secret spaceship for bonus missions:
Enter BLUENSF as the code to unlock the Experimental N-1 Fighter. Alternately, earn a gold medal in the Naboo Proving Grounds, The Royal Escort, Taking The Offensive, Midnight Munitions Run, Rescue On Solleu, and The Final Assault missions.

Multi-player levels:
Enter ANDREW as the code to unlock the two multi-player levels.

Disable cockpit displays:
Enter NOHUD as the code.

Enemy ship gallery:
Enter SHIPS as the code.

Spaceship and cast pictures:
Enter HEROES as the code.

Pre-production art:
Enter PLANETS as the code.

Reversed controls:
Enter JARJAR as the code. The message "Jar Jar Mode" will appear to confirm correct code entry.

Programmer message:
Enter LTDJGD as the code.

Default screen:
Enter SHOTS, SIZZLE, or HOTEL as the code.

View programming team:
Enter TEAM as the code.

Pictures of Simon:
Enter SIMON as the code.

James' day of work:
Enter JAMES as the code.

View credits:
Enter CREDITS as the code.

Christmas FMV sequence:
Enter WOZ as the code.

Alternate camera angles:
Enter DIRECTOR as the code. The message "Director Mode" will appear to confirm correct code entry. Hit Select to cycle camera views or R1 to zoom in.

Charm's Way mission:
Earn a bronze medal in The Royal Escort, Contract Infraction, Piracy Above Lok, Taking The Offensive, The New Resistance, and The Final Assault missions.

Outpost Attack mission:
Earn a bronze medal in all default missions.

Canyon Sprint mission:
Earn a silver medal in the Naboo Proving Grounds, The Royal Escort, Taking The Offensive, Midnight Munitions Run, Rescue On The Solleu, and The Final Assault missions.

Space Sweep mission:
Earn a silver medal in all default missions.

Guardian Mantis ship:
Earn a gold medal in the Contract Infraction, Secrets On Eos, and The New Resistance missions.

Havoc ship:
Earn a gold medal in the Piracy Above Lok, Valuable Goods, Eye Of The Storm, The Crippling Blow, and Last Stand On Naboo missions.

Darth Maul's Infiltrator ship:
Earn a gold medal in all default missions.

Giant hot-rod:
In the Canyon Sprint bonus level, finish before Essara and get a gold medal. A giant hot rod will appear when the canyon opens up after the finish line.

Robot riding a missile:
In the Charm's Way bonus level, quickly get near the second Trade Federation missile frigate. Look carefully to see some missiles being launched. Cycle your targets until one missile identified as "ChrisCorrpedo" appears. Quickly fly towards it to see a robot riding on top of a missile.

Robot making hamburgers:
In the Fighter Training bonus level, fly to one of the nearby asteroids when the level begins to see a robot making burgers. To find it easier, enable the "Alternate camera angles" code and wait a few seconds after the level begins.

Hidden pictures:
In the Naboo Proving Ground level, ignore Essara's instructions to follow her and boost in the opposite direction. When you see a blue wall, go through it. You will end up in the gallery featuring characters from the LucasArts game Outlaws.

STAR WARS: SUPER BOMBAD RACING

Unlock Boba Fett:
Hit ■, ●, ▲, ●, ■ at the main menu. Hit ■, ● x2, ■ to disable this code. The message "Boba Fett has left the building" will confirm correct code entry.

Unlock AAT battle tank:
Hit ●, ■, ●, ■ at the main menu. Hit ●, ■, ▲, ●, ■ to disable this code. The message "Hocus pocus! The tank is gone" will confirm correct code entry.

Unlock Power Queen Amidala:
Hit ⇩, SELECT, ⇧, SELECT, ⇦, ⇨, SELECT at the main menu.

Unlock Naboo Kaadu racers:
Hit L1, R1, L2, R2 at the main menu.

Unlock Shaak racers:
Hit ⇧, ⇨, ⇩, ⇦, SELECT at the main menu.

Unlock Unlimited boost:
Hit L1, R2, L1, R2, ■, SELECT at the main menu.

Unlock Space Freighter arena:
Hit L1, R1, SELECT, ● at the main menu.

Unlock Arena Battle tracks:
Hit ⇧ x2, ⇩ x2, ⇦, ⇨, ⇦ at the main menu.

Unlock Death Star mode:
Hit R1 x4, ⇧, ⇦ at the main menu. A message will confirm correct code entry.

Unlock Super honk:
Hit ● x4, L2, SELECT at the main menu.

Unlock Race backwards:
Hit L2 x4, ●, SELECT at the main menu.

Unlock Fast and small racers:
Hit L1 x4, R2, ■ at the main menu.

Unlock Spinning mode:
Hit ⇧, ⇦, ⇩, ⇨, ⇦, ⇧, ⇩ at the main menu.

Unlock Slippery mode:
Hit ⇦, ⇨, ■, ●, L1, L2 at the main menu.

Unlock Switch language to German:
Hit SELECT x3, L1 at the main menu.

Unlock Switch language to Spanish:
Hit SELECT x3, R1 at the main menu.

Unlock Switch language to French:
Hit SELECT x3, R2 at the main menu.

Unlock Switch language to Italian:
Hit SELECT x3, L2 at the main menu.

Unlock Switch language to English:
Hit SELECT x3, ● at the main menu.

Unlock Switch language to Jawa:
Hit SELECT x3, ■ at the main menu.

Unlock Switch language to Battle Droid:
Hit SELECT x3, ⇧ at the main menu.

Reverse mirror tracks:
Win the Gold Cup in the Galaxy circuit as any racer.

Hidden racers:
Win the Gold Cup in the Galaxy circuit race as Anakin to unlock additional racers, including Darth Vader.

Galaxy circuit:
Finish in first, second, or third place on each track.

Quick start:
Hold ✖ + R2 (accelerate and jump) a moment before the final start light illuminates to get a jumping boost off the starting line.

STATE OF EMERGENCY

Unlock Invincibility:
Hit L1, L2, R1, R2, ✖ during the game.

Unlock Unlimited time in Kaos mode:
Hit L1, L2, R1, R2, ● during the game.

Unlock Unlimited ammunition:
Hit L1, L2, R1, R2, ▲ during the game. You cannot be holding a weapon for this to work.

Unlock All weapons:
Hit L1 x2, R2 x2, ✖ during the game.

Unlock Pistol:
Hit ⇦, ⇨, ⇩, L1, ▲ during the game.

Unlock Tazer:
Hit ⇦, ⇨, ⇩, L1, ● during the game.

Unlock Pepper Spray:
Hit ⇦, ⇨, ⇩, L1, ■ during the game.

Unlock Tear Gas:
Hit ⇦, ⇨, ⇩, L1, X during the game.

Unlock Shotgun:
Hit ⇦, ⇨, ⇩, L2, ▲ during the game.

Unlock Minigun:
Hit ⇦, ⇨, ⇩, R1, ▲ during the game.

Unlock Flame Thrower:
Hit ⇦, ⇨, ⇩, R1, ● during the game.

Unlock Grenade Launcher:
Hit ⇦, ⇨, ⇩, R1, ■ during the game.

Unlock Rocket Launcher:
Hit ⇦, ⇨, ⇩, R1, ✖ during the game.

Unlock AK47:
Hit ⇦, ⇨, ⇩, R2, ▲ during the game.

Unlock M16:
Hit ⇦, ⇨, ⇩, R2, ● during the game.

Unlock Grenade:
Hit ⇦, ⇨, ⇩, R2, ■ during the game.

Unlock Molotov Cocktail:
Hit ⇦, ⇨, ⇩, R2, ✖ during the game.

Unlock Mission skip:
Hit ⇦ x4, ▲ during the game.

Unlock Mission select:

Hit L1, L2 x3, L1, ✖ during the game.

Unlock Punches decapitate:
Hit L1, L2, R1, R2, ■ during the game.

Unlock Little player:
Hit R1, R2, L1, L2, ✖ during the game.

Unlock Big player:
Hit R1, R2, L1, L2, ▲ during the game.

Unlock Normal player:
Hit R1, R2, L1, L2, ● during the game. Alternatively, hit R1, R2, L1, L2, ■ during the game.

Unlock Looting on the rise:
Hit R1, L1, R2, L2, ▲ during the game.

Unlock Bull:
Hit ⇨ x4, ✖ during the game in Kaos mode. Alternatively, successfully complete the East Side level in Revolution mode to unlock Bull in Kaos mode.

Unlock Freak:
Hit ⇨ x4, ● during the game in Kaos mode. A message will confirm correct code entry. Alternatively, successfully complete the Chinatown level in Revolution mode to unlock Freak in Kaos mode.

Unlock Spanky:
Hit ⇨ x4, ▲ during the game in Kaos mode. A message will confirm correct code entry. Alternatively, successfully complete the Mall level in Revolution mode to unlock Spanky in Kaos mode.

Unlock Policeman:
Hold L1 then hit R2 x2, L2, R1 during the game.

STITCH: EXPERIMENT 626

Finding Film Strips:
Always look for Film Strips throughout the levels. Use the Right Analog-stick during game play to find Film Strips that are hidden in hard to see locations.

STREET FIGHTER EX3

Unlock Fight as Evil Ryu:
Successfully complete the game in original mode as Ryu eight times without continuing. Highlight Ryu, then hold Select and hit ✖, ■, or ● at the character selection screen.

Unlock Fight as Bison II:
Successfully complete the game in original mode as M.Bison eight times without continuing. Highlight M.Bison, then hold SELECT and hit ✖, ■, or ● at the character selection screen.

Unlock Fight as Dark Kairi:
Highlight Zangief at the character selection screen then hit ⇩/⇦.

Unlock Fight as Vega II:
Get all ten silver medals in original mode. Highlight Vega, then hit Select at the character selection screen.

Fight as True Vega:
Get all ten platinum medals in original mode. True Vega will be unlocked in arena mode.

Hidden characters:
Complete original mode with a regular character without continuing under the normal or hard difficulty setting to unlock one of the hidden characters. Another character will be unlocked each time the game is completed, in the following order: Sagat, Vega, Garuda, Shadow Geist, Kairi, Pullum, Area, Darun, and Vulcano. A different character must be used to complete the game to unlock a new hidden character.

Fight against Evil Ryu:
Win all matches in original mode with a Meteo Combo, Meteo Tag Combo, or Character Parade as Sagat, Ken, Sakura, Vega, or Vega II.

Fight against Kairi:
Win all matches in original mode with a Meteo Combo, Meteo Tag Combo, or Character Parade as Hokuto or Nanase.

Fight against Shadow Geist:
Win all matches in original mode with a Meteo Combo, Meteo Tag Combo, or Character Parade as Skullomania or Sharon.

Fight against Vega II:
Win all matches in original mode under the normal difficulty setting with a Meteo Combo, Meteo Tag Combo, or Character Parade using no continues. You must also have over 500,000 points You will fight Vega II in the last match in original mode. Alternately, win all matches using no continues under the hard difficulty setting.

Unlock Narrator Sakura:
Successfully complete the game in original mode as Sakura eight times without continuing. Highlight Sakura, then hit Select at the character selection screen.

STUNTMAN

Unlock All driving games, cars and toys:
Enter BiNdErS as a case-sensitive driver's name at the "New Game" menu.
Unlock All toys:
Enter Turnips as a case-sensitive driver's name at the "New Game" menu.
Unlock All trailers:
Enter BonNeTT as a case-sensitive driver's name at the "New Game" menu to unlock all trailers at the "Filmography" menu.
Unlock All cars:
Enter spiDER as a case-sensitive driver's name at the "New Game" menu. In the PAL version of the game, enter Sez4Jnr as a case-sensitive name.
Quick start
Hold R1 during the pre-race countdown.
A Whoopin' And A Hollerin':
Jumping through train
On the scene where you have to jump through a gap in the train, stop before the ramp and allow the train pass. Then, go over the ramp to easily complete the scene.
Conspiracy: Speed boost:
On the second stunt when the microlite is chasing you, if you time passing the first explosion precisely, it will give you a speed boost which will make getting to the other explosions much easier. Repeat the process to gain more speed at the other explosions.

SUMMONER 2

The White Lady statue:
After you beat the Sepulchre, you can enter a place called Miridian's Pass. Once inside the area, follow the right wall. You will find a trail that leads up into the mountains to a statue called "The White Lady". Equip Sangaril with a crossbow and enter first person view. Aim at the colored gongs in a specific order to raise the bridge up to the statue. Once you get there, you will get 15000 experience points. Shoot the gongs in the following order.
First bridge: Red, Yellow, Blue
Second bridge: Orange, Green, Yellow, Red
Third bridge: Blue, Orange, Red, Yellow, and Green

SUPER BUST-A-MOVE

Unlock Another World In Puzzle Mode:
Hit ▲, ⇦, ⇨, ▲ at the "Push Start button" screen.

Unlock Secret characters:
Hit ▲, ⇨, ⇦, ▲ at the "Push Start button" screen.

SUPERMAN: SHADOW OF APOKOLIPS

Unlock Master code:
Enter MXYZPTLK at the cheat codes screen at the options menu.
Unlock Unlimited superpowers:
Enter JOR EL at the cheat codes screen at the options menu.
Unlock Unlimited health:
Enter SMALLVILLE at the cheat codes screen at the options menu.
Unlock All FMV sequences:
Enter LANA LANG at the cheat codes screen at the options menu.
Unlock All biographies:
Enter LARA at the cheat codes screen at the options menu.

Unlock Expert mode:
Enter BIZZARO at the cheat codes screen at the options menu.

SURFING H3O

Unlock Tyrone King, Lara Barcella, Gareos, and six more boards:
Successfully complete the game under the normal difficulty setting.

Unlock Morsa, Serena Knox, Jojo, and six more boards:
Successfully complete the game under the semi-pro difficulty setting.

Unlock Mikey Sands, Largo, Lyco Sassa, and five more boards:
Successfully complete the game under the pro difficulty setting.

Unlock Surfoid and three more boards:
Successfully complete the game under the master difficulty setting.

SWING AWAY GOLF

Unlock All golfers:
Hit L2, R2, L2, R2, ⇧, ⇨, ⇩, ⇦, L1, L2 at the main menu.

Unlock Left-handed golfers:
Highlight a golfer, then hold L2 + SELECT and hit ✖ at the character selection screen.

Unlock Alternate sounds:
Hit L1, R1, L2, R2, L1, R1, L2, R2, L1, R1 at the main menu.

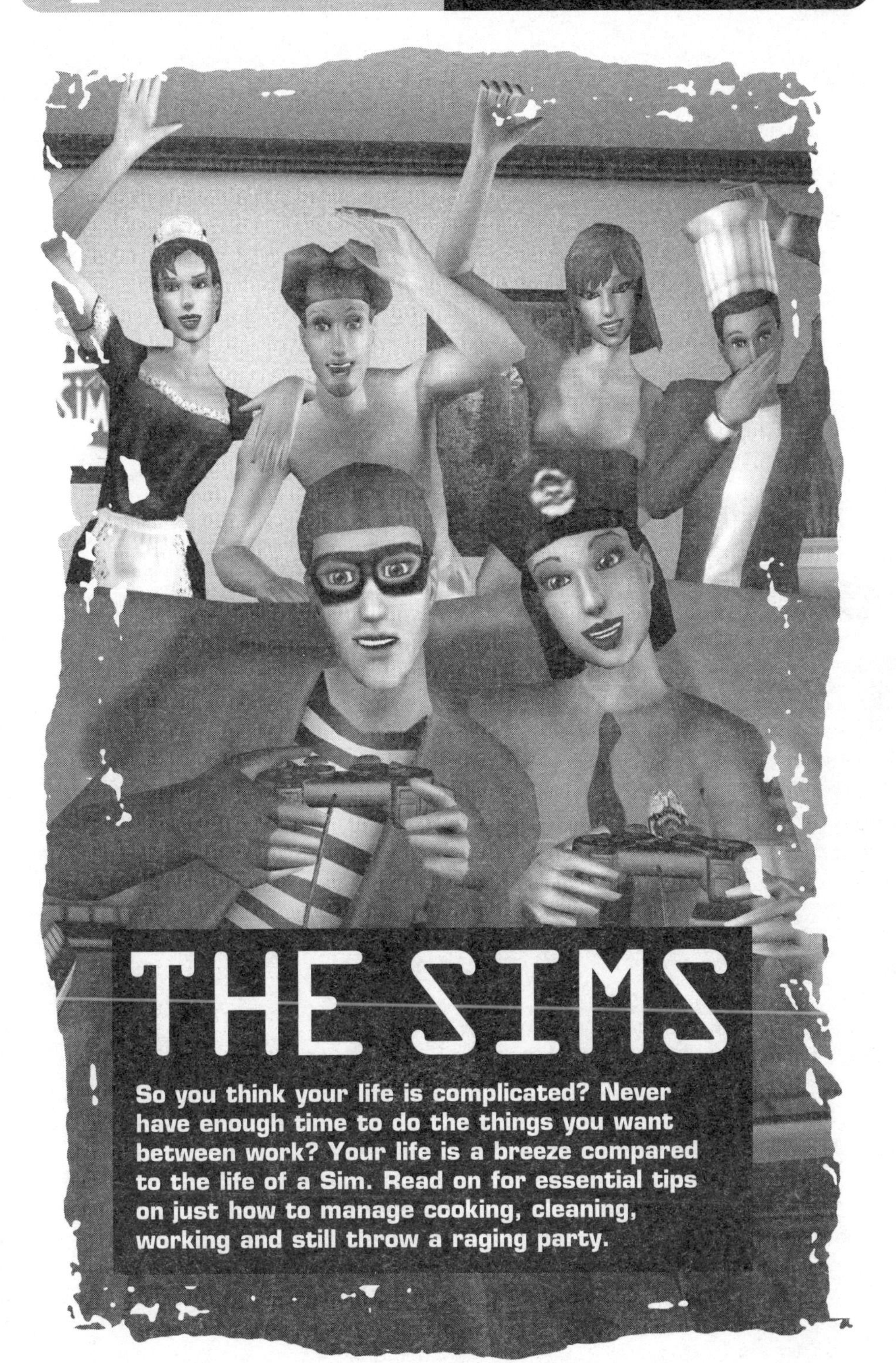

THE SIMS

So you think your life is complicated? Never have enough time to do the things you want between work? Your life is a breeze compared to the life of a Sim. Read on for essential tips on just how to manage cooking, cleaning, working and still throw a raging party.

A SIM-PLE TASK

First things first, choose your Sim's outfit from top to bottom. It is totally up to you if you go for a wild and wacky outfit or a drab suit. Besides, you can always change it later. After that comes choosing his or her personality, and this is where a bit of attention is needed.

Shy or Outgoing?

Being outgoing really will help you make friends and is very useful on some of the more people friendly career tracks. However, if you fail to keep up to date with your social calendar, you will notice the drop in popularity much faster than if you were a bit of a wallflower. Also consider that making friends is a sure fire way of unlocking new items. In our opinion, outgoing is better, especially for later levels where parties play a big part.

Lazy or Active?

Again, certain career tracks (X-Treme sports for example) will be a lot easier to excel in if you have an active Sim, rather than a couch potato. If you want your Sim to enjoy swimming, dancing and exercising (exercising is important for building the Body meter), pump up the active bar. If you want them to be content just reading a book and watching TV, go for a lazy so and so.

Messy or Neat?

Not an essential character trait, but one which can make you life a bit easier when looking after a houseful of messy Roomies. Tidiness gives no real social or career advantages, but tidy Sims will clean stuff away automatically rather than just leaving plates on the table, etc. Set it too high however, and you will constantly be stopping your Sim cleaning to do other important chores.

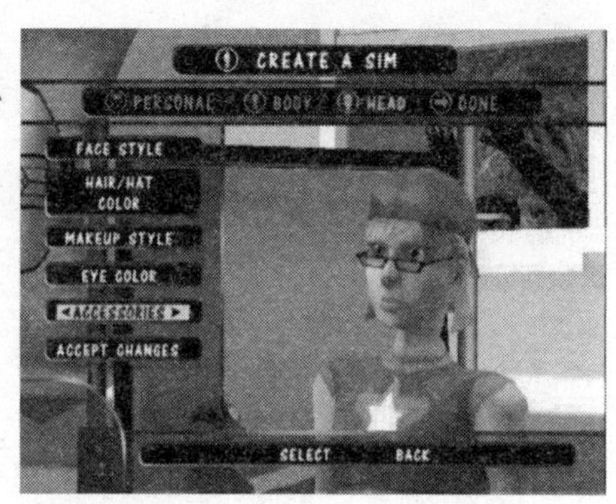

Serious or Playful?

Playful Sims love to tickle and joke and would prefer to watch cartoons on TV and play video games on their PCs. Being playful can help you make friends by allowing you to tickle and joke with them. Serious Sims will enjoy playing chess, reading the paper or books and generally not joining in with silly fun. This can make it harder to make friends, but means they will be happier on their own.

Mean or Nice?

Create a Nice Sim, and he or she will find it very easy to build friendships and will be easier to live with and therefore a more appealing Roomie when the time comes. If you combine nice with outgoing you will have a better chance of making those all important Roomie friends. Mean Sims will find it difficult to make friends with anyone who is not also mean. They will enjoy bragging to, scaring and insulting other less mean Sims and making them cry. Boo Hoo!

WORK HARD

The first major thing you will need to do in the game (no, we don't mean the dishes), is get a job. There are several different career tracks you can follow, from slacker (not as great as it sounds) to criminal. Choosing the right career for you is important, as changing jobs later on will mean starting from the bottom of the ladder.

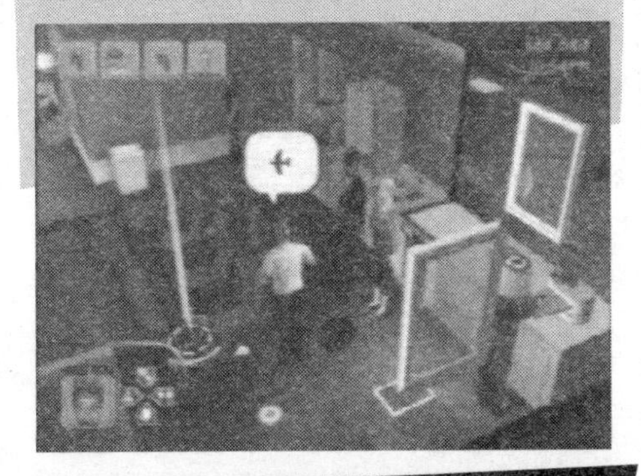

DREAM HOUSE

Fancy building your dream home? Well, in the Play the Sims mode you can do just that. But first you need to know what makes a dream house!

Size

The first time you have a go at building a house, you will probably want to make a huge mansion with a games room, swimming pool and all the mod cons. However, doing this will almost certainly mean you cannot afford to buy it and move in. For a one or two Sim family, a kitchen, living room, bathroom and bedroom are sufficient. An additional bedroom may be needed for each extra Sim added to the family.

Layout

You can really go to town with the design of your house (as long as you don't want a second floor), build it around a central garden, make all "designer" and cool. It is worth remembering that a well laid-out house will be much easier to control your Sims in and a few rules are worth noting. The living room should be the largest room in the house with enough space for a sofa, TV,

bookcase and maybe a stereo and side table. Having no wall between the kitchen and living room will make moving around easier. The bathroom should be next to the bedroom for those early morning calls of nature.

Decorating

It is tempting to spend huge amounts on carpets and wallpaper for your house, but these all add to the value. The cheaper stuff will do to start with, although it is a good idea to think about colour schemes that match. Stick with the Aluminium for the outside, you can always upgrade later. Go for the cheapest doors and make sure you have plenty of windows (Sims like light).

Garden

Don't worry too much about the outside space at the beginning. Gardens are not essential but are good for entertaining party guests and especially if your Sim family has kids. Remember that if you have a garden, it will need watering and tending, otherwise it will look terrible and effect your Room level. Bear in mind that you can hire a gardener to do this for you.

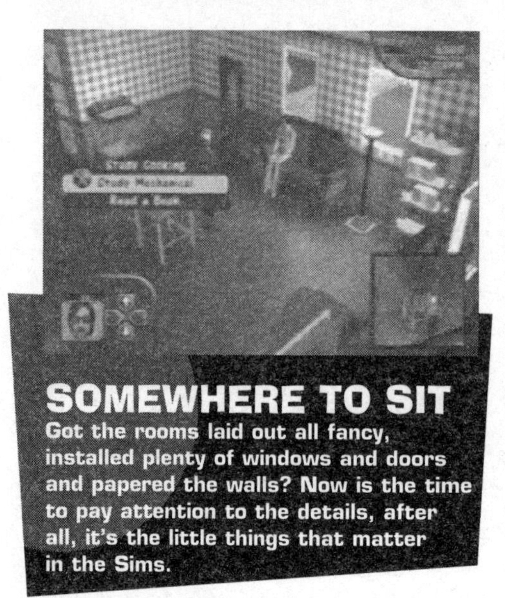

SOMEWHERE TO SIT

Got the rooms laid out all fancy, installed plenty of windows and doors and papered the walls? Now is the time to pay attention to the details, after all, it's the little things that matter in the Sims.

Living Room

Sofa: somewhere to sit to watch TV is important. As watching TV is a group activity, a two-seater is recommended.
TV: A television is a easy source of fun, and since it is a group activity, benefits multiple Sims at once.
Lamps: Light is essential for your Sims mood. A lamp in each room is essential, two or three if the room is large.
Telephone: Essential for maintaining social relationships, calling for Services and even for some jobs.
Stereo/table: Music is another group activity that will improve the Room rating. Listening and dancing to music is also fun.
Computer/desk: Not as important as the other item on this list but a useful tool both for finding a job and boosting your fun rating.

Kitchen

Refrigerator: Your Sims will starve without it. You cannot even get a snack without a fridge.
Kitchen table/ 4 chairs: Any table will do, just as long as you have four chairs around it for guests.
Cabinet/sink: Until you can afford a dishwasher, the sink will have to do for all those dishes. Obviously you need a counter to put it in.
Cooker: Important for cooking. However, it is well worth gaining some cooking skills or you might burn the kitchen down.
Rubbish Bin: Fill it with rubbish and take it to the dustbin when full. Easy.
Smoke alarm: If a fire breaks up, it will call the fire department for you and possibly save your house.

Bathroom

Toilet: The cheapest toilet will do until you have more spare cash.
Shower/Bathtub: Showers are faster but do not clean as well as a good long bath.
Medicine cabinet: Provides a mirror to boost Charisma and a toothbrush for Hygiene.
Lamp: As with every other room, light is essential to keep your Sims happy.

Bedroom

Beds: Without adequate beds, your Sims' Energy and Comfort will not regenerate. Buy one for each Sim in the house to begin with, at least until they are friends.
Lamps: Put at least one in the bedroom, preferably two.
Dresser: If you want to change clothes, you need a dresser. It contains Formal wear as well as Normal wear.

LIVE LONG AND PROSPER

Okay, so your Sim is looking good and feeling fine, it is now up to you to keep them that way. He or she will soon become a tired, cranky mess without careful watching, ordering and steering by you. Pressing up on the D-Pad will show you how your Sim is doing, Green bars = Good, Red bars = Bad.

Hunger

Fairly obviously affected by lack of food. Head over to the fridge and choose Snack, Quick meal, Full meal or Serve meal. Snacks are the fastest but recover only a small amount on the hunger bar. Quick meals recover about a quarter of a bar and full meals just over half a bar. Serving a meal means you can feed more than one person and help yourself to seconds or even thirds. Make sure you have at least one cooking point (Down on D-Pad to check) or you will burn the kitchen down. The higher your cooking skill, the more nourishing the meal. Serving a meal is also great for making friends.

Comfort

The comfort bar is generally the one you need to worry about least as it is usually replenished at the same time as one of the more important bars. Having a bath will increase it, as will sleeping and sitting in any chair or sofa.

Hygiene

Making friends will become difficult if your Sim stinks to high heaven. That said, you don't need to bathe or shower every day,

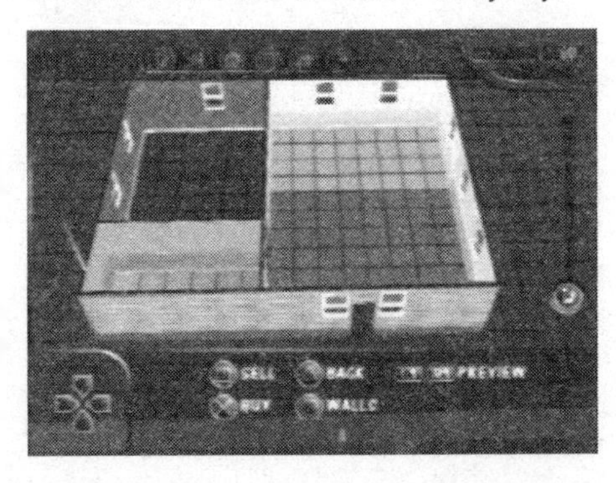

but do make sure you really have a good scrub every two days and wash your hands as often as possible (i.e. after taking out the rubbish, using the loo, etc).

Bladder

Eating and drinking both speed the rate at which your bladder bar fills. Let it get too low and your Sim will start hopping around and letting you know they need to go. Failing to do so will result in a puddle on the floor and a massive drop in both comfort and hygiene. It will also put off any friends you have around at the time. Neat Sims will take themselves off to the loo unless they are in the middle of something.

Energy

Fail to let your Sim sleep a good eight hours a night will result in a cranky sim who will

have difficulty concentrating. Being overly tired will also make your Sim refuse to do exercise of any kind and in some cases fall asleep in a heap on the floor, lowering your comfort bar quickly. If your Sim has a job, remember to allow enough time to wash and eat after waking, as your hunger, hygiene and bladder bars all drop during sleep.

Fun

Between working, eating, sleeping and bathing, you also need to find the time for your Sim to have some fun. Without some sort of down time, your Sim will quickly become difficult to deal with, refusing to study, exercise or socialise. Take some time out to watch TV, listen to music, play video games or read a book. Even better, save up for a pool table or virtual reality headset.

Social

Socialising and making family friends is essential for your success. With friends you will become depressed and find it impossible to get promoted at work. When meeting a new friend, start by talking to them for a while before joking or complimenting them. Inviting people over and serving a meal is a good way to build bridges. When your friendship bar (check with Right on D-Pad) is above 50, you can call them a real friend.

Room

Sims like plenty of light in their houses. Make sure there is at least one light in a small room and two in a larger room (living room, etc). Nice wallpaper and carpets will also help keep them happy with their lot. When you can afford it, splash out on a nice painting and some potted plants. Fail to keep your rooms nice and Sims will turn cranky and unresponsive.

CAREER TRACKS

Entertainment

Pros = Good pay at high levels
Cons = Long-ish working days

Level 1 - Waiter/Waitress
Hours: 9am - 3pm
Pay: $100
Skills: none
Friends: none
Level 2 - Extra
Hours: 9am - 3pm
Pay: $150
Skills: Charisma +2
Friends: [none]
Level 3 - Bit Player
Hours: 9am - 3pm
Pay: $200
Skills: Body +2
Friends: 2
Level 4 - Stunt Double
Hours: 9am - 4pm
Pay: $275
Skills: Charisma +1, Body +1, Creativity +1
Friends: 4
Level 5 - B-Movie Star
Hours: 10am - 5pm
Pay: $375
Skills: Mechanical +1, Charisma +1, Body +1, Creativity +1
Friends: 6
Level 6 - Supporting Player
Hours: 10am - 6pm
Pay: $500
Skills: Charisma +2, Body +1, Creativity +1
Friends: 8
Level 7 - TV Star
Hours: 10am - 6pm
Pay: $660
Skills: Mechanical +1, Charisma +2, Body +1, Creativity +1
Friends: 10
Level 8 - Feature Star
Hours: 5pm - 1am
Pay: $900
Skills: Charisma +1, Body +1, Creativity +3
Friends: 12
Level 9 - Broadway Star
Hours: 10am - 5pm
Pay: $1,100
Skills: Charisma +1, Body +1, Creativity +3
Friends: 14
Level 10 - Superstar
Hours: 10am - 3pm
Pay: $1,400

Life of Crime

Note: You unlock this career path by first catching a burglar in 'Get a Life' mode!
Pros = You usually get your days free to make friends, etc.
Cons = You will need a wide range of skills to make the top.

Level 1 - Pickpocket
Hours: 9am - 3pm
Pay: $140
Skills: none
Friends: none
Level 2 - Bagman
Hours: 11pm - 7am
Pay: $200
Skills: Body +2
Friends: none
Level 3 - Bookie
Hours: 12pm - 7pm
Pay: $275
Skills: Charisma +1, Creativity +1
Friends: 2
Level 4 - Con Artist
Hours: 9am - 3pm
Pay: $350
Skills: Mechanical +2, Creativity +1
Friends: 3
Level 5 - Getaway Driver
Hours: 5pm - 1am
Pay: $425
Skills: Mechanical +1, Charisma +1, Body +1, Logic +1
Friends: 4
Level 6 - Bank Robber
Hours: 3pm - 11pm
Pay: $530
Skills: Body +2, Logic +1, Creativity +1
Friends: 6
Level 7 - Cat Burgular
Hours: 9pm - 3am
Pay: $640
Skills: Mechanical +2, Logic +1, Creativity +2
Friends: 8
Level 8 - Counterfeiter
Hours: 9am - 3pm
Pay: $760
Skills: Charisma +3, Body +1, Creativity +1
Friends: 10
Level 9 - Smuggler
Hours: 9am - 3pm
Pay: $900
Skills: Charisma +2, Logic +1, Creativity +2
Friends: 12
Level 10 - Criminal Mastermind
Hours: 6pm - 12am
Pay: $1,100

Military

Pros = Fairly low hours once past the recruit stage.
Cons = Poor money, even when you make general!

Level 1 - Recruit
Hours: 6am - 12pm
Pay: $250
Skills: none
Friends: none
Level 2 - Elite Forces
Hours: 7am - 1pm
Pay: $325
Skills: Body +2
Friends: none
Level 3 - Drill Instructor
Hours: 8am - 2pm
Pay: $400
Skills: Mechanical +1, Charisma +2
Friends: none
Level 4 - Junior Officer
Hours: 9am - 3pm
Pay: $450
Skills: Cooking +1, Body +2
Friends: none
Level 5 - Counter-Intelligence
Hours: 9am - 3pm
Pay: $500
Skills: Mechanical +1, Charisma +2, Logic +1
Friends: 1
Level 6 - Flight Officer
Hours: 9am - 3pm
Pay: $550
Skills: Mechanical +1, Charisma +1, Logic +2
Friends: 3
Level 7 - Senior Officer
Hours: 9am - 3pm
Pay: $580
Skills: Mechanical +3, Charisma +1, Logic +2
Friends: 5
Level 8 - Commander
Hours: 9am - 3pm
Pay: $600
Skills: Mechanical +3, Body +3, Logic +1
Friends: 6

Level 9 - Astronaut
Hours: 9am - 3pm
Pay: $625
Skills: Mechanical +1, Charisma +2, Body +2, Logic +3
Friends: 8
Level 10 - General
Hours: 9am - 3pm
Pay: $650

Xtreme

Pros = The hours allow you time to socialise.
Cons = $925 dollars a day for an international Spy?

Level 1 - Daredevil
Hours: 9am - 3pm
Pay: $175
Skills: none
Friends: none
Level 2 - Bungee Jump Instructor
Hours: 9am - 3pm
Pay: $250
Skills: Body +2
Friends: 1
Level 3 - Whitewater Guide
Hours: 9am - 3pm
Pay: $325
Skills: Body +2, Mechanical +1 Friends: 2
Level 4 - Xtreme Circuit Pro
Hours: 9am - 3pm
Pay: $400
Skills: Cooking +1, Mechanical +1, Logic +1
Friends: 3
Level 5 - Bush Pilot
Hours: 9am - 3pm
Pay: $475
Skills: Mechanical +2, Body +2 Friends: 4
Level 6 - Mountain Climber
Hours: 9am - 3pm
Pay: $550
Skills: Mechanical +1, Charisma +2, Creativity +3
Friends: 5
Level 7 - Photojournalist
Hours: 9am - 3pm
Pay: $650
Skills: Mechanical +1, Charisma +1, Body +1, Logic +2, Creativity +1
Friends: 7
Level 8 - Treasure Hunter
Hours: 10am - 5pm
Pay: $725
Skills: Charisma +2, Logic +2, Creativity +3
Friends: 9
Level 9 - Grand Prix Driver
Hours: 10am - 4pm
Pay: $825
Skills: Cooking +1, Charisma +3, Body +1, Logic +1, Creativity +2
Friends: 11
Level 10 - International Spy
Hours: 11am - 5pm
Pay: $925

Musician

Pros = Great money at the top level
Cons = Usually required to work evenings.

Level 1 - Subway Musician
Hours: 3pm - 9pm
Pay: $90
Skills: none
Friends: none
Level 2 - Piano Tuner
Hours: 3pm - 8pm
Pay: $120
Skills: Creativity +2
Friends: none
Level 3 - Wedding Singer
Hours: 9am - 3pm
Pay: $190
Skills: Creativity +3
Friends: 2
Level 4 - Lounge Singer
Hours: 8pm - 4am
Pay: $250
Skills: Mechanical +2, Creativity +1
Friends: 2
Level 5 - High School Band Teacher
Hours: 7am - 2pm
Pay: $325
Skills: Mechanical +3, Creativity +1
Friends: 5
Level 6 - Roadie
Hours: 11am - 8pm
Pay: $400
Skills: Body +4
Friends: 8
Level 7 - Back-up Musician
Hours: 12pm - 9pm
Pay: $550
Skills: Charisma +2, Body +1, Creativity +2
Friends: 9
Level 8 - Studio Musician
Hours: 11am - 6pm
Pay: $700
Skills: Charisma +5, Body +2 Friends: 12
Level 9 - Rock Star
Hours: 5pm - 2am
Pay: $1,100
Skills: Charisma +3, Logic +4
Friends: 15
Level 10 - Celebrity Activist
Hours: 10am - 3pm
Pay: $1,400

Slacker

Pros = You can get to be a non-stop party guest!
Cons = The pay is terrible, terrible, terrible!

Level 1 - Golf Caddy
Hours: 5am - 10am
Pay: $90
Skills: none
Friends: none
Level 2 - Convenience Store Clerk
Hours: 10am - 3pm
Pay: $110
Skills: Body +2
Friends: 1
Level 3 - Life Guard
Hours: 9am - 3pm
Pay: $150
Skills: Charisma +2
Friends: 2
Level 4 - Record Store Clerk
Hours: 12pm - 5pm
Pay: $180
Skills: Charisma +2
Friends: 4
Level 5 - Party D.J.
Hours: 11pm - 4pm
Pay: $220
Skills: Mechanical +3
Friends: 6
Level 6 - Projectionist
Hours: 6pm - 1am
Pay: $280
Skills: Mechanical +2
Friends: 7
Level 7 - Video Editor
Hours: 12pm - 6pm
Pay: $350
Skills: Charisma +3, Body +1
Friends: 10
Level 8 - Freelance Photographer
Hours: 12pm - 5pm
Pay: $400
Skills: Charisma +1, Body +3
Friends: 12
Level 9 - Personal Tour Guide
Hours: 2pm - 7pm
Pay: $450
Skills: Charisma +2, Body +3
Friends: 15
Level 10 - Permanent Celebrity Party Guest
Hours: 10pm - 2am
Pay: $600

WALKTHROUGH

fixer upper

DREAM HOUSE

GOALS
Get in the hottub

Once either Roxy or Randy have appeared in a puff of smoke, you can explore the house and try out the toys and gadgets. To leave this tutorial, all you need to do is join Roxy or Randy in the hot tub. The next thing you hear is your Mom yelling at you to wake up.

MONEY FROM MOM

GOALS
Fix the TV
Make dinner without starting a fire
Borrow 800 Simoleons from Mom
Pay the bills
Get a job

It turns out, that you are actually living with your Mom in a house with only one bed!
Obviously, the sooner you can get out of there, the better. Go straight to the bookcase and choose to study mechanics. As soon as you have one skill point in this subject, select the broken TV and choose Repair. Mom can now settle down for her soaps, while you study cooking so you don't burn the kitchen down when cooking her tea.
As soon as you have one skill point in this subject, head to the refrigerator and choose Serve Dinner/Lunch/Breakfast. After eating, have a chat to Mom and build up your friendship bar. Even though you cook and clean for her, she still won't lend you money unless you compliment and boost her ego. She will give you $100 each time, but don't try to get it all in one go. If you really want to unlock the guitar, you can always just sell something in the house to speed the whole thing up. Next thing to do is to get a job so you can move out of this grief hole. Head down to the mailbox and search the latest paper for a job. Check the career guide elsewhere in this solution, to see which job you might want to take. If you prefer, you can forget the job and just take it slow and use the

time at moms to learn some more skills. You can even splash out on treadmill and work on your body. If you do choose to do this, you will have to pay the bills after every three days.

Unlockables

Aroma Machine - Cook your first meal.
Vanity Mirror - Fix Mom's TV
Treadmill - Get a job
The Museum (2-player mini-game) - Borrow $800 from Mom.
Beejaphone Electric Guitar - Get through the level in 24 Hours or less.

REALITY BITES

GOALS
Clean up the house
Fix the broken objects
Get promoted to career level 2
Get promoted to career level 3

After your relatively easy life at Moms house, you are now thrown in at the deep end with your own place...plus your own chores, problems, bills, etc to go with it. Aside from trying to juggle a job, bills, cooking, cleaning, bathing and socialising, you also need to find the time and money to upgrade the house to a sufficient level. Your first job should be to clean the fish tank, unclog the toilet and mop the bathroom floor. Now head to the kitchen and sweep up the smouldering remains of the floor and walls and fix the Espresso machine. Now to tackle the lounge. First job is to pick up any piles of rubbish lying around and fix the TV and computer. As soon as the house is clean and the appliances fixed, the Maid and Handyman Services (Phone menu) become available. With the house clean and in good shape, and your Sim in a daily routine, you need to spend some money on the house to increase its value. Buying a nicer TV will increase the value of the house, and you'll have more fun watching it. An exercise machine of some sort may also be important, depending on your career choice. You need to get promoted up to job level 3, so after each promotion have a look at the career panel elsewhere in this guide to see what skills you need and how many friends are required. Go to work happy and when you have been promoted twice and the house has risen in value to around $36000, you will get a visit from Dudley and be invited to move in with him.

Unlockables

Ice Chest – Get promoted to Career level 2
Teppanyaki Table – Get promoted to Career Level 3
Bug Zapper: Increase the house value
The Frat House (2-Player game) – Complete the level
Repairman – Fix all broken objects
Maid – Clean up the house
Coat of Arms – complete the level in 4 days or less

PARTY ANIMALS

GOALS
Get promoted to Career level 4
Get promoted to Career level 5
Upgrade the house
Throw a raging party
Move out with one of Dudley's / Mimi's friends at a party

Dudley or Mimi can be a real nightmare to live with. They don't clean up much but do cook and are usually up for a chat. The first thing to do is hire a maid as soon as you arrive, she will have twice the work to do now. Devote a bit of time and energy to building a friendship with your roommate, cook them a meal and chat about stuff. When the house is clean and you have some spare time before work, get on the phone and Throw a Party. Make sure, before your guests arrive, to cook and serve a meal ready for them to eat when they do. With the party in full swing, choose a guest to approach and start chatting, you will certainly need at least four friends to get promoted to level 5, so keep it moving. It is also a good idea to invite guests into the hot tub for some easy friendship points. If the party runs on and the police turn up to complain about the noise, stop it or you will be fined $200. You will need your cash to upgrade the house, which should be done like last time, only buying things useful to your career or mood. When you have been promoted to level 5, thrown a raging party and upgraded the house, you can start concentrating on someone to move out with. Pick any one of the Roomies and really suck up to them, building your friendship meter to at least 60. Then ask them if you can move in with them. If they say no first time, just keep complimenting them, talking and being nice until they do give the answer you are looking for.

Unlockables

Strip Poker Table: Get promoted to Career Level 4
Spa System: Get promoted to career level 5
Tree Swing: Increase the house value
The Motel (2-player) – Throw a raging party
The Park – Greet and feed Bobo the bum.

Head in Curio Jar – Complete level in eight days or less.

HOT TO TROT

GOALS
Get promoted to Career level 6
Get promoted to Career level 7
Throw a raging party
Try and "score" with a party guest
Raise the house value

The first thing to do is to pick your new Roomie a job and make sure they get to it for the first few days. Unlike Mimi and Dudley, your new Roomie will actually be able to de well at his/her job as long as they can get used to going on time. The job goals are very similar to those on the previous level. There are also the usual friend requirements to meet on each level, so throw a few parties to meet some hip and happening new people. Work on increasing the right skills and never leave for work in a bad mood, as this will stop any promotion chances. To throw a raging party in this house, you will first need to raise its value enough to keep the landlord happy, if not, the landlord will shut it down before it starts. Hot tubs are one of the best items to have during a party, as it will entertain four guests quite well for quite a while. The next thing on your agenda should be to "get it on" with a likely female. Once it is clear you are in love with her and she is in love with you, have a go at scoring with her. If at first you don't succeed, try and try again. Cook her a meal, compliment her, give her a back rub and entertain her. Hit it off and a new house is on the cards.

Unlockables

Sonic Shower – Get promoted to career level 6
Carving Block – Get promoted to career level 7
Love Bed – Upgrade your house.
Club Abhi and Taylor's Place (Two-Player) – Throw a Raging party.
The Park (Two-Player) – Feed Bobo if he appears.
Wurl 'N Hurl Jukebox – Complete the level in eight days or less

WHO LOVES YA BABY

GOALS
Get promoted to Career level 8
Get promoted to Career level 9
Raise the house value
Take care of the babies
Keep your kids in school
Have two babies
Get married (if your partner leaves you)

The tricky thing here is to raise two children in this house. All of the other objectives you have tackled before, so we will concentrate on this one. For a baby to be born, you firtst need to make your Sims have a bit of fun in either the hot tub or Vibromatic Love Bed. Once your baby is born, there are few things you need to watch out for. For the sake of the baby (and the other Sim in the house), keep the cot next to the bed and be quick to act when it cries. Otherwise, social services might pay you a visit and you will have to start again. Once the first baby has grown into a child, you can try for a second. Once both the kids are of school age, you will need to make sure that they always leave for school in a good mood. Bad moods will result in bad grades, and if they get an F they will be sent off to military school. Make sure they have plenty of fun at home but also remember to make your kids study, either with the bookcase, computer, telescope or other educational item. If you are feeling particularly lazy, you can make your eldest child look after the new baby, saving you a heap of time. If your current partner leaves you, you will have to build a new relationship with someone else and get married before you can move on to the next level.

Unlockables

Sand Box – Raise your first baby to childhood.
Lawn Sprinkler – Raise your second baby to childhood.
Maid's House (Two-Player) – Get promoted to career level 8.

Two New Swimming Pools – Get promoted to career level 9
The Park (Two-Player) – If you haven't already, greet and feed Bobo.
Bearskin Rug – Complete level in eight days or less.

THE LAST SIMOLEON

GOALS
Get promoted to Career level 10
Send kids to Prep School with straight A's
Save 20,000 Simoleons to retire
Throw one last raging party before you retire

Getting that level ten promotion should be fairly easy by now (as long as you don't decide to change jobs). You will probably need 12 friends and a whole host of skills to make it, but you should be high up on the social ladder by now. To reach the $20,000 retirement fund quickly, you can just sell anything you don't need (no upgrade objective here). The trickiest thing is getting the kids into prep school. They will need straight A's, which means study must take priority over fun. Once they come home with their A's, you can send them off to prep school at a cost of £1,500 each. If you have lost one of your kids to military school, you will need to have a new baby, as you need to get at least two kids into the Prep school. The retirement party is also pretty tough. It has a higher requirement for the overall mood level of your guests than your previous parties. Follow the same steps as before and make sure everything is perfect. If you can afford it, two hot tubs is a great way to go. Once you've successfully thrown the retirement party, sit back and relax. You have successfully made it through a Sim's life.

Unlockables

Monkey Butler –Send your children off to Prep school.
The Park (2-player) – Greet and feed Bobo.
Rhino Trophy – Complete the level in eight days or less.

NEW THREADS

To unlock these pieces of clothing, simply make friends with the correct person. The house where you will first meet the characters is listed, though once you've met them, you can invite them to later houses and earn their clothing then.

Reality Bites House

Pauline Peacock's purple skirt
Pierre Peacock's purple hip-huggers

Party Animals House

Dudley's camo pants
Mimi's ponytail hair style
Fran Foofaraw's hair style
Freddy Foofaraw's mullet hairstyle
Zara Roomies' red camisole
Betty Roomies' backwards baseball cap
Bingo Roomies' "Liberty Spikes"
Carlos Roomies' mohawk hairstyle
Layla Roomies' fishnet stocking
Leon Roomies' bowling shirt

Hot to Trot House

Thomas Thimblewit's top hat
Theresa Thimblewit's geisha hairstyle
Pamela Party Girls' dyed-ends hairstlye
Ginger Party Girls' cat-eye sunglasses
Debbie Party Girls' "genie" blouse
Candy Party Girls' tiger-striped skirt
May Party Girls' bell-bottom jeans
Rod Party Guys' cowboy shirt
Peter Party Guys' striped sweater
Randy Party Guys' gold-rimmed sunglasses
Woody Party Guys' orange sunglasses
Ziggy Party Guys' cornrows hairstyle

Who Loves Ya Baby House

Charles Cheeky's red blazer
Chantal Cheeky's Egyptian headdress

TWO PLAYER MODES

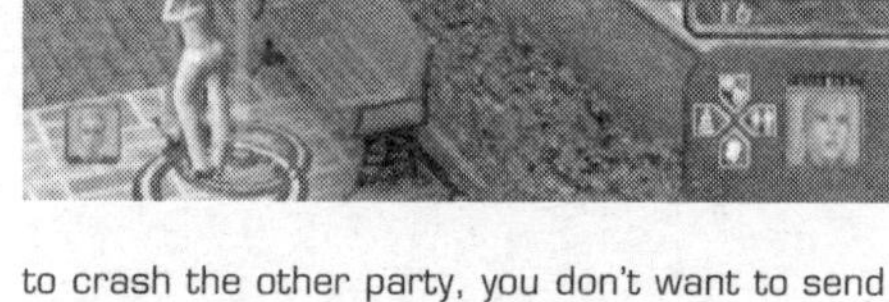

Access to the two player games is unlocked after borrowing the money from Mom in the first house. More and more two-player games are then unlocked as you work your way through the various Get a Life missions.

The Museum

How to unlock = Borrow 800 Simoleans from Mom

You had better get your talking head on, because this game is all about talking people out of their hard earned cash. Build yourself a nice, friendly relationship with someone and then tap him or her for some dosh. Blagging a loan will certainly make your relationship level drop, but a few nice words or a compliment between wads of cash should do the job of bringing it back up to scratch. Focus on trying to borrow as much money as possible from a single Sim rather than flitting between several.

The Frat House

How to unlock = Get invited to live with Dudley or Mimi

Easy, just find three people and make friends with all of them (friends have smiley faces next to them on the relationship meter). Too easy, so what's the catch. Well the catch is that your opponent can spread rumours about you to put off any potential friends. Of course, you can do the same to him or her and you had better make sure you do just that. You will need to find a nice medium between making friends and spreading rumours. If you spread rumours, try to tell them to as many Sims as possible. Once you leave one Sim who you've told the rumour to, they will hopefully go and tell another, and so on.

The Motel "Bash N' Smash"

How to unlock = Throw a raging party

Throw the biggest, baddest, most debauched party and stop your opponent at the same time. As with the Frat House game, you don't just need to rely on your own party throwing skills, you can also put a big spanner in the works of your opponents bash by sending your troops (guests) over to cause a bit of mayhem. Your guests will leave your party if they're in a bad mood, so you'll have to keep them entertained. As always, hot tubs are great for keeping the party mood high, as well is the essential food and drink. Serve your guests as soon as the game starts to keep them happy while you get yourself organized. When you send people over to crash the other party, you don't want to send everyone, but less guests mean less trouble to look after.

Club Abhi and Taylor's Place

How to unlock = Throw a raging party in the Hot to Trot house

Think yourself a bit of a ladies man? Like to strut your stuff for the fairer sex? Well now's the chance to test out hose pulling techniques, as you battle you opponent to see who can pull the most totty and have them fall in love with you. Apart from your probably terrible chat-up lines, there are other problems to consider when wooing multiple ladies. If you have two women falling in love with you, showing affection to either one when the other is in the room will obviously not go down too well. Instead, move into another room or out into the garden and call over the lucky lady. When you have made firm her love for you, leave her and do the same for lucky lady number two. You can also interfere with your opponent's progress with the chicks by constantly talking to him until he loses his rag. This will make it harder for him to charm the ladies in his life.

The Maid's House and The Handyman's House

How to unlock = Get promoted to job level 8 (any career)

Like Club Abhi and Taylor's Place, these two houses have the same goal. As the titles suggest, you will either be in the Maid's or Handyman's house, with objective to clean the house better than your opponent. The Maid (or Handyman) will come by periodically to check on the progress of the cleaning jobs. If your house is cleaner than your opponent's, you'll get a heart. You'll also get a heart if the child you are watching is happier than the other child. Like the party game, breaking stuff is a good tactic. Run over to your opponent's house and break stuff to slow them down. Preferably break something that will take a while to fix or clean, like something that will leak. Note that the Maid will only give you hearts if you are home when she drops by. Make sure she's not about to show up before you take off to cause havoc.

SPLINTER CELL

Splinter Cell is not about running in all guns blazing. To play this game to it's full potential, you really need to know the finer points of stealth. Forget Solid Snake, Sam Fisher has all the moves and we are here to show you them all.

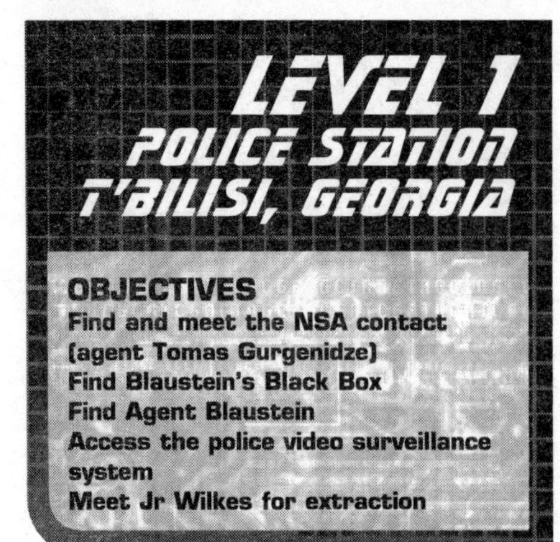

1ST CHECKPOINT

To get started, head up onto the veranda on your right and climb to the top of the ladder. When you reach the small room, pull open the trapdoor and drop through into the passageway below. Equip your night vision goggles and follow the dark tunnel to its end. Climb the drainpipe onto the roof and use the cable to reach the burning building on the far side of the street. Once you have received the radio call, head through the door leading out to the corridor.

2ND CHECKPOINT

Head right, down the corridor and descend the stairs. At the bottom, jump up to the pipe hanging from the ceiling and monkey swing across the hole. Once safely on the far side, take the first left and enter the room on the right. Head through this room

and up the stairs on the other side.
In the first room on the left, you can find Gurgenidze, talk to him and then exit through the door on the right. Head left, along the corridor and through the next door on the right. Shoot out the skylight to let the smoke out of the room, before heading in and opening the door on your right.

3RD CHECKPOINT

Open the door and head over to the break in the fence. You can shoot out the light in the ceiling to keep things dark. Jump over to the balcony across from you and start moving to your right, towards the plant-covered fence. Quickly kill the guard on the radio before he sounds an alarm. Hide his body before heading into the house and killing his mate by the computer. Head through the house and into the bedroom, slide the portrait across and collect Blaustein's Black Box. After the conversation is over, head over to the keypad by the closed door. The code is 091772. Head out onto the balcony. Grab the cable on your left and slide down onto the opposite roof. Open the door on your left and look at the wire holding the elevator. Jump over to grab it and then slide all the way down to top of the elevator. Open the trapdoor below you and drop down into the elevator. Enter the small courtyard and use your lock pick on the door at the top of the stairs. Once it is open, pass through to reach the checkpoint.

4TH CHECKPOINT

Don't head down the steps, instead, drop off of the balcony onto the bin below. Pick up a can and throw it down the stairs to distract one of the guards. When he walks down to investigate, sneak behind him and knock him out. Knock out the guard talking to the drunk, before hiding both their bodies somewhere dark. Follow the alleyway around and head up the stairs at the end to reach a large courtyard with a fountain. Walk over to the large gate and crawl under the bush to the right into a small room with a laptop.

5TH CHECKPOINT

Take the medi kit and ammo, and then use the laptop to open the gates back out in the courtyard. Crawl back into the courtyard, but be careful of the guard waiting in the courtyard. Either avoid him or wait until his back is turned and then knock him out. Follow the alleyways avoiding contact with civilians and knocking out any Police officers you see. After passing through the vine covered walkway, climb onto the skip on the far side of the small courtyard and do a wall jump to reach the high wall. Climb over into the grounds of the Precinct.

6TH CHECKPOINT

After you've saved your game, follow the wall on your left and head down the stairs. At the bottom will be a door with a keypad. The key code is 5929. Punch it into the keypad and open the door. There is a guard patrolling the hallway, so be quiet. Wait for him to walk away and then find a place between two cells where you can do a split jump. Then wait in position as the guard comes back through the hallway. When he's underneath you, drop down and take him out. Then pick up his body and head for the door on the left side of the wall. Once inside, dump the body and use the computer. Head out through the door and down the hallway. Ignore the door on the left and crouch below the window so the chap inside doesn't see you. Head through the sliding glass door on your left and make your way around the room to the door on the other side, making sure the lab guy doesn't see you. From behind the curtain, shoot out the

security camera before entering completely. Move over to the bodies to get your next objective and then pick up the medkit on the wall and head out the way you came in. Take a left when you get out to the hallway and go through the door and up the stairs.

7TH CHECKPOINT

Proceed through the door and walk into the small office and quickly kill the guard at the reception. Next enter the main foyer and go through the door on your right. Now head up the stairs into the main Police control room.

8TH CHECKPOINT

Eliminate, knock out, or if you are very careful, sneak past the two guards working at the computer terminals and then go through the second door on the right into a small surveillance room. Sneak up behind the guard on the other side of the curtain and knock him out. Accessing the computer will give you a car registration number. Now simply head back into the main foyer and go through the main door leading into the courtyard, to finish the mission.

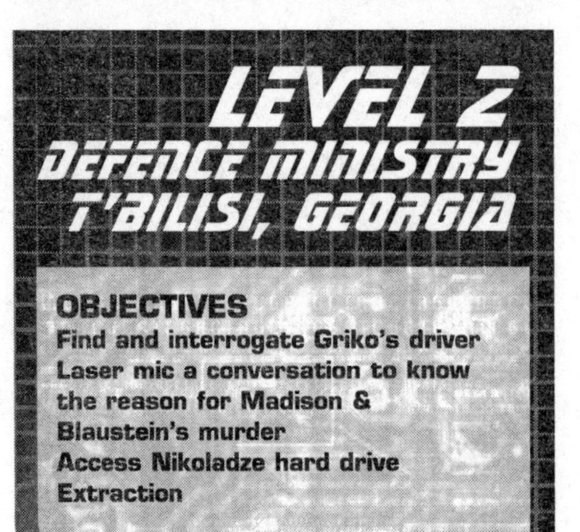

1ST CHECKPOINT

Walk over to the chimney pipe and start rappelling down the wall. When you reach the window, press Y to swing inside the building. Put on your night vision goggles if you need to. Slowly walk up to the edge of the bookshelf and wait as the guard heads your way. Wait for him to sit back down before sneaking up behind him and grabbing him. Drag him over to the shadows and then knock him out. Now shoot the camera on the wall and use the computer. Open the next door and position the camera so you that you can see the two guards. While the one patrolling is walking the other way, head over to the door on the left wall and sneak inside. Head up the stairs to pick up a medkit before heading down the stairs. When you hear the whir of a camera, make your way slowly around the corners until you see the camera. Shoot it out while you are still one staircase above it. Do the same with the next few cameras. At the bottom of the stairwell you will see a door. Approach it and save your game.

2ND CHECKPOINT

Head into the car park and use the shadows to make your way around to the left. When you can see the limousine, hide and wait for the driver to turn away before quickly grabbing him. Make sure you interrogate him before knocking him out. Now head back up the stairs you entered the car park by. Once you reach the hallway at the top, knock out the patrolling guard and the stationary guard. Hide both bodies before breaking into the office at the left end of the hallway. Before walking in, knock out the camera above the door. Now walk through the office to the door on the opposite side of the room and use the lock pick to open it.

3RD CHECKPOINT

Using the drainpipe, climb around to the open window and drop quietly through the kitchen window. Wait for the guard to leave and then quickly lure the two cooks into the freezer with a carefully thrown bottle. With the guards out of the way, head into the canteen. Quickly knock out the guard in the lobby and then sneak down the stairs to the first floor. Sneak up behind the guard between the pillars so you can knock him out. After doing so, head slowly down the stairs on the left side. Once you reach the bottom, make a quick left around the staircase and sneak up behind the guard at the computer. Knock him out, hide the bodies and use the computer. Do this and you'll be

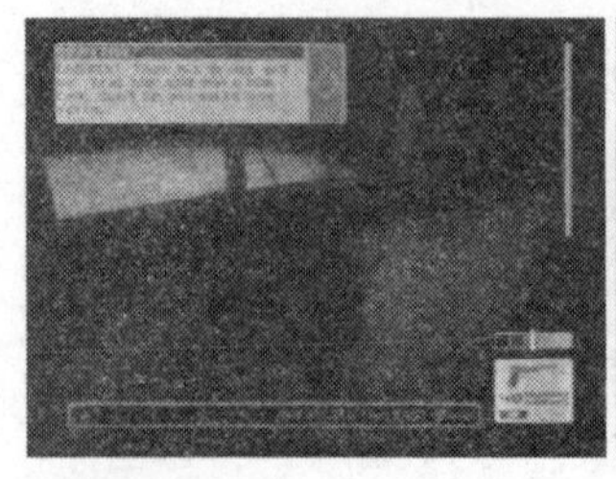

informed that a Colonel is heading towards you. Walk back up the stairs and wait for the Colonel to stop moving. Quickly grab him from behind and drag him to the retinal scanner and use him to open the door for you. Once it is open, knock out the Colonel and head through the door.

4TH CHECKPOINT

Sneak past the surveillance camera (you can't take it out) and go through the double doors into the main courtyard. Walk over towards the far left corner and use the laser-Mic on the glass elevator to listen in on the conversation of Masse and Grinko. A red square means you're getting a good signal. When the conversation ends, quickly climb up the mesh fence on the right side of the doors in front of you and climb through the window at the top.

5TH CHECKPOINT

Quickly enter the store cupboard to the left of the elevator and wait for the two guards to walk past you. When they both have their backs to the elevator, quickly sneak in and ride it up to the top floor.

6TH CHECKPOINT

Exit the elevator and use your lock pick to enter the room on the left. Switch off the light and wait for the nosey guard to investigate. Give him a crack on the back of the head and then use the desk to reach the open ventilation shaft. Crawl around until you can drop down into the u-shaped corridor. Watch out for the camera on the far wall; avoid its gaze and head into the storeroom to the left of the stacked boxes. Collect the medi pack and ammo, before climbing the ladder onto the roof. Once on the roof, walk over to the ventilation pipe to reach the checkpoint.

7TH CHECKPOINT

Using the pipe, rappel down the wall until you reach the large window of Nikoladze's office. Inside is a single guard to take out before you can enter. Once inside the office, use the computer. This will set off an alarm and guards will quickly approach the room. To avoid them, hang out of the window. Climb back inside when the coast is clear and access the computer again to retrieve all the data you require. With all the info acquired, head over to the door and save your game.

8TH CHECKPOINT

After saving your game, take a left outside the door and go through the open door on the left. Head down the stairs, picking up the Medi pack at the bottom. Go through the door and then run across the roof to the elevator shaft on the other side. Jump into shaft to grab the pipe in the centre and slide all the way down. When you can't slide down any further, jump down and head left through the parking garage. Now simply walk around to where Grinko's driver was earlier and talk to Wilkes to complete the mission.

1ST CHECKPOINT

Climb the ladder in front of you to reach the high platform. Once at the top, head right and follow the pipes to the barbed wire fence. To get past this obstacle, drop off of the ledge, grabbing the edge as you fall, and shimmy past the barbed wire. Climb back up and continue right until you come to another obstacle, a large container. Use the same trick to get past it and reach the checkpoint.

2ND CHECKPOINT

Walk onto the platform to your right and slide down the cable to the platform below. As you do so, the rig explodes. Next, head under the large pipe and climb up the pole to the right and drop onto the top of the pipe. Once on top of the pipe, drop through the large hole and follow the inside of the pipe to the next checkpoint.

3RD CHECKPOINT

Climb up the ladder and open the trap door. Once out, avoid the technician and head over to the ladder on the right and climb all the way to the top. Quietly walk around the gantry until you can see a long platform across from you. When the technician has moved out of sight, kill the lonely guard and climb down from the gantry. Now use the large metal girders to reach the far platform. Once across, head up the stairs and continue up onto the main section of the rig. Three warplanes will now attack the rig. When they have gone, slowly follow the bodyguards around the corner to the next checkpoint.

4TH CHECKPOINT

You job is still to follow the technician, so do so until he and his guards enter one of the structures. Now kill the guard outside and hide the body as best you can. Hide and wait for the technician and guards to enter the main control room. Once they are safely inside, follow the outside of the building until you reach a massive fire.

5TH CHECKPOINT

Climb onto the large generator to your right and use the cable to crawl through the small window across from you. Once through, hang down from the pipe and shoot the guard from your elevated position before dropping into the room. Leave via the door to your right and head up the stairs, take down the guard and follow the technician down the stairs around the corner. Kill the guard at the bottom of the stairs and head through the door opposite your position.

6TH CHECKPOINT

Using your lock pick, head through the door and into the corridor. Continue through the door at the far end and follow the next passage until you reach the main section of the rig. Here you will see the mercenary technician making a crafty run for it. Quickly follow him down the staircase and grab him when you're close enough. Interrogate him, knock him out and grab the suitcase to complete the mission.

OBJECTIVES

Retrieve your SC-20k from storage
Access the CIA central server
Locate Mitchell Dougherty's computer
Kidnap Mitchell Dougherty
Incapacitate the CIA security
Rendezvous for extraction

1ST CHECKPOINT

Follow the corridor to a t-junction; take the left and head through the door at the end into the security room. Turn off the lights and knock out the guard inside at the reception. Now head back out and now follow the corridor all the way around to the left until you are faced with a coke machine. Wait until there are no guards looking and go through the door to your right using the code 7687 to unlock it. Begin by taking out the agent on the left before knocking out the maintenance guy. Hide both the bodies and turn off the lights. Now go through the door on the far side of the room and unlock the door at the end of the small passage using the code 110598.

2ND CHECKPOINT

Head quietly down the steps and take out the two maintenance workers before they have chance to sound the alarm. Switch off the lights in the storeroom and head along the small corridor to the staircase. At the top, collect the SC-20k Assault Rifle and other items off of the shelf and continue forward to the checkpoint.

3RD CHECKPOINT

Shoot the agent talking on the mobile and carry his body into the shadows to hide it. Follow the corridor around to the left and knock out the guard patrolling inside the partitioned office. Hide his body before moving into the blue corridor. Follow this corridor to the end to reach the next checkpoint.

4TH CHECKPOINT

Unlock the door on your right with the code 2019 and head out onto the gantry.

Quietly sneak down the stairs and knock out the maintenance worker at the bottom. Continue into the server room and find the main computer. After accessing it, head back out of the room and back to the office area. Once there follow the corridor around to the left until you reach a small reception area, guarded by one guy.

5TH CHECKPOINT

Take out the single guard in the reception area and then climb out through the open window. Switch off the lights and head into the corridor on the other side. Go through the door on the other side into the lobby, and make your way to the door on the other side staying close to the right wall. Sneak past the agent in the office and head down the stairs at the end making sure to shoot out the light at the bottom to avoid detection from the camera. Using the code 110700 will unlock the door and let you proceed into the next room.

6TH CHECKPOINT

Shoot out the lights, hide and wait for the guard to approach to see what happened. Knock the nosy chap out and head over to the door and the end of the room to your left.
Once inside the shooting range, use your lock pick on the door leading into the small lobby. Pass through the now open door and enter the elevator and ride it up to the 1st floor.

7TH CHECKPOINT

Head down the corridor and enter the room at the end, but do not confront any of the guards inside. Pass around the back of the computers behind the large partitions and quietly walk towards the door on the other side of the room. Enter the computer room, wait for Dougherty to leave his office and head inside. Access his computer and then leave his office and quietly follow him down the corridor to reach the next checkpoint.

8TH CHECKPOINT

Still following Dougherty, head into the projection room on your left just before the security guard. Sneak over to the door on the far right side and knock out the guard before using your lock pick to open it. Once you are back out in the main corridor, sneak past the canteen and go through the door at the very end using the code 0614. Enter the smoking room at the end of the corridor and wait for Dougherty to walk inside. Quickly grab him and drag him outside onto the rooftop courtyard.

9TH CHECKPOINT

Drag Dougherty across the roof, down the stairs and across the metal walkways past the thermal vents. At the bottom of the stairs, drop him and open the door on your left.

10TH CHECKPOINT

Head down the stairs, still clutching Dougherty, and carry him through the small warehouse silently eliminating any guards in your way. On the other side, walk down the stairs and take out the guard peering over the balcony. Now simply pick up Dougherty and make your way down to the car park below. There should be one final guard to incapacitate before carrying Dougherty over to the van for extraction.

OBJECTIVES

Deactivate the wall mines
Disarm the bomb planted in the storage room
Restore power to the fire door
Access Kalinatek's fire emergency system
Find Ivan
Clear the roof of Georgian mercenaries

1ST CHECKPOINT

Carefully make your way across the car park and hide yourself behind the yellow car on the left. Take careful aim and shoot the two terrorists in the head as they walk through the door. Head into that door once they are dead and make your way up the stairs to the second floor. At the top, take careful aim and shoot all three of the guards by the white van. With the three guards out of the way, climb up the stack of crates in front of you until you reach the checkpoint.

2ND CHECKPOINT

Line yourself up and jump over to the crate hanging in front of you. Grab the cable above it and slide down to the crane. Another jump is needed to reach the roof of the Kalinatek building. Use the chimney to rappel down the side and into the glass corridor below. Quietly make your way over to the double doors and wait for a guard to walk out. Kill him and head through the

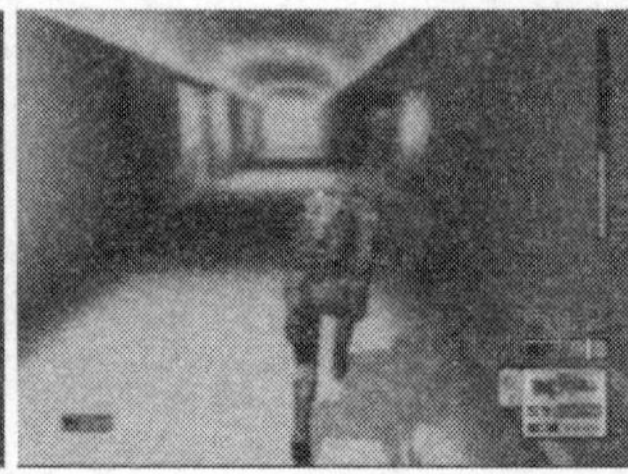

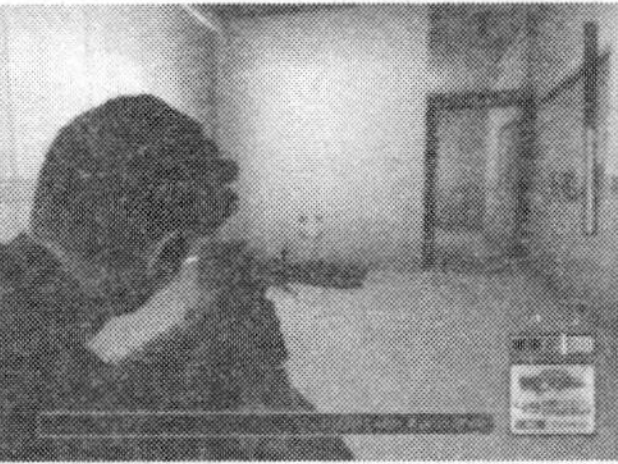

doors. Using the code 97531, open the door on your left and head through the office to the opposite door. Climb through the open ventilation hatch and slowly follow the vent around to another open hatch. Drop down through the hole to reach the next checkpoint.

3RD CHECKPOINT

Carefully open the door behind the fish tank and use your zoom on the rifle to shoot out the wall mine to the right of the two guards. This will usually kill them all in one fell swoop. Proceed to the end of the corridor and kill the guard around the corner before entering the damaged elevator.

4TH CHECKPOINT

Exit the elevator shaft and head right. Pick up the frag grenades on the coffee table then head left, past the office where the guys are shooting. When you reach the end of the blue wall, pull out your SC-20K and go into sniper mode. Ahead of you on the corner of the next set of blue walls, there is a wall mine. Two guards will enter the far hallway and begin walking in your direction. As they move closer to the wall mine, shoot it, letting the explosion take out both guards. Now head to the office directly to your left. There are two programmers hiding behind two wall mines. Walk up the each wall mine very slowly and deactivate them.

5TH CHECKPOINT

Quickly leave the office and make your way to the end of the corridor. Head through the door using the code 33575. Now quickly run through the blazing offices avoiding the exploding wall mines until you safely reach the other side. Now use your lock pick on the door with Archives written on it and enter the blazing office. Climb over the filing cabinet and disarm the bomb on the on the wall.

6TH CHECKPOINT

Exit the Archives office and head into the auditorium. Shoot the two guards from the doorway before continuing down the steps and towards the stage on the opposite side of the area. Continue into the basement through the stairs on the left and take out the three guards inside (use the rifle). To reach the checkpoint, walk around to the end of the room and activate the breaker switch, before heading back up to the auditorium.

7TH CHECKPOINT

At the top of the stairs, get your rifle out and use the sniper mode to whack the guards up in the viewing gallery. With the coast clear, head over to the door on the far right of the room and use 1250 as a code to unlock it. Once through to the lobby on the other side, quietly walk up the stairs and around the balcony to reach the door on the other side. Inside the recreation room, you will find two guards. Kill them both and head through to the medical room. Speak to the technician inside and head back out. Follow the corridor around to the small computer

room and kill the guard inside. Use the computer to open the fire doors, before heading through them to the checkpoint.

8TH CHECKPOINT

Open the door in front of you and head to the top of the stairwell. Open the door and move into the shadows you see in front of you. Wait for the two guards to finish talking. One will go to the restroom, while the other will head for the counter area. When the guard reaches the counter, sneak up behind him and knock him out. Next, head past the flames and into the door that leads to the toilets. Sneak up behind the guard inside and knock him out. Climb into the large air duct above the urinals. Crawl through and you'll hear Ivan talking with someone. Pull out your gun and shoot the guard in the head before he kills Ivan. Hop out of the duct and talk to Ivan. After listening to Ivan, exit the restroom and head right. Hop into the elevator and press the up button.

9TH CHECKPOINT

Once out of the elevator, quietly walk up to the wall on the left and throw a grenade through the wooden slats to hopefully blow up the three guards on the other side. Walk past the blaze and through the open door. Climb the stacked building materials and drop down into the dark room on your left. Enter the adjacent room and walk towards the door at the end. Two guards will then enter the room and attack you. Kill them both as quickly as possible, collect the ammo and medical packs, and continue through the door to reach the checkpoint.

10TH CHECKPOINT

Upon entering the room, you will quickly be attacked by three guards. Kill the guard who climbs the ladder first and then the other two. Now walk across to the other side of the room and follow the corridor until you find a small staircase. Head up the stairs to reach the next checkpoint.

11TH CHECKPOINT

Another three-guard ambush awaits you at the top of the stairs, so be ready. Take out the chap in the window first and then turn your wrath on to the other two. A grenade should take them both out in one go. With all three dead, walk up the stairs and take a left at the top. Continue through the door at the end to reach the checkpoint.

12TH CHECKPOINT

First things first, take out the lights in the room ahead and wait in the doorway. Fire a grenade to take out the three guards who appear at the end. Now proceed along the corridor and follow it around into an unfinished room full of wooden slats. From here, head through the doorway in front of you to reach the next checkpoint.

13TH CHECKPOINT

Follow the corridor until you reach a large courtyard area. Head through the door to your right, go up the stairs and out onto the balcony. Quickly kill the guard on the balcony and then shoot the oil drums, blowing them up and hopefully killing the remaining guards. Now climb down the ladder and walk around the corner to the edge overlooking a large courtyard under construction. Jump down and take out the two guards shooting at Jr Wilkes, and then climb up the scaffolding onto the large platform at the top. When all of the guards are dead, jump into the back of the large chopper to complete the mission.

LEVEL 6
NADEZHDA NUCLEAR PLANT KOLA PENINSULA, RUSSIA

OBJECTIVES

Stow away on the waste train for extraction
Retrieve the Cooling Rod Room access code from the mercenary technician Esfir
Infiltrate the Cooling Rod Room and trigger a meltdown alert
Retrieve the FlashRAM shipping log for the power plant's waste disposal train
Investigate the Nadezhda communications centre
Locate the Georgian microwave relay
Tap the Georgian microwave relay

1ST CHECKPOINT

Walk straight to the far side of the room and take a look over the edge. Snipe the camera first and then the guard walking up the stairs. Hide his body and drop down. Head through the open gate and open the window so you can jump out into the snow. Head around to the right and use the sniper scope to shoot the guard next to the big tank. Now it is safe to enter the building, head inside and shoot the guard. Use the lock pick to open the fire doors at the end of the room.

2ND CHECKPOINT

Walk out into the courtyard and quickly climb the large red pipe to your left. When you reach the top of the red pipe, climb a second pipe to reach the small ledge. Turn around and take out the spotlight and the two guards with the sniper rifle. Make your way around the ledge and climb a third pipe to the top. Follow this ledge and enter the ventilation shaft. At the far end, you will emerge onto a rooftop. From here, snipe the next two guards and the camera above the door. Enter the door on the far side. Use your lock pick to open the door inside the small room. Enter the next room and drop down into the ventilation system and drop onto the elevator to reach the next checkpoint.

3RD CHECKPOINT

After listening in on the elevator conversation drop off the far side of the elevator and climb into the ventilation shaft to reach the next checkpoint.

4TH CHECKPOINT

Before moving anywhere, take out the camera. Then climb up through the small gap in the corner of the room. Quickly and quietly, take out the guard in the corridor and snipe the camera at the far end. Knock out (but don't kill) the technicians, before continuing around the corner to the left. Take out the third camera and drop down through the gap on your left. Follow this passage until you reach the generator room.

5TH CHECKPOINT

Quickly knock out the civilian and hide his body. Sneak up on the technician and interrogate him to get the cooling chamber access codes. Head through the door on the left near to where you came in and follow the corridor. Kill the guard and hide

his body in the nearby staff room and then knock out the civilians (or they will alert more guards). With the civilians out of the way, continue to follow the corridor until you reach the next checkpoint.

6TH CHECKPOINT

Access the cooling room using 560627 as the code. Head down the stairs and use the four big computers to trigger the meltdown alert. Quickly take out the guard that enters the room and head back into the corridor via the staircase. Follow the corridor around to the left, through the security door and up another staircase.

7TH CHECKPOINT

Follow the corridor and run into the computer room to avoid a hail of bullets from the mounted gun. Continue through the door at the end into a large generator room and quickly take down the guard standing on the stairs. Find the technician and interrogate him until he tells you about the nuclear waste. Now head back up onto the gantry and climb through the ventilation shaft. Drop down into the office on the other side and go through the door on the left side of the room. Keep going until you find yourself back in a familiar corridor. Take a left and disable the IFF on the sentry gun and watch it kill the two guards before disabling the gun itself. Now turn around and walk towards the glass door. Use the keypad and enter 151822 for the code. Follow the corridor beyond to the checkpoint.

8TH CHECKPOINT

Continue around the corridor into a small office complex. Use the broken cubical to get close to the sentry gun and disable it (stay to the left of the office). Now take the corridor on the left and follow it around going through the door at the end to reach another checkpoint.

9TH CHECKPOINT

As soon as you open the door, start to shoot the guards in the Comms centre. When they are all dead, make your way into the communication room and through the door at the end. Sneak up behind the technician and interrogate him fully, before knocking him out and using his computer. When you have finished, head through the door next to the computer to reach the checkpoint.

10TH CHECKPOINT

Go through the door on the other side of the room and head up the staircase. In the corridor at the top, shoot the guard and

hide his body somewhere safe before continuing. Take out the next guard and using the code 795021, go through the door at the end to reach the checkpoint.

11TH CHECKPOINT

Finally, drop carefully down through the open grate onto the platform below. Use the large red pipe to slide down into the main train depot. Take out the two remaining guards with your rifle, before going through the door on the far right of the room.

LEVEL 7
CHINESE EMBASSY YANGON, MYANMAR

OBJECTIVES
Meet NSA contact
Laser-mic the Ambassador's office
Trail Kong Feirong
Extraction

1ST CHECKPOINT

Immediately head over to the alley on your right. Climb on top of the dumpster and then over the wall. Hide the alcove in the left wall. When Lambert is finished talking, a guard should make his way down the alley. When he passes you, knock him out and then hide his body somewhere dark. Now head back down the alley and pick up the glass bottle by the fence. Hide behind the dumpster on the right side and throw

the bottle against the wall to your left and behind you. This should lure the second patrolling guard down the alley. Knock out the guard as he passes you and hide his body. As soon as you come out to the street, head to your left, towards the building with the burning oil drum in it. Inside the building to your right is a ladder. Climb up it to reach the first checkpoint.

2ND CHECKPOINT

Very quietly, walk through the building and out onto the scaffolding. At the end of the wooden plank is a ladder. Climb the ladder to the next level and then slowly walk across it to the end of the plank, being careful not to alert the guards below. When you reach the end of the plank, look up. Jump up to grab the wire, lift your legs up, and then shimmy your way across to the other side.

3RD CHECKPOINT

Carefully shoot out the light above you and then shoot the guards in the street below you with the sticky shocker. When they have all been taken care of, use the ladder to climb down and then climb the pipe directly opposite the ladder. Follow the second rooftop into a large clearing. Drop into the street and proceed around the fence in front of you. Finally, climb down into the sewers through the manhole.

4TH CHECKPOINT

Walk straight ahead and then take the first left, at the end of the sewer pipe. Get close to the next junction and several guards will appear and stop in front of you. Use a diversion cam and gas all three of

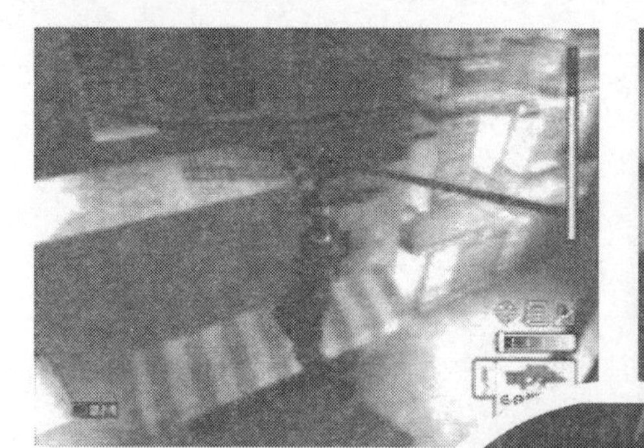

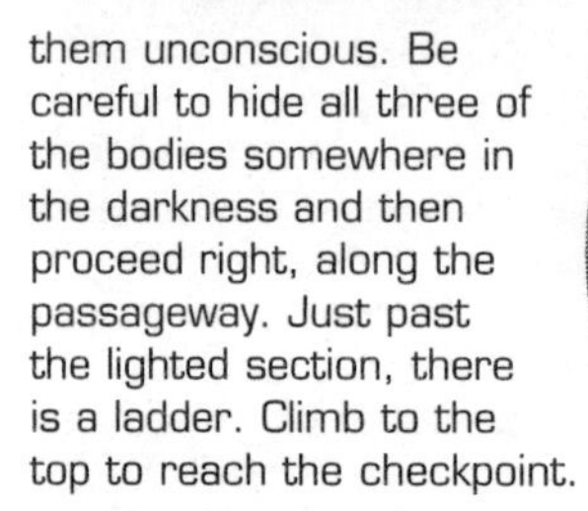

them unconscious. Be careful to hide all three of the bodies somewhere in the darkness and then proceed right, along the passageway. Just past the lighted section, there is a ladder. Climb to the top to reach the checkpoint.

5TH CHECKPOINT

Clamber carefully out into the street and silently walk over to the scaffolding nearby. Head up the ladder and swing along the cable to the other side, staying off the scaffolding as you do so. Finally, climb through the window into the abandoned building.

6TH CHECKPOINT

In the corner of this room, you will find a pipe to climb up. At the top, climb onto the roof and talk to your contact. When you have the info you need, jump up onto the metal gantry at the edge of the roof and use the chimney to rappel down the wall to the next checkpoint.

7TH CHECKPOINT

Quickly move inside the small building on your right and wait for the guard to walk inside. Quickly knock him unconscious. Next, follow the alley into the large clearing and wait for the second guard to turn his back and walk away down the street. When he does this, climb the ladder onto the scaffolding directly in front of you and scramble through the window. Inside, quietly follow the corridor around to the next checkpoint.

8TH CHECKPOINT

Shoot the guard on the balcony and stash his body, now climb up onto the stacked crates and use the cable to slide down onto one of the awning. Drop onto the floor and head down the alleyway on the other side of the street. Follow it to the ladder at the end. Climb the ladder and quietly walk around the gantry. Wait for the guard to walk beneath you, climb down the second ladder and follow the small alleyway to the end, and walk behind the silver van to save you game.

9TH CHECKPOINT

Making careful use of the shadows, sneak slowly into the embassy compound. Walk around the truck to the right and head under the large trailer. Knock out the nearby guard with an airfoil round, remembering to hide his body. Now select a diversion cam and fire it near the second guard patrolling the embassy grounds. Knock him out, and then simply walk around the compound grounds, over the small stream and into the darkened bushes to reach the next checkpoint.

10TH CHECKPOINT

Listen in on the first part of Kong Feirong's conversation with your laser-mic. After he leaves the embassy, use the laser-mic again on his car to hear the second part of the conversation. Once his car drives off, clear the courtyard of enemy troops using diversion cams. Next, walk over to the wall

on the other side of the courtyard, climb up the pipe and drop down on the other side to complete the mission. Easy!

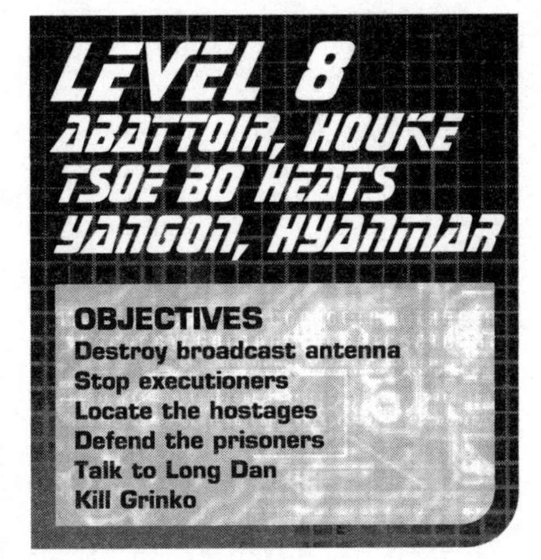

1ST CHECKPOINT

Climb over the fence on your right and use your sniper scope to take out the three guards in the courtyard beyond. When all three are dead, hide their bodies and then head through the door on the other side, which leads into the main abattoir courtyard.

2ND CHECKPOINT

Quickly but quietly, kill the guard talking on the walkie-talkie. Equip your sniper scope and look up onto the balconies to see two more guards. Snipe them both, equip your thermal goggles and then carefully make your way across the courtyard. You need to watch out for both searchlights and mines. Once you are at the far side, enter the small rubbish area and use the bin to pull of a wall jump into the small ventilation duct above you.

3RD CHECKPOINT

Once out onto the rooftop, deliberately make a bit of noise to attract the attention of the nearby guards. Before they appear, hide beneath the metal walkway. From here, use the sniper scope to pick them both off. Drag their prone bodies under the walkway to hide them and then walk over to the radar. Use the small control box to disable its broadcasting capabilities.

4TH CHECKPOINT

Once out onto the veranda, select you snipe scope and wait. When the two guards run out onto the roof, shoot them both (ideally with headshots) and hide their bodies. Lock pick the door they came through and enter the main abattoir. Head down the stairs and collect all the items from the table. Return back up the stairs and open the door on the left. Follow the stairs down, go through the door at the bottom and out onto the balcony above the toilets. Use the pole to shimmy across the partition until you are above the sinks. From here, drop down onto the guard below and kill them. Now take out the second guard at the door and exit the toilets. Head through the door to your left once you are out in the corridor. Continue

to follow the corridor around and go through the next door on the left. Interrogate the guard inside, knock him out and then head back out into the corridor. Drop into the ventilation duct to reach the checkpoint.

5TH CHECKPOINT

Crawl through the vent to the end and climb the pipe you see there. At the top, crawl onto the ceiling and follow it along to a small opening. Fire a frag/smoke grenade down and take out the three guards before dropping down. When the area is clear, head towards the freezer to reach the next checkpoint.

6TH CHECKPOINT

You will need to use your thermal goggles to see clearly here. Walk towards the first door behind the partition, wait for the guard to walk through and take him down with a slick shot to the head. Walk into the next room and take out the second guard before walking over to the opposite side of the room. Climb over the machine to your left and quietly drop down next to the sentry gun, activate the control panel and disable it. Enter the next freezer and quickly and quietly take out all three guards and then walk alongside the machine on your left until there is a break in the middle. Grab onto the pipe, tuck up and shimmy into the next freezer as a sentry gun guards the entrance. Drop down on the other side, walk up to the control panel and disable the sentry gun and then take out the guards before enter the corridor to the right of where you came in.

7TH CHECKPOINT

Walk around into the final freezer room, take out the remaining three troops and drop into the ventilation duct and follow it to the end.

8TH CHECKPOINT

Climb out of the vent, grab the medical pack and quietly walk down the stairs. Kill the guard patrolling the area at the bottom using your rifle. Now activate the switch on the right side of the large grate to open it and drop down inside.

9TH CHECKPOINT

Crawl to the end of the small passageway and head straight into the shadows. Kill the two guards who enter the room and then head out into the corridor from where they came. Take the first right in the corridor and enter the second stables. Sneak up behind the first sentry gun at the end on the right, disable it and then quickly kill the guard that enters the room. Now exit the room and follow the next corridor into the final stables. Sneak into the second stable and deactivate the two sentry guns before proceeding. You'll now have two guards to finish off. Finally, run past the final sentry gun on your left at the end and enter the corridor. Follow the corridor to the right to reach the next checkpoint.

10TH CHECKPOINT

From where you start, wait for two guards to walk around the corner at the end. Use your scope to kill them both. When they are both dead, hide their bodies and follow the corridor into the final stables. Disable the sentry gun on the right and walk through the doorway to find the Chinese dignitaries.

11TH CHECKPOINT

Unfortunately, Grinko's men will now attack you. Quickly head back into the main stable and walk towards the main entrance. Hide behind one of the partitioned walls. From here, you should easily be able to take out all of the guards who approach. Do not let any of them get past you or they will certainly blow up the hostages. Kill the Colonel and Grinko will come down himself. Luckily, he is extremely easy to defeat. Take careful aim and hit him with one headshot to kill him. The mission is now over.

LEVEL 9
CHINESE EMBASSY
YANGON, MYANMAR

OBJECTIVES
Access the Embassy's server
Destroy the Nuclear material
Force Feirong to access the computer

1ST CHECKPOINT

Carefully head into the alley next to the van. Shoot out the light above the door and open it. Turn off the light switch in the kitchen and then head past the table on its left side as the cook walks to turn the light

back on. Climb the ladder into the small storeroom and then climb the second ladder. Walk across the wooden beams into the derelict building on the other side. When the patrolling guard goes right, into the hallway with the broken windows, head into the building towards the back wall and then take a right down the far hallway. Head out onto the balcony, climb the drainpipe and then slide down onto the wall of the embassy. From here, shimmy around the corner, drop down onto the roof and sneak across to the other side. Stand on the small ledge and follow it around to a drainpipe. Climb the drainpipe and drop through the hatch at the top leading into the embassy.

2ND CHECKPOINT

Walk straight into the small storeroom and through the hole in the wall on your left. Flatten yourself against the wall to squeeze through the next gap. At the end, slide down the pipe into the wall space below. Slide across until you can release yourself from the wall. Wait for all three guards to walk into the main server room and then fire a smoke grenade through the door to knock them all out in one fell swoop. Access the computer, listen to what Lambert has to say and then go through the door into the maintenance corridor.

3RD CHECKPOINT

At the top of the stairs, shoot the guard, wait for his partner to investigate and shoot him as well. Take out the camera and hide both of the guard's bodies somewhere dark before heading around to the right. Stop at the first door you reach,

walk into dormitory and silently kill the two guards. Collect any useful items from next to their beds. Now wait for the guards in the corridor to enter the main hall and quickly access the control panel. Use the thermal goggles to retrieve the code (1436). Sneak behind the sentry gun on the right side of the room and disable it before it can shoot you. Next, jump up onto the shelf above you and climb through the broken banister and disable the sentry gun. Now use your scope to eliminate the two guards at the end. Next equip your pistol

and shoot out every light in the room and the grab on the large pole with the flag and shimmy across to the other side of the room. Wait until the Colonel has used the retinal scanner, quietly drop down next to him and force him to open the door for you. Enter the small office, eliminate the guard inside, open the window and drop down into the small courtyard below.

4TH CHECKPOINT

Your first job is to snipe the lights in this area, and then use your scope to take out all of the guards and dogs in the large Oriental garden. Hide all of their bodies and then make your way to the far side of the gardens. Head through the gate on the right. Open the second gate and have a look into the small loading bay. Quickly take out the guard and the camera before an alarm is sounded. Now enter the building and walk towards the door inside to reach the next checkpoint.

5TH CHECKPOINT

Grab the medical pack if you need to, before heading through the door into the first warehouse. Slowly make your way to the other side, ensuring that the guard doesn't spot you. Wait for him to enter the room, and then head for the control panel and enter the code 9753 and enter the small staff room.

6TH CHECKPOINT

Enter the second, larger warehouse and start to eliminate all of the guards inside (make sure to take out the surveillance cameras other the alarm will be sounded). Now walk around to the right until you come across a single box. Use the box to climb up onto the top of the stacked crates and then follow the gantry along to the end where you'll see two fuel trucks. Use you scope and shoot the fuel tank to send both truck in a ball of flames. Now walk down the stairs, open the large hatch and drop down into the sewers below.

7TH CHECKPOINT

Begin to walk to wards the end of the passageway taking out the guard in front of you first. Now when the second guard appears, do not let him see you, as he must remain alive in order for you to reach Feirong. When he runs off, follow him through the passageway, wait for him to go through the first door and activate the keypad and input the code 1456, pass through the door and hop onto the elevator and ride it upwards. Exit the elevator when it stops, run to the end of the corridor and head through the door using the code 1834, and then open the final door On the right with the code 7921 and enter Feirong's office.

8TH CHECKPOINT

Talk to Feirong and wait for him to challenge you with his gun. Grab him from behind and force him to access the information in his computer, upon which he'll keel over and die. All you need to do now is follow the flaming corridor to a large staircase. Head down the stairs, slide the window open and drop down into the garden below. Once in the garden walk over to the helipad to complete the mission.

LEVEL 10
GEORGIAN PRESIDENTIAL PALACE T'BILISI, GEORGIA

OBJECTIVES
Ark interrogation file
Use Nikolaze for retinal scanner
Use laser mic to identify which shadow is Nokolaze, then snipe him using the thermal vision.
Final extraction

1ST CHECKPOINT

Make your way around the outside with a series of jumps. Perform a wall jump and grab onto the ledge in front of you, and then lower Sam down on the other side carefully without dropping. Next jump up onto the ledge and then perform a wall jump, grab onto the drainpipe and climb up to the ledge above you. Grab onto the horizontal pipe and shimmy across until you are directly above the next ledge and drop down. Now grab onto the next pipe and shimmy all the way around the corner and grab onto the ledge on the other side. From here perform two running leaps to reach the final platform. Drop off the edge and shimmy past the protruding wall. Climb up on the other side and begin to climb the drainpipe in front of Sam.

2ND CHECKPOINT

Use the drainpipe to reach the top and wait for the spotlight to pass before climbing up onto the wall. Run to the far right and begin by using your rifle to snipe the sniper in the tower. Next take out the two dogs and then finally the two guards (although ensure both guards aren't in the way of the spotlight otherwise the alarm will be sounded). Next head through the maze into a small courtyard with a fountain unlock the gate on the other side with the code 2126 and take a left. Now slide open the cellar window and drop through it.

3RD CHECKPOINT

Immediately proceed up the stairs into the study and go straight into the gallery. Unlock the door on the far side of the room, head inside and shoot out the light. Next wait for the four guards to enter the gallery, and then quickly pick them all of with your scope. Hide their bodies and then pass through the door from where they came. Now head up the stairs (use your thermal goggles to avoid the laser wires) and open the door at the top.

4TH CHECKPOINT

Quickly dart into the small alcove to the right and then arm your scope. Kill the Georgian elite guards first as they will cause you the most problems. When the two guards run up the stairs, take them both down quickly and then proceed to shoot out all of the lights in the room. Now simply go to the door on the top balcony and unlock the door the code 70021 and passing through.

5TH CHECKPOINT

Take out the nearby lights, and then proceed to kill the two guards and the Georgian Elite troops in the corridor. Hide their bodies and then head up the corridor. Take the second left and go through the door at the end on the left into the Presidential Office.

6TH CHECKPOINT

Use you thermal goggles to see the laser wires and navigate your way past into the office. Eliminate the guard who comes through the door and then access the computer to learn more info on the ARC. With this intelligence, exit the office back out into the main corridor. Go through the double doors on your left and then proceed through the large double doors at the end of the second corridor to reach the next checkpoint.

7TH CHECKPOINT

Unlock the door on the side of the room with the code 66768 and enter the corridor. Take out the light above you, and then quickly and efficiently take out the three Georgian elite troops patrolling the elevator (remembering that only headshots are effective for instant kills). When all of the troops have been killed, enter the elevator and ride it down into the library.

8TH CHECKPOINT

As soon as the elevator stops you will be ambushed by four Georgian elite troops. Begin by killing the first troop that enters the library and then exit the elevator and hide behind the bookcase to the left. Two will now attempt to kill you, but as they come around the corner they will leave themselves open enough for you to get two clean headshots in and kill them both. Finally use you scope through the bookcase and snipe the fourth troop on the staircase. When they are all dead make your way into the basement and grab Nikoladze and interrogate before forcing him to open the safe. Cristavi's men will now hold you up and release Nikoladze.

9TH CHECKPOINT

Activate your night vision goggles and use the blackout to your advantage by eliminating all five troops in the basement before they can get their bearings (remember that these guys also have night vision goggles. Once you have killed all of the guards, head back up into the library and go through the large double doors into the garden.

10TH CHECKPOINT

Eliminate the two guards in the garden and climb up the drainpipe on the far side onto the balcony at the top.

11TH CHECKPOINT

Collect the ammo on the ledge and use your scope to aim up at Cristavi's office. Nikoladze is the man on the left and one shot to the head will take him out. Once he is dead, wait for the guard to come through the door to your right. Eliminate him quickly and go through the door.

12TH CHECKPOINT

Quickly run down the stairs and enter the kitchen and shoot out the two lights plunging the place into darkness. Wait for two of the guards to investigate and kill them both with headshots. Finish off the remaining guard in the dining room and go through the door at the end leading into a small foyer. Two armed guards are watching each set of doors. Open one of the doors and quickly fire a grenade through, which will hopefully finish off two of them. Now use your rifle to clean up the remaining guards and then finally pass through the main door to complete the mission and the game!

TEKKEN TAG TOURNAMENT

Start match with second character selected:
Hold Tag and hit START.
Gallery mode:
Unlock Devil and Angel to access gallery mode.
Tekken Bowl mode:
Unlock True Ogre to access Tekken Bowl mode. You can hit Dr. Boskonovitch in the background while playing Tekken Bowl.
Tekken Bowl mode: Hit Dr. Bostonovitch:
Aim at Dr. Bostonovitch at the left hand side of your screen and bowl into him. You will knock him out, and the announcer will yell "K.O." To make this easier, choose a robot fighter and use its ability to aim to your advantage.
Tekken Bowl mode: Juke Box:
Score more than 200 points in Tekken Bowl. Hit Start, select "Bowling Options", and choose a song.
Tekken Bowl mode: Hit man:
When in the Tekken Bowl tournament round, aim for the man on the right side wearing the purple and white outfit and stop the power at the max. The screen will rattle and "K.O." will appear. The message "Caution: Do not try this at home" will appear at the bottom of the screen.
Theatre mode:
Successfully complete the game in arcade mode under any difficulty setting once to unlock Theatre mode. This allows the FMV sequences to be viewed.
Fight as Alex:
Highlight Roger and hit ✖ at the character selection screen.
Fight as Angel:
Complete arcade until Devil is unlocked. Then, highlight Devil and hit Start at the character selection screen.
Fight as Gold Tetsujin:
Win ten matches in versus mode.
Fight as Heihachi:
Complete arcade mode under the normal difficulty setting with two rounds, without losing any rounds, in less than 5 minutes, 30 seconds.
Fight as Tiger:
Highlight Eddy's screen and hit Start.
Fight as Tetsujin and Unknown in arcade mode:
Unlocked Tetsujin and/or Unknown. Select arcade mode, then scroll down the character list to the bottom left corner (Wang). Hit Left and will appear and can be selected.
Angel FMV sequences:
Select Angel with Start and successfully complete arcade mode with her.
Devil FMV sequences:
Select Devil with ■, ▲, ✖, or SELECT and successfully complete arcade mode with him.
Eddy FMV sequences:
Successfully complete arcade mode once as Eddy after choosing him with ●, ■, ▲, or ✖ at the character selection screen. Then complete arcade mode again after choosing him with Start at the character selection screen. Note: Make sure you choose him as your first player and not your partner.
Kuma FMV sequences:
Successfully complete arcade mode as Kuma after choosing him with ■ or ▲ at the character selection screen. Then, complete it again after hiting ● or ✖ at the character selection screen (Panda).
Ling FMV sequences:
To view two FMV sequences featuring Ling, successfully complete arcade mode as Ling, and complete it again in her school costume.

TEKKEN 4

Fight as Eddy Gordo:
Successfully complete the game in story mode as Christie Monteiro. Then, highlight Christie and hit ▲ at the character selection screen. Eddy Gordo plays exactly like Christie.
Fight as Miharu:
Successfully complete the game in story mode as Ling Xiaoyu . Then, highlight Ling Xiaoyu and hit ● at the character selection screen. Miharu looks like Ling in her schoolgirl outfit from Tekken 3 and Tekken Tag Tournament and plays just like her.
Fight as Ling Xiaoyu in school uniform:
Successfully complete the game in story mode as Ling Xiaoyu. Highlight Ling Xiaoyu and hit ▲ at the character selection screen.
Fight as Panda:
Highlight Kuma at the

character selection screen, then hit ▲ or ●.
Fight as Violet:
Highlight Lee at the character selection screen, then hit ●.
Dojo stage:
Successfully complete the game in Tekken Force mode.
Theater mode:
Successfully complete the game in Story mode.
Ranking password:
Successfully complete Time Attack, Survival, Tekken Force, or Training mode. Hold ■ + ▲ and hit ⇧/⇨ to display a password that corresponds to your rank.

TERMINATOR: DAWN OF FATE

Control introduction sequence:
During the opening screens, press L1 and R1 to zoom in the image in the background.
Turret gun zoom:
When you get to use a turret gun in certain parts of a level, press L3 to zoom in 3x. This will help you see what you are shooting at, and result in better aim.
Weapon zoom:
On most weapons, you can zoom in by 3x pressing R1.
Easy Skynet Tech points:
While zoomed in, aim for the neck of most enemies and their heads will pop off. Each head is worth Skynet Tech points.
T-400 Threat data:
Finish all the training missions under the time limit, then press L1 at the mission complete screen to see what you have unlocked.
Easy kills
Aim for a terminator's head while in battle. If you shoot its head, it will pop off, and you will get a lot of Skynet Tech points. Sometimes when you shoot its head off, it will run around shooting its gun in the air and then explode.

TEST DRIVE

Master code:
Hit ⇦ x2, ⇨, ■, ⇧, L2 x2, R1 at the main menu.
All cars and tracks:
Hit ⇨ x2, ⇦, ■, ⇧, L2 x2, R1 at the main menu.
Bonus cars:
Select the San Francisco Drag Race and use the Dodge Concept Viper to set a new time record. Then, enter SOUNDMAX as a name at the high score screen. The Jaguar XK-R

TENCHU 3: WRATH OF HEAVEN

Unlock All characters:
Press L1, L2, R1, ⇨, ⇦, L3, R3 at the title screen.
Unlock All missions:
Press L1, R1, L2, R2, ⇨, ■, L3, R3 at the mission selection screen.
Unlock All mission layouts:
Press R3, L3, R2, L2, R1, L1 at the mission selection screen.
Unlock Bonus stage:
Press L1, ⇧, R1, ⇩, L2, ⇨, R2, ⇦ at the title screen.
Unlock Recover health:
Pause game play and press ⇧, ⇩, ⇨, ⇦.
Unlock Unlock all items:
Press and hold R1 + L1 and press ⇧, ■ x2 , ⇦, ■ x2 , ⇩, ■ x2 , ⇨, ■ x2 at the item selection screen .
Unlock Increase items:
Press and hold R2 + L2 and press ■ x3, ⇧, ⇦, ⇩, ⇨ at the item selection screen
Unlock Hidden level:
Press ⇧, ⇩, ⇨, ⇦, ✖ x3 at the title screen.

"SoundMAX SPX", Jaguar XK-R "Analog Devices", and the Aston Martin DB7 "SoundMAX SPX" will be unlocked.

TIP: G4 TV car:
Select the San Francisco Drag Race and set a new time record. Then, enter PLWCBF as a name at the high score screen. The G4 TV Viper will now be unlocked.

Alternate replay views:
Hit Select during replays to change the camera effects.

Unlock Dodge Viper GTS:
Win the track 27 race in story mode.

Unlock Dodge Viper GTS-R Concept:
Defeat Clark in all races. Alternately, win the track 45 race in story mode.

Unlock Ford GT:
Defeat Vasily in all races.

Unlock Ford Mustang:
Win the track 7 race in story mode.

Unlock Jaguar XJ220:
Win the track 33 race in story mode.

Unlock Reese's Chevrolet Camaro:
Win the track 9 race in story mode.

Unlock Shelby Cobra 427 SC:
Win the track 5 race in story mode.

Skeeter's Chevrolet Chevelle:
Win the track 26 race in story mode.

TEST DRIVE: OFF-ROAD WIDE OPEN

Unlock Pro class trucks:
Successfully complete the first nine tracks in single race mode.

Unlock Unlimited class trucks:
Successfully complete the first twenty-seven tracks in single race mode.

Unlock Monster truck:
Successfully complete the all twenty-seven tracks in single race mode in first place. Try using Moon Buggy or the Rod Hall Hummer after they are unlocked.

Unlock Humvee:
Finish in first place in the first three seasons of career mode in all divisions.

Unlock Shelby Dodge Durango:
Finish in first place in season four of career mode in the speed division.

Unlock Dodge T-Rex:
Finish in first place in season four of career mode in the power division.

Unlock Rod Hall Hummer:
Finish in first place in all divisions in career mode. The Rod Hall Hummer is good for speed. It handles poorly and is average in climbing. It can be a power vehicle if needed. It works well for single race on the blitz races.

Unlock Moon level and Moon Buggy:
Collect all nine Blue Moon cafe signs in free roam or career mode. There are three signs in each level. The Moon Buggy is the best all around vehicle and is able to reach speeds of 132 mph. It is the vehicle to use on all the other races in single race.

Unlock Controlled landing:
Hold R1 after a jump, then use the Left Analogue-stick to steer your descent.

Unlock Flip or barrel roll:
Go off of a large jump and when in the air, hold R1 (default controls) + ⇦ or ⇨ to do a barrel roll. To flip, hold R1 + ⇧ or ⇩.

THEME PARK ROLLER COASTER

All purchases are free:
Hit (⇦, ⇩, ✖, ●) eight times while in the park.

Golden Tickets:
Hit (⇧, ⇩, ⇦, ⇨, ●, ⇨, ⇦, ⇩, ⇧, ●) four times while in the park.

All items researched:
Hit (⇧, ⇩, ⇧, ⇩, ⇦, ⇧, ⇩, ⇧, ⇩, ⇨) eight times while in the park. Note: This only works for the park you are in at the time you entered the code.

All awards:
Hit (⇧, ⇩, ⇦, ⇨, ●, ⇨, ⇦, ⇩, ⇧, ●) five times while in the park.

Rollercoaster Test Park:
Create 10 roller coasters with an ultimate rating to unlock a Rollercoaster Test Park when a starting a new game or reloading a saved game.

THE THING

Persuade a person:
When someone's trust is in the orange and they will not do anything for you, enter first person mode and aim the gun at their head for three seconds. They will now do things for you without good trust.

Skip first Boss battle:
When you encounter the first Thing Boss, hold ⇧/⇦ to run diagonally and you should run under it before it can hit you. This will also aim you directly at the junction box. Immediately start fixing it. As soon as it is almost fixed, hold ⇨ to run through the door. Since he will still keep fixing it as long as you do not release the button, with luck it will be fixed before the Boss attacks for the third time. At the intermission sequence you tend to take off in a random direction, so this may take a few attempts. Save immediately before trying this. If successfully completed, you will lose only about half a bar of health and

no ammunition, making the next area much easier.
Defeating the third Boss:
Run around the Boss in a circle while shooting it with the machine gun. When it is low on health, use the flamethrower to finish it off. If done correctly, you can kill it without being hit. After you kill the Boss, the Thing in the glass in the room will break out, and the door will be opened with a few guards.
Shutting doors:
Always shut the door of the room you walk into, if you have the chance. For example, on the level where you have to kill all the walkers, a walker will enter from the front door if you do not shut it.
Keeping your team together:
Listen to your team. They will tell you how they feel. If you hear someone say something similar to "We're gonna die", check the team menu and see how he is doing. If there is an X across his face while he is shaking uncontrollably, bring out the Tazer and shock him. Wait for him to calm down, move out of the area, and give him back his gun. He might be bitter, but after you kill a few more things he will be fine. Otherwise, he might start shooting you and your team, ending with himself in the head.
Blood Test Kits:
Save Blood Test Kits for showing your team that you are not infected to gain trust. Using them on a team member is useless because they get infected randomly, and usually break out within a minute of infection.
Medi-Packs:
Always try to keep medics alive because medical packs can be few and far between. If you want your medic to heal a member of the team, tell your team to stay, then push your medic into the wounded team member. If he is hurt enough, the medic will heal him.

THIS IS FOOTBALL 2002

Unlock Africa All-stars team:
Win the Africa Cup to unlock the Africa All-Stars.
Unlock North American All-stars team:
Win the North American Cup to unlock the North America All-Stars.
Unlock South American All-stars team:
Win the South American Cup to unlock the South America All-Stars.
Unlock Asia All-stars team:
Win the Asia Cup to unlock the Asia All-Stars.
Unlock German League All-Stars team:
Win the German League to unlock the German League All-Stars.
Unlock All Time 22 and all Superteams:
Win the Super Team Championship in World Class mode.
Unlock Square Pitch:
Win the European Cup to unlock the Square Pitch.
Unlock Semi Pro Pitch:
Win the World Cup in World Class mode.
Unlock Credit FMV sequence:
Win the Timewarp Cup to unlock an option for the game's credits at the main menu.
Double pass:
Hit ✖ x2 during a game to a nearby teammate.
Spin around:
Tap L1 when you have the ball.
Step-Over and Kick Ahead:
Hold L1 when you have the ball.
Shimmy:
Tap L2 when you have the ball.
Shimmy and Kick Ahead:
Hold L2 when you have the ball.
Kick Ahead:
Hit R1 x2 when you have the ball.
Recommended players:
The two best players in the game are Alfredo di Stefano and Johann Cruyff.

THUNDERHAWK: OPERATION PHOENIX

Unlock Level select:
Enter the options screen. Set "Vibration" to "1" and "Sound effects" and "Music" to "0".. Then, hold L1 + L2 + R1 + R2 + ● + ■. The message "Spooky Cat" will appear in the middle of the screen to confirm correct code entry.

TIGER WOODS PGA TOUR 2001

Unlock Faster CPU turn:
Hold L1 + ▲ when the CPU hits the ball.
Red shirt:
Successfully complete all 21 courses in "Play Now" mode. Tiger Woods' red shirt is now unlocked, which allows the ranges on all clubs to match his actual stats.
Good drives:
You can hit almost every green in the game with a driver (400) yard drive average. Hit R2 to tee up the ball. Perform your swing with the Right Analogue-stick while holding D-pad Up. Once your ball gets into the air, you can put more spin on the ball

with spin control. The sooner you hit it and the longer you hold it, the further the ball will go. Also, for those tough par fours, you may want to try hitting the ball while using the topspin during your swing and using backspin on the spin control to get the ball to sit down.

TIGER WOODS PGA TOUR 2002

Unlock All golfers and courses:
Enter ALLORNOTHIN as the code.
Unlock All courses:
Enter GIVEITUP as the code.
Unlock Brad Faxon:
Enter ENOXAF14D as the code.
Unlock Cedric "Ace" Andrews:
Enter TSWERDNA120 as the code.
Unlock Colin Montgomery:
Enter EYTNOMO9E as the code.
Unlock Erika "Ice" Von Severin:
Enter RVESNOVO8G as the code.
Unlock Jasper Parnevik:
Enter OKIVENRAPO2U as the code.
Unlock Jim Furyk:
Enter OKYRUFO5R as the code.
Unlock Justin Leonard:
Enter RDRANOAEL130 as the code.
Unlock Kellie Newman:
Enter SNAMWEN172 as the code.
Unlock Lee Janzen:
Enter INEZNAJ11W as the code.
Unlock L'Mo:
Enter P2UTAVAAT15S as the code.
Unlock Melvin "Yosh" Tanigawa:
Enter WAWAGINATO7I as the code.
Unlock Moa "Big Mo" Ta'a Vatu:
Enter O1UTAVAATO6T as the code.
Unlock Notah Begay III:
Enter DYAGEBO4E as the code.
Unlock Stuart Appleby:
Enter UYBELPPA16O as the code.
Unlock Solita Lopez:
Enter GZEPOL1OR as the code.
Unlock Super Tiger:
Enter 2TREPUSO1S as the code.
Unlock Vijay Singh:
Enter SHGNISO3P as the code.
Unlock Advance time:
Hold ✖ after the ball is in the air to fast forward its movement.
Unlock Slow time:
Hold Triangle after the ball is in the to slow down time.
Unlock Skip tutorial mode:
Hit L1 during the tutorial.
Unlock Control ball spin:
Hold Triangle while the ball is in the air to slow time, then hold a direction + L2 to control its spin.
Bonus golfers:
Defeat a golfer in the Tiger Challenge to unlock that person in other game modes.
Aces Wild trophy ball:
Shoot a hole in one in the Tiger Challenge.
Back-to-Back trophy ball:
Shoot two consecutive eagles in the Tiger Challenge.
Birdie Buster trophy ball:
Shoot over twelve consecutive birdies in the Tiger Challenge.
Birdie Streak trophy ball:
Shoot six consecutive birdies in the Tiger Challenge.
Eagle Extravaganza trophy ball:
Shoot four eagles in a round in the Tiger Challenge.
Eagle Hunt trophy ball:
Eagle all par 5 holes in the game in the Tiger Challenge.
Fairway Challenge trophy ball:
Hit all the fairways in a round in the Tiger Challenge.
GIR Challenge trophy ball:
Hit all the greens in regulation in the Tiger Challenge.
Long Distance Drive trophy ball:
Hit a drive over 350 yards in the Tiger Challenge.
Long Putt trophy ball:
Sink a putt from over 55 feet in the Tiger Challenge.
Low Round trophy ball:
Shoot under 60 in a round in the Tiger Challenge.
One Time trophy ball:
Tee off and hit a par 5 green in the Tiger Challenge.
Pin Seeker trophy ball:
Hit the pin in the Tiger Challenge.
Scenario Challenge trophy ball:
Successfully complete all scenarios in the Tiger Challenge.
Tiger Challenge Completion trophy ball:
Successfully complete the Tiger Challenge.
Top of the Tournaments trophy ball:
Win first place in all tournaments in the Tiger Challenge.

TIME CRISIS 2

Unlock Mirror mode:
To activate the Mirror Mode, you must clear the Story Mode without using a "Continue".
Unlock Stage Trial 2:
To reach Stage Trial 2, clear Stage 1 of the Story

Mode on any difficulty level.
Unlock Stage Trial 3:
To reach Stage Trial 3, clear Stage 2 of the Story Mode on any difficulty level.
Unlock Music Player:
To access the Music Player, you must clear the final mission of the Crisis Mission.
Unlock Additional Quick and Crash Game Modes:
To access the additional Game Modes, "Chain Hit Game", "One Shot Game" and "10 Second Game", you must achieve higher than fifth place in the Standard Difficulty level.
The Target will change in the "Chain Hit Game" as follows:

0 - 48:	A cup
49 - 98:	A piggy bank
99 - 148:	A filament light bulb
149 - 173:	Pac - Man
174 - 198:	Cosmo
199 - 223:	Mappy
224 - 253:	Pooka
254 - 255:	Bacura

If you shoot Bacura, the counter will stop at 255 points. There will be no further increase in your points after this, regardless of how many targets you continue to hit.
Unlock Auto Bullets:
Clear the Story Mode twice at any difficulty level to unlock the capacity to fire 20 bullets in one trigger.
Unlock Auto Reload:
Clear the Story Mode at any difficulty level using your Auto Bullets and you will then be entitled to unlimited firepower with your gun.
Unlock Wide Shots:
Clear the Story Mode at any difficulty level with the Auto Reload function to enable your firearm to shoot wide shots (shot-gun type with 9 bullets per reload).
Unlock Shoot Away 2 Extra Mode:
To access Extra Mode, you must score good points in the Arcade Original Mode (Retro).

Unlock Shoot Away 2 arrange mode:
To access arrange mode, you must score very high points in the arcade original mode (Retro). You will receive bonus points if you hit two clay pigeons with one bullet. Your points will double, so if you hit a 30 points clay and a 40 points clay with one shot, you will get 140 bonus points.

TIMESPLITTERS 2

ENDING BONUSES
Cardboard Cutouts and Streets
Successfully complete the game in story mode under the easy difficulty setting to unlock the Cardboard Characters cheat and the Streets multi-player level in arcade mode.

Big Heads and Cloaked characters
Successfully complete the game in story mode under the normal difficulty setting to unlock Big Heads and All Characters Cloaked cheats and the Compound multi-player level in arcade mode.

Unlimited ammo and Site Level
Successfully complete the game in story mode under the hard difficulty setting to unlock the Unlimited Ammo cheat and the Site multi-player level in arcade mode.

Paintball mode
Successfully complete all challenges with at least a Bronze rank to unlock the Paintball cheat.

TOCA RACE DRIVER

Unlock All cars:
Enter XKIMCF or LEZEJD as the code at the bonus screen.
Unlock All tracks:
Enter QTRIKX or TMYTKO as the code at the bonus screen.
Unlock Pro Race Driver tracks:
Enter LQJFFA as the code at the bonus screen.
Unlock Realistic handling:
Enter SIM as the code at the bonus screen.
Unlock Alternate car handling:
Enter VIBAKH as the code at the bonus screen.
Unlock Better damage:
Enter DAMAGE as the code at the bonus screen.
Unlock No damage:
Enter IHHBIV or OATRYU as the code at the bonus screen.
Unlock View credits:
Enter CREDITS as the code at the bonus screen.

TONY HAWK'S PRO SKATER 3

Unlock Cheat menu:
Enter backdoor to unlock the cheat menu.

Unlock Master code:
Enter MAGICMISSILE as the code to unlock all mode options.

Unlock All characters:
Enter Yohomies (case-sensitive) to unlock all characters.

Unlock Level select:
Enter RoadTrip (case-sensitive) to unlock all levels.

Full stats:
Enter PUMPMEUP for maximum stat points.

Unlock All decks for current skater:
Enter givemesomewood (case sensitive) to unlock all decks for the current skater

Unlock All FMV sequences:
Enter Peepshow (case-sensitive) to unlock all FMV sequences.

Tony Hawk's sons as created skaters:
Enter Riley Hawk or Spencer Hawk as a name at the "create a skater" screen and their stats will appear.

Hidden created skaters:
Enter one of the following names at the "create a skater" screen and their stats will appear.
062287
80's Mark
Braineaters
Crashcart
DDT
Eastside
Frogham
GMIAB
Gorilla
Grass Patch
Mini Joel
Pimpin Frank
Rastapopolous
Skillzilla (or by entering Gi Skillz)
Stacey D

Perfect record:
To get a perfect record for a skater, enable the following codes in order: "Level select", "All characters", "All FMV sequences", and "Cheat menu".

Unlock Perfect balance for manuals:
Complete all the goals in the game and get gold medals in all three competitions seventeen times in career mode with a different skater each time.

Unlock Perfect balance for rails:
Complete all the goals in the game and get gold medals in all three competitions thirteen times in career mode with a different skater each time.

Unlock Unlimited specials:
Complete all the goals in the game and get gold medals in all three competitions twelve times in career mode with a different skater each time.

Unlock Super Stats:
Complete all the goals in the game and get gold medals in all three competitions fourteen times in career mode with a different skater each time.

Unlock Slow motion:
Complete all the goals in the game and get gold medals in all three competitions sixteen times in career mode with a different skater each time.

Unlock Moon physics:
Complete all the goals in the game and get gold medals in all three competitions nineteen times in career mode with a different skater each time.

Unlock Snowboard mode:
Complete all the goals in the game and get gold medals in all three competitions eleven times in career mode with a different skater each time.

Unlock Expert mode:
Complete all the goals in the game and get gold medals in all three competitions twenty times in career mode with a different skater each time.

Unlock Neversoft mascot:
Complete all the goals in the game and get gold medals in all three competitions twenty-one times in career mode with a different skater each time.

Unlock Officer Dick:
Complete all the goals in the game and get gold medals in all three competitions three times in career mode with a different skater each time.

Unlock First person mode:
Complete all the goals in the game and get gold medals in all three competitions twenty-two times in career mode with a different skater each time.

Unlock Demoness:
Complete all the goals in the game and get gold medals in all three competitions ten times in career mode with a different skater each time.
Unlock Darth Maul:
Complete all the goals in the game and get gold medals in all three competitions one time with any character in career mode.
Unlock Kelly Slater:
Complete all the goals in the game and get gold medals in all three competitions eight times in career mode with a different skater each time.
Unlock Ollie the magic bum:
Complete all the goals in

the game and get gold medals in all three competitions seven times in career mode with a different skater each time.
Unlock Private Carrera:
Complete all the goals in the game and get gold medals in all three competitions five times in career mode with a different skater each time.
Unlock Wolverine:
Complete all the goals in the game and get gold medals in all three competitions two times in career mode with a different skater each time.
Unlock Small skater:
Complete all the goals in the game and get gold medals in all three competitions eighteen times in career mode with a different skater each time.
Unlock Huge skater:
Complete all the goals in the game and get gold medals in all three competitions fifteen times in career mode with a different skater each time.
Unlock Burnside level:
Complete all the goals in the game and get gold medals in all three competitions six times in career mode with a different skater each time.
Unlock Roswell level
Complete all the goals in the game and get gold medals in all three competitions nine times in career mode with a different skater each time.
Unlock Warehouse level
Complete all the goals in the game and get gold medals in all three competitions three times in career mode with a created skater.
Unlock Cruise Ship level:
Get any medal on all three competition levels.
Unlock All highlight tapes:
Get gold medals in all three competitions in career mode with a skater to unlock his or her tape.

TOP GEAR DAREDEVIL

Unlock Alternate colours:
Hit ⇩, ■, ⇩, R1, ⇨ x2, ⇧, ⇦, ● x2, L2, L1 at the main menu, then begin game play.

TONY HAWK'S PRO SKATER 4

Unlock Hidden skaters:
Enter the options menu, then select "Cheats" and then enter homielist to unlock Eddie, Jango Fett, and Mike Vallely.
Unlock Moon physics:
Enter the options menu, then select "Cheats" and then enter superfly for moon physics.
Unlock Matrix mode:
Enter the options menu, then select "Cheats" and then enter nospoon for Matrix mode. All ollies and aerial tricks will be in slow motion.
CHEATS:
Big Head mode:
Spend $1,000 at the store to unlock heads of giant proportions.
Cool Specials mode:
Spend $1,000 at the store to unlock so bullet time-esque camera tricks.
Disco mode:
Spend $1,000 at the store to unlock the sprit of the 70's on your PS2.
Flame mode:
Spend $1,000 at the store to unlock a trail of flames when you grind.
Gorilla mode:
Spend $1,000 at the store to unlock yet more horrific freaks.
Hoverboard mode:
Spend $1,000 at the store to lose your wheels and float instead.

Invisible mode:
Spend $1,000 at the store to make yourself invisible, simple really.
Kid mode:
Spend $1,000 at the store to relive the bygone days of your youth.
Sim mode:
Spend $1,000 at the store to make the game too damn hard.
Slow motion mode:
Spend $1,000 at the store to slow things down to a snail's pace.
Super Blood mode:
Spend $1,000 at the store to unlock so much gore, Jason would puke.
Custom Skater Parts:
If you have any spare cash burning a hole why not invest of some of this lot...
Clown's hair:
Buy it at the store for $250.
Clown's head:
Buy it at the store for $300.
Clown's pants:
Buy it at the store for $250.

Unlock Motion blur effect:
Hit ⇧, ⇦, ●, ⇩, ⇨, ■, ⇧, ⇩, ⇦, ⇨, ●, ■. A "Blur" setting will appear on the options screen.
Unlock All cars:
Hit ■, ⇧, ⇩, ⇨, ⇦, ✖, ●, ■ while the main screen is loading.
Unlock P-nut car (Mini Cooper):
Collect all coins in Rome level 2.
Unlock Froggy car:
Collect all coins in Rome level 3.
Unlock Super Genius car (Smart Car):
Collect all coins in London level 1.
Unlock Turtle car (VW Beetle Convertible):
Collect all coins in London level 2.
Unlock Ricochet car (Audi TT):
Collect all coins in London level 3.
Unlock Fang car (Mazda MR2 Spyder):
Collect all coins in London level 4.
Unlock Road Shark car (Honda S2000):
Collect all coins in London level 5.
Unlock Portabello car (Lotus Elise):
Collect all coins in Tokyo level 1.
Unlock Street Eagle car (Porsche 911):
Collect all coins in Tokyo level 2.
Unlock Black Widow car (Plymouth Prowler):
Collect all coins in Tokyo level 3.

Clown's shoes:
Buy it at the store for $150.
Eraser hair:
Buy it at the store for $250.
Heart boxers:
Buy it at the store for $150.
Kenny's head:
Buy it at the store for $150.
Kilt:
Buy it at the store for $150.
King glasses:
Spend $100 at the store.
Metal head:
Buy it at the store for $300.
Officer Dick's head:
Buy it at the store for $150.
Officer Dick's shirt:
Buy it at the store for $250.
Ollie's coat:
Buy it at the store for $250.
Ollie's head:
Buy it at the store for $150.
Ollie's pants:
Buy it at the store for $250.
Paper bag:
Buy it at the store for $300.
Smiley boxers:
Buy it at the store for $150.
Hidden created skaters:
Hidden with THPS 4 are over 60 pre-made Custom Skater models to access them, you must enter one of the following names at the create a skater screen.

Aaron Skillman
Adam Lippman
Andrew Skates
Andy Marchal
Angus
Atiba Jefferson
Ben Scott Pye
Big Tex
Brian Jennings
Captain Liberty
Chauwa Steel
Chris Peacock
ConMan
Danaconda
Dave Stohl
DDT
DeadEndRoad
Fakes The Clown
Fritz
Gary Jesdanun
grjost
Henry Ji
Jason Uyeda
Jim Jagger
Joe Favazza
John Rosser
Jow
Kenzo
Kevin Mulhall
Kraken
Lindsey Hayes
Lisa G Davies
Little Man
Marilena Rixfor
Mat Hoffman
Matt Mcpherson
Maya's Daddy
Meek West
Mike Day
Mike Lashever
Mike Ward
Mr. Brad
Nolan Nelson
Parking Guy
Peasus
Pete Day
Pooper
Rick Thorne
Sik
Stacey D
Stacey Ytuarte
Stealing Is Bad
Team Chicken
Ted Barber
Todd Wahoske
Top Bloke
Wardcore
Zac ZiG Drake

Better control
When you start, do not drive with the Analogue-stick. This will help you stop swerving all around the lanes.

TUROK EVOLUTION

Unlock Master code:
Enter FMNFB as the code at the cheat menu.

Unlock Invincibility:
Enter EMERPUS as the code at the cheat menu.

Unlock All available weapons:
Enter TEXAS as the code at the cheat menu. All weapons available in the current level will be unlocked.

Unlock Unlimited ammunition:
Enter MADMAN as the code at the cheat menu.

Unlock Level select:
Enter SELLOUT as the code at the cheat menu. Load a saved game and all levels will be unlocked.

Unlock Invisibility:
Enter SLLEWGH as the code at the cheat menu.

Unlock Big head mode:
Enter HEID as the code at the cheat menu.

Unlock Zoo mode:
Enter ZOO as the code at the cheat menu. You will be able to kill any animal in the game with the war club as a weapon.

Unlock Demo mode and target mini-game:
Enter HUNTER as the code at the cheat menu. Besides starting demo mode, you will also be able to play the Target mini-game at the main title screen. Use the D-pad to move the pointer and Fire to shoot.

TWISTED METAL BLACK

Unlock Invincibility:
Set the control option to "Classic". Hold L1 + R1 + L2 + R2 and quickly hit ⇧, ⇩, ⇦, ⇨ x2, ⇦, ⇩, ⇧ during game play. Repeat the code to disable its effect. This works in story, endurance, challenge, and multi-player modes.

Unlock Unlimited health and turbo:
Set the control option to "Classic". Hold L1 + R1 + L2 + R2 and quickly hit ⇨, ⇦, ⇩, ⇧ during game play.

Unlock Mega machine guns:
Set the control option to "Classic". Hold L1 + R1 + L2 + R2 and quickly hit ✖ x2, ▲ during game play.

Unlock One hit kills:
Set the control option to "Classic". Hold L1 + R1 + L2 + R2 and quickly hit ✖ x2, ⇧ during game play.

Unlock God mode:
Set the control option to "Classic". Hold L1 + R1 + L2 + R2 and quickly hit ⇧, ✖, ⇦, ● during game play. You will have unlimited weapons, health, turbo, and energy.

For health:
Set the control option to "Classic". Hold L1 + R1 + L2 + R2 and quickly hit ▲, ✖, ■, ● during game play.

Unlock No opponents:
Select challenge mode. Then, hit L2 + R2, L2 + R2, L2 + R2 + ● at the opponent selection screen.

Alternate weapon view:
Hit SELECT + ⇨ during game play.

Alternate view:
Hold Select and hit ⇩ during game play. Hold SELECT and hit ⇦ to change to yet another view.

Character preview:
Hit ● at the character selection to zoom into the driver of the vehicle. During the zoom, hit ● again and the view will freeze.

Unlimited weapons:
Enable the "God mode" code, then the "Invincibility code". You will disable unlimited health but you will have unlimited weapons.

TY THE TASMANIAN TIGER

Unlock Unlimited health:
Quickly press L1, R1, L1, R1, ▲(4), ● x2 at the "Press Start" screen.

Unlock gallery and movies:
Quickly press L1, R1, L1, R1, ▲ x2, X x2, R2, ■, R2, ■ at the "Press Start" screen.

Unlock Show objects:
Press L1, R1, L1, R1, ▲ x2, ●, ■ x2, ●, R2 x2 during game play.

Unlock Technorangs:
Press L1, R1, L1, R1, ▲ x3, ■, ▲, ■ during game play.

UEFA CHAMPIONS LEAGUE

Eliminated teams:
Successfully complete the UEFA Champions League scenarios to unlock the "Eliminated Teams" option at the team selection screen in exhibition mode.

UFC THROWDOWN

Unlock Big John McCarthy:
Successfully complete all challenges and unlock all hidden moves as Mario Yamasaki. Then, highlight Mario Yamasaki and hold L1 at the character selection screen.

Unlock Bruce Buffer:
Win the Gold belt in UFC mode with a default character.

Unlock Dana White:
Successfully complete all challenges and unlock all hidden moves as Lorenzo Fertita. Then, highlight Lorenzo Fertita and hold L1 at the character selection screen.

Unlock Lorenzo Fertitta:
Win the Gold belt in UFC mode with a created character.

Unlock Mario Yamasaki:
Win the Gold belt with a default lightweight character. Alternately, get to the game over screen fifty times.

Unlock Ring Card girl 1:
View the complete between-round highlights and card girls walk around octagon 100 times.

Unlock Ring Card girl 2:
Successfully complete all challenges and unlock all hidden moves as Ring Card girl 1. Then, highlight Ring Card girl 1 and hold L1 at the character selection screen.

Unlock Kung-Fu fighting style:
Successfully complete career mode with a kick boxer.

Unlock Karate fighting style:
Successfully complete career mode with a created Sumo fighter.

Unlock Nin-Jitsu fighting style:
Successfully complete career mode with a karate fighter.

Silver belt:
Complete UFC mode with a default or created character to win the Silver belt.

Gold belt:
Win the Silver belt with a character, then enter UFC mode. Select the Free Weight option, then select the character with the Silver belt. Complete UFC mode again to win the Gold belt.

Unlock Bonus moves:
Accomplish one of the following tasks to unlock another move:
Complete UFC mode and get the Silver belt.
Complete UFC mode in the Open Weight class and get the Gold belt.
Complete the game in Arcade mode.
Complete the game in Tournament mode.

UNREAL TOURNAMENT

Unlock Level skip:
Hit Start to pause game play, then hit ⇧, ⇩, ⇦, ⇨ x2, ⇦, ●.

Unlock Level select:
Save the game and return to the main menu. Select the "Resume Game" option, then highlight the previously saved game and hit ⇧, ⇩ x2, ⇧, ⇦, ⇧, ⇨, ⇩.

Unlock Invincibility:
Hit Start to pause game play, then hit ■, ●, ⇦, ⇨, ●, ■.

Unlock Full ammunition:
Hit Start to pause game play, then hit ⇦, ⇨, ● x3, ⇨, ⇦.

Unlock All characters:
Hit Start to pause game play, then hit ⇦ x2, ● x2, ⇨, ⇦, ✖.

Unlock All weapons:
Hit Start to pause game play, then hit ⇦, ●, ⇨, ■, ⇨, ⇦.

Unlock Fatboy Mutator:
Hit ● x3, ⇧, ⇩ x2, ⇧, ● x3 at the main menu.

Unlock Stealth Mutator:
Hit ■ x2, ● x2, ■ x2, ● x2 at the main menu.

Unlock Big head mode:
Hit ⇦, ⇨, ⇦, ⇨, ⇦, ⇨, ● x3 at the main menu.

VAMPIRE NIGHT

Free play:
Successfully complete all of the training missions (every icon has three things under it) to unlock free play for arcade mode.

VIRTUA FIGHTER 4

Classic victory poses:
Use a created fighter to reach the Second Kyu level. Hold Punch + Kick + Guard during the replay after winning a match to do a classic victory pose from Virtua Fighter 1.. Use a created fighter to reach the Third Dan rank. Hold Punch + Kick during the replay after winning a match to do another classic victory pose.

Alternate main menu background:
Enter the "Game Option" menu, then hit R1 to cycle forwards or L1 to cycle backwards through the list of backgrounds for the main menu.

Alternate costumes:
Each character has two appearances. Most are just two different sets of clothes. To see the alternate costume, hold Start at the character selection screen. Hit ✖ to select that character while holding START to wear that costume.

Virtua Fighter 1 fighter model:
Use a character fighter to reach at least the First Dan rank. Select that fighter, then hold Punch + Kick until the match begins.

Training Stage 1 in versus mode:
Use a created fighter to reach the First Dan rank to unlock the first training stage in versus mode.

Training Stage 2 in versus mode:
Use a created fighter to reach the Fifth Dan rank to unlock the second training stage in versus mode.

Training Stage 3 in versus mode:
Use a created fighter to reach the Champion rank to unlock the third training stage in versus mode.

Dural's stage in versus mode:
Use a created fighter to reach the Emperor or High King rank to unlock the hangar stage in versus mode.

Fight as Dural:
Defeat Dural in in Kumite mode to unlock her in versus mode.

Training trophy:
Successfully complete the trial events in training mode with a created fighter. A small

Keep a winning streak in Kumite mode:
If you have a good winning streak going in the Kumite mode and are about to lose, pause game play and return to the main menu. The game will save. Once you return into Kumite, you will still have your winning streak and no losses.

Special items:
Get a 100 consecutive wins in Kumite mode and your character will be awarded a special item. Note: The item varies with the fighter you use.

Orb items:
Once you reach the Conqueror rank in Kumite mode you will begin to face several opponents who are ranked as High Kings. Each High King has a colored orb that you can collect by defeating them. There are seven orbs in the following colors: crimson, green, purple, blue, black, orange, and white. After you collect them all, watch the screen and you will see the orbs merge together, forming an item chest.

V RALLY 3

Unlock Floating cars:
Enter 210741974 MARTY as a name.

Unlock Small cars:
Enter 01041977 BIGJIM as a name.

Unlock Squishy cars:
Enter 25121975 PILOU as a name.

Unlock Smashed cars:
Enter 25121975 PILOU as a name.
Unlock Jelly cars:
Enter 07121974 FERGUS as a name.

Unlock Flat cars:
Enter 21051975 PTITDAV as a name.

Unlock Stretched cars:
Enter Gonzales SPEEDY as a name.

Mitsubishi Lancer Evolution VI:
Select career mode and win the 1.6L championship.

SEAT Cordoba Repsol:
Successfully complete the game in challenge mode.

Subaru Impreza 2000:
Select career mode and win the 2.0L championship.

Toyota Corolla V-Rally:
Set a record time in all circuits.

Reversed tracks:
There are four tracks in each country. Beat the record of a track to unlock the next one. Unlock all of them to access the four reversed tracks for that country.

WACKY RACES

Unlock All cars:
Enter MONKEYSPOILERS at the cheat code screen.

Unlock Kid mode:
Enter THOSEWACKYKIDS at the cheat code screen.

Unlock Dastardly difficulty setting:
Enter FASTCARSAGOGO at the cheat code screen.

Unlock All tracks:
Enter CHIMPGIVEAWAY at the cheat code screen.

Unlock All gadgets:
Enter GADGETCLEAROUT at the cheat code screen.

WARRIORS OF MIGHT AND MAGIC

Unlock All weapons:
Hit L1, R2 x2, L1, R1, L2, L1, R2, L2, R2 during game play.

WAY OF THE SAMURAI

Restore health:
Hit START to pause game play, then hold L1 + L2 and hit ⇩, ⇧, ⇩, ⇧, ⇨, ⇦, ●.

Increase sword durability:
Hit START to pause game play, then hold R1 + R2 and hit ⇨ x2, ⇦ x2, ⇩, ⇧, ●. The main player's currently equipped sword will increase in hardness by one. Repeat as needed to reach the maximum hardness of five.

All sword skills:
Hit START to pause game play in versus mode, then hold R1 and hit R2 x2, L1 x2, L2 x2, release R1, and hit R2.

Random sword:
Hold L1 + R1 then hit ●, ⇩ x2, ⇧ x2, ⇩, ⇧, ● at the sword inventory screen. One random sword will be added to your inventory, with random attributes.

Increase brightness:
Hold L2 then L1 and rotate the Left Analogue-stick several times in either direction while both buttons are held. Your character's eye will begin to flash and will illuminate your surroundings at night.

Change characters:
Hit L1, R1 x2, L2 x3, R2 x2, R2 + ■ at new game menu with the face, clothes, and sword options. Hit ⇦ or ⇨ to choose a character.

Battle mode:
Hold L1 + R1, then hit ● + ■ at the title screen.

Control title screen:
Hit ■ at the title screen after the cherry blossoms stop to have more fall. Hold L1 + L2 + R1 + R2 and hit ■ to have a large number of blossoms fall.

WILD WILD RACING

Cheat mode:
Hold ■ and hit ⇧, ●, ⇩, ●, ⇦, ⇨, ⇦, ⇨, ● at the options screen.

Quick start
Hit ✖ to accelerate when "1" appears during the pre-race countdown.

Better engine
Successfully complete the game in time attack mode to unlock a better engine.

WINBACK: COVERT MISSIONS

Unlock Trial mode:
Quickly hit ⇧, ⇩ x2, ⇨ x3, ⇦ x4, then hold ▲ and hit Start at the "Hit Start" menu to unlock trial mode.

Unlock All multi-player characters:
Quickly hit ⇧, ⇩ x2, ⇨ x3, ⇦ x4, then hold ● and hit Start at the "Hit Start" menu.

Unlock Max power mode:
Quickly hit L1, R2, L2, R2, L2, ▲, ●, ▲, ●, then hold L1 and hit START at the "Hit Start" menu to unlock max power mode.

Unlock Sudden death mode:
Quickly hit L2, R2, L2, R2, ●, ▲, ●, ▲, then hold L1 and hit START at the "Hit Start" menu to unlock sudden death mode.

Unlock Max power, sudden death, trial modes:
Successfully complete the game on the hard difficulty setting to unlock max power, sudden death and trial modes.

Easy Bot mode:
In Bot mode, go to the settings and under "Team 1" change "Handicap" to "250%" and "Med kit" to "100%". Then, under "Team 2" set them down to "1%". Your enemies will die quicker and the med kits will put your health up to 100%.

Killing machine gunner:
When someone is behind a machine gun, take out your missile launcher and aim over the machine gun.

WIPEOUT FUSION

Unlock Features unlocked:
Select "Extras" at the main menu, and then select "Cheats". Then, enter ✖, ▲, ●, ▲, ● as the code.

Unlock Unlimited weapons:
Select "Extras" at the main menu, and then select "Cheats". Then, enter ▲, ●, ✖, ●, ■ as the code.

Unlock Unlimited shields:
Select "Extras" at the main menu, and then select "Cheats". Then, enter ▲, ▲, ■, ■, ■ as the code.

Unlock Retro ships:
Select "Extras" at the main menu, and then select "Cheats". Then, enter ✖, ●, ▲, ■, ✖ as the code.

Unlock Mini ships:
Select "Extras" at the main menu, and then select "Cheats". Then, enter ●, ■, ■, ✖, ● as the code.

Unlock Animal ships:
Select "Extras" at the main menu, and then select "Cheats". Then, enter ▲, ●, ●, ▲, ✖ as the code.

Unlock Time Trial Mode:
Complete 60% of the game.

Unlock Better cornering:
Collect and save an Auto-Pilot power-up. When you reach a tricky corner, get as around it as well as possible, then activate the Auto-Pilot power-up at the last moment.

Unlock Auricom Team:
Complete the Franco Gonzales Challenge with a gold medal.

Unlock EG-r Team:
Complete the Alex Reece Challenge with a gold medal.

Unlock Tigron Team:
Complete the Sveta Kirovski Challenge with a gold medal.

Unlock Xios Team:
Complete the Zala Woolf Challenge with a gold medal.

Unlock Piranha Team:
Complete the Jann Shlaudecker Challenge with a gold medal.

Unlock Zone Challenge:
Complete 30% of the game.

WORLD CHAMPIONSHIP SNOOKER 2001

Fine shot adjustment:
Hold L2 while adjusting the shot direction to move the pointer more precisely.

Look around table:
Hold R1 while adjusting the shot direction.

Adjust camera angle:
Hold L1 while adjusting the shot direction.

Overhead view:
Hold ▲ while lining up a shot.

Backspin:
Hold ● + ⇧ or ⇩ to put backspin on the ball.

Side spin:
Hold ● + ⇦ or ⇨ to put side spin on the ball.

Change shot height:
Hold ■ while lining up a shot. This also can be used to make illegal shots. For example, hit the ball very far past the middle to chip

it or break very fast to hit a ball off the table.

WORLD CHAMPIONSHIP SNOOKER 2002

Overhead view:
Hold ▲ while lining up a shot.

Backspin:
Hold ● + ⇧ or ⇩ to put backspin on the ball.

Side spin:
Hold ● + ⇦ or ⇨ to put side spin on the ball.

Fine shot adjustment:
Hold L2 while adjusting the shot direction to move the pointer more precisely.

Look around table:
Hold R1 while adjusting the shot direction.

Adjust camera angle:
Hold L1 while adjusting the shot direction.

Change shot height:
Hold ■ while lining up a shot.

WORLD DESTRUCTION LEAGUE: THUNDER TANKS

Destroying blimps
Use a satellite or artillery strike to blow up the blimp in levels with them.

WORLD DESTRUCTION LEAGUE: WAR JETZ

All codes and levels unlocked:
Enter SPRLZY as the code.

All codes unlocked:
Enter TWLVCHTS as the code.

Level select:
Enter JMPTT as the code.
Invincibility:
Enter DNGDM as the code.
Shields when rolling:
Enter SCRW as the code.
Top gun mode:
Enter DH as the code.
Overlords mode:
Enter VRLRDS as the code.
Valhalla mode:
Enter WNRLFST as the code.
Super armour:
Enter MRRMR as the code.
Faster jets:
Enter ZPPY as the code.
Big guns:
Enter HMMR as the code.
Huge guns:
Enter QD as the code.
Rapid fire:
Enter FRHS as the code.
Speed shots:
Enter NSTNT as the code.
Dual fire:
Enter NDBMBS as the code.
Spin shots:
Enter DZZY as the code.
Ghost mode:
Enter SNKY as the code.
Double Bux:
Enter TWFSTD as the code.
Add 10 Bux:
Enter WNNNGS as the code.
Weapon level-up at 3:
Enter PYRS as the code.
Switch planes:
Enter NDCSN as the code.
Instant win:
Enter SMSHNG as the code.
Slow down to hover:
Enter SSPNDRS as the code.
Show boxes:
Enter BXDRW as the code.
Show waypoints:
Enter WYPNT as the code.
All FMV sequences:
Enter GRTD as the code.

WORLD RALLY CHAMPIONSHIP

Overhead camera:
Choose the "Extra" option at the main menu, and then select "Codes". Enter DOWNBELOW or DOWNUNDER as the code.

Reversed camera:
Choose the "Extra" option at the main menu, then select "Codes". Enter ONTHECEILING as the code.

Underwater graphics:
Choose the "Extra" option at the main menu, and then select "Codes". Enter WIBBLYWOBBLY as the code.

Psychedelic graphics:
Choose the "Extra" option at the main menu, and then select "Codes". Enter IMGOINGCRAZY as the code.

Master code:
Choose the "Extra" option at the main menu, and then select "Codes". Enter OPENSESAME as the code.

Greater acceleration and maximum speed:
Choose the "Extra" option at the main menu, and then select "Codes". Enter EVOPOWER as the code.

Great Britain challenge:
Choose the "Extra" option at the main menu, and then select "Codes". Enter YJFTRS as the code.

Monte Carlo challenge:
Choose the "Extra" option at the main menu, and then select "Codes". Enter L5020K as the code.

Portugal challenge:
Choose the "Extra" option at

the main menu, and then select "Codes". Enter PHY8ZP as the code.

Sweden challenge:
Choose the "Extra" option at the main menu, and then select "Codes". Enter 745MJJ as the code.

All bonus challenges:
Choose the "Extra" option at the main menu, and then select "Codes". Enter GIMMEBONUS as the code.

High pitched commentary:
Choose the "Extra" option at the main menu, and then select "Codes". Enter HELIUMAID as the code.

Cars with no chassis:
Choose the "Extra" option at the main menu, and then select "Codes". Enter THATSSTUPID as the code.

Flying cars in replays:
Choose the "Extra" option at the main menu, and then select "Codes". Enter FLOATYLIGHT as the code.

WORLD RALLY CHAMPIONSHIP 2 EXTREME

Master cheat code:
Go to the "Archives" and enter the "Secrets" section. Press ✖ to enter a cheat code, and enter EVOS.

Turbo mode:
Go to the "Archives" and enter the "Secrets" section. Press ✖ to enter a cheat code, and enter NITRO.

UFO vehicle:
Go to the "Archives" and enter the "Secrets" section. Press ✖ to enter a cheat code, and enter UFOPTER.

Chrome paint:
Go to the "Archives" and enter the "Secrets" section. Press ✖ to enter a cheat code, and enter CHROME.

Overhead view:
Go to the "Archives" and enter the "Secrets" section. Press ✖ to enter a cheat code, and enter SATALITE.

Low gravity:
Go to the "Archives" and enter the "Secrets" section. Press ✖ to enter a cheat code, and enter LUNAR.

Bouncing cars:
Go to the "Archives" and enter the "Secrets" section. Press ✖ to enter a cheat code, and enter KANGAROO.

Swaying objects:
Go to the "Archives" and enter the "Secrets" section. Press ✖ to enter a cheat code, and enter SWAY.

High pitched co-driver:
Go to the "Archives" and enter the "Secrets" section. Press ✖ to enter a cheat code, and enter HELIUM.

Disco lighting:
Go to the "Archives" and enter the "Secrets" section. Press ✖ to enter a cheat code, and enter DISCO.

Motion blurred graphics:
Go to the "Archives" and enter the "Secrets" section. Press ✖ to enter a cheat code, and enter MOBLUR.

WORMS BLAST

Unlock Bonus characters:
Hold L1 and hit ⇧ x4, ⇩ x3, ⇧ x5 at the start screen.

Unlock All tournament modes:
Hold L2 and hit ⇧ x2, ⇩ x6, ⇧ x3 at the start screen.

WRECKLESS

Earn Gold rank on all missions:
Highlight the "Unlimited time" option at the main menu then press L2 + R1 + Right + Circle as the game loads.

Unlock Missions A-2 to A-4:
You must complete mission A-1.

Unlock Missions B-2 to B-4:
You must complete mission B-1.

Unlock AUV:
You must complete mission A-9.

Unlock Dragon-SPL Car:
You must complete mission A-1.

Unlock Super Car:
You must complete mission B-1.

Unlock Tank-90:
You must complete mission B-8.

Unlock Tiger-SPL:
You must complete mission A-8 to unlock the car that Tiger Tagachi drives.

Unlock Yakuza Car:
You must complete mission B-9.

Unlock Music test:
You must complete all twenty missions to unlock the "Music Test" selection at the options screen.

WWF SMACKDOWN! JUST BRING IT

Unlock New SmackDown! arena:
Choose Slobber Knocker mode. Choose The Rock. Defeat 15 wrestlers in the 10 minutes.
Unlock WWF title:
Refuse Vince McMahon's offer to form a tag team. Talk trash on the microphone to the first superstar that goes to the ring. Tell Michael Cole you want to "Kick his butt all over the arena" and find Vince in the parking lot to get the match. Win that match. Show up on stage when the superstar calls you out and defeat him in any of the three matches he offers. Whichever one you pick will unlock that match type. This will take you to a title shot with the current WWF champion.
Unlock Fred Durst:
Choose Slobber Knocker mode. Choose Undertaker and defeat over 15 wrestlers in the ten minutes.
Unlock Jerry Lynn:
Choose anyone who does not hold a title. Say that you do not want to form tag team to Vince. Talk trash on mic. Say that you were just messing. Let time run out. Win the battle royal. Let time run out. Win the battle royal. Show up on stage. Win the match and the match that follows. Jerry Lynn will now be unlocked.
Unlock Mick Foley:
Choose anyone who does not hold a title. Say you do not want to form tag team to Vince. Talk trash. Say that you want to kick his ass. Go to parking lot to find Vince. Win the match. Show up on stage. Win the match. Lose the match at Wrestlemania. Foley appears and makes it a hell in a cell. Win the hell in a cell match. Mick Foley will now be unlocked.
Unlock Rhyno:
Choose anyone who does not hold a title. Answer that you do not want to form tag team to Vince. Run down and attack. Lose the match, stay backstage, and then go to Earl Hebner. He will be near the vending machines in the lobby. Tell him you are going after hard-core title. Defeat Rhyno to unlock him.
Unlock Spike Dudley:
Accept a tag team match. Find anyone, and then win the match. Get your partner to find the third partner for six-man tag. Go to the corridor where the APA office is located (door opposite vending machines in lobby). Help Spike, and then win the tag table match. Win the tag team title match and Spike Dudley will be unlocked.
Unlock Shane McMahon and Stephanie McMahon Helmsley:
To use them, you need to unlock all the SmackDown cards. If you have unlocked them all, go through one of them again to get to Wrestlemania. You will unlock about three to four cards each time. Another way to do it is to defend a belt. Each time you defend, you unlock a card.
However, when you are left with about three cards remaining you will need to go through story mode and win the WWF title at Wrestlemania. To do this, choose anyone who does not hold a title. Say that you do not want to form tag team to Vince. Talk trash on mic. Say you want to kick his ass. Go to the parking lot to find Vince. Win the match. Show up on stage. Win the match. Then, win the match at Wrestlemania.
Unlock Tajri:
Choose anyone who does not hold a title. Answer that you do not want to form tag team to Vince. Talk trash on mic, then say you were messing. To get to Regal's office, go down stairs on left, and then go into the door on left before the vending machines. The first on the left is Regal's office. Say that you do not want the Euro title match. Defeat Tajiri to unlock him.
Unlock InsurreXtion arena:
Choose anyone who does not hold a title. Say that you do not want to form a tag team to Vince. Run up and attack. Go talk to the ref, Earl Hebner and ask "Hi Earl how are you?" He will say that Regal wants you, and that he will take you there. Tell Regal that you want to go for the European title. Win the European title, and the match that follows.

Unlock WWF Womens Title:
Make the same choices as in the WWF Title with a woman and you will win the WWF Women's Title.
Unlock WWF Hardcore title:
Choose anyone that does not hold a title. Answer that you do not want to form a Tag Team to Vince. Run down and attack. Lose the next match. Stay backstage, and then go to Earl Hebner. He will be

near the vending machines in the lobby. Tell him you are going after the Hardcore title. Defeat the Hardcore champion to get the title.

Unlock WWF
Intercontinental title:
Choose anyone that does not hold a title. Answer that you do not want to form a Tag Team to Vince. Run down to the ring and attack. Lose the match. During the next match the Intercontinental champion will hit you with a chair. Stay backstage, and then go to Earl Hebner. He will be near the vending machines in the lobby. Ask him to take you to Regal's office, or go there when you stay backstage.

Unlock WWF European title:
Choose anyone who does not hold a title. Answer that you do not want to form a Tag Team to Vince. Talk trash on mic, and then say you that you were messing with him. Then, go to Regal's office. Tell him that you want a European Title match.

WWF SMACKDOWN! SHUT YOUR MOUTH

UNLOCKING IT ALL:

When You Win the Undisputed Championship you can UNLOCK:
RVD Special movie
Smackdown SYM Special movie

When You Win a match at Backlash PPV you can UNLOCK:
The Rock's attire
Christian's attire
Create Parts 1
Backlash arena
Foam Hands A

When You Win a match at Judgement Day PPV you can UNLOCK:
RVD's attire
Vince McMahon's attire
Eddie Guerrero's attire
Undertaker's attire
Create Parts 2
Judgment Day arena

When You Win a match at King of the Ring PPV you can UNLOCK:
Kurt Angle's attire
Edge's attire
Moves 2
Create Parts 8
King of the Ring arena
Plaza B backstage area.

When You Win a match at Vengeance PPV you can UNLOCK:
Lance Storm's attire
Raven's attire
Billy Kidman's attire
Create Parts 3
Vengeance arena A
Vengeance arena B

When You Win a match at SummerSlam PPV you can UNLOCK:
Booker T's attire
Torrie Wilson's attire
Moves 4
Moves 6
Create Parts 9
SummerSlam arena

When You Win a match at Unforgiven PPV you can UNLOCK:
Chris Benoit's attire
Trish Stratus's attire
Moves 3
Create Parts 5
Unforgiven arena or Foam Hands B

When You Win a match at Backlash PPV you can UNLOCK:
Shawn Michaels attire
Stephanie McMahon's attire
Rikishi's attire
D-Von's attire
Molly Holly's attire
No Mercy arena

When You Win a match at Survivor Series PPV you can UNLOCK:
Matt Hardy's attire
Hardcore Holly's attire
Moves 7
Moves 8
30 Ability Points
Survivor Series arena

When You Win a match at Armegeddon PPV you can UNLOCK:
Ric Flair's attire
Chuck's attire
Billy's attire
Armageddon arena
Winter Plaza area
Winter Times Square area

When You Win a match at Royal Rumble PPV you can UNLOCK:
Triple H's attire
Steve Austin's attire
Bubba Ray's attire
Create Parts 6
Royal Rumble arena
WWE Superstar Special Movie

When You Win a match at No Way Out PPV you can UNLOCK:
Kevin Nash (for Season Mode)
X-Pac (for Season Mode)
Big Show's attire
The Big Valbowski's attire
Moves 5
No Way Out arena

When You Win a match at WrestleMania PPV you can UNLOCK:
Hulk Hogan (for Season Mode)
Faarooq's attire
Bradshaw's attire
Moves 1
Create Parts 7
WrestleMania X8 arena

When You Win a match at Insurrection PPV you can UNLOCK:
Jeff Hardy's attire
William Regal's attire
Moves 9
Create Parts 4
Insurrextion arena

When You Win a match at Rebellion PPV you can UNLOCK:
Chris Jericho's attire
Stacy Keibler's attire

Brock Lesnar's attire
Moves 10
Rebellion arena

X-MEN: NEXT DIMENSION

Unlock Master code:
Remove the memory card before activating this code. Hold L1, and then press ⇨ x2, ⇦ x2, ⇩, ⇧, ● at the main menu.

Fight as Bastion:
Successfully complete the game in the story mode as Magneto without losing any matches to face Bastion.

Fight as Bishop:
Successfully complete the game in the arcade mode as Gambit to unlock Bishop as a selectable character.

Fight as Blob:
Successfully complete the game in the arcade mode as Bishop to unlock Blob as a selectable character.

Fight as Psylocke:
Successfully complete the game in the arcade mode as Betsy to unlock Psylocke as a selectable character.

Fight as Dark Phoenix:
Successfully complete the game in the arcade mode as Phoenix to unlock Dark Phoenix as a selectable character.

Fight as Sentinel A:
Successfully complete the game in the arcade mode as Cyclops.

Fight as Sentinel B:
Win twenty matches in the survival mode.

X SQUAD

Defeating the Flamethrower Boss:
When he uses his flame gun, always stay away from it as it can set you alight. Kill any guards who jump down, then face him again. Once his yellow bar is empty, he will die.

Unlock Master of X-Squad rank:
Hit ● x4, ▲, ■ x4 at the main title screen, then start a new game. This results in a game with a level 3 shield, level 3 sensor, radar, no weight limit, master level of all weapons, 99 clips for each, and bonus points displayed when earned.

Unlock Private rank:
Hit ■, ●, ▲ at the main title screen, then start a new game. This results in a game with Michaels 9mmS, 99 clips, and bonus points displayed when earned.

Unlock Sergeant rank:
Hit ▲, ●, ■ at the main title screen, then start a new game. This results in a game with no weight limit, Taylor M82, Michaels 9mmS, 99 clips and bonus points displayed when earned.

Unlock Lieutenant rank:
Hit R1, L2, L1, R2 at the main title screen, then start a new game. This results in a game with a level 2 shield, no weight limit, Taylor M82, Michaels 9mmS, 99 clips, bonus points displayed when earned, and a 10,000 point bonus when a level is completed.

Unlock Captain rank:
Hit ●, R1, ●, L1, ▲, R2 at the main title screen, then start a new game. This results in a game with radar, no weight limit, Taylor M82, Michaels 9mmS, 99 clips and bonus points displayed when earned.

Unlock Major rank:
Hit L2, ■, R2, ▲, L1, ●, R1 at the main title screen, then start a new game. This results in a game with a level 3 shield, Level 3 sensor, radar, no weight limit, Taylor M82, Michaels 9mmS, 99 clips and bonus points displayed when earned.

Unlock Colonel rank:
Hit ▲, ■, ●, ■, ▲, ● at the main title screen, then start a new game. This results in a game with a level 3 shield, level 3 sensor, radar, no weight limit, beginner level of all weapons, 99 clips for each, and bonus points displayed when earned.

Unlock General rank:
Hit L1 x2, L2 x2, R1 x2, R2 x2 at the main title screen, then start a new game. This results in a game with a level 3 shield, level 3 sensor, radar, no weight limit, intermediate

level of all weapons, 99 clips for each and bonus points displayed when earned.

Buying weapons:
Hit the acquire button and select "Weapons". You can get a rocket launcher, flame gun, assault rifle, and sniper rifle including a grenade gun.

Z.O.E.

Unlock Refill ammunition and health:
Pause game play, then hit L1 x2, L2 x2, L1, R1, L1, R1, R2, R1. Note your level will be penalized each time this code is activated. This does not make the Jehuty invincible.

Unlock Versus mode:
Hit ●, ✖, ⇨, ⇦, ⇨, ⇦, ⇩ x2, ⇧ x2 at the "Hit Start" screen. A sound will confirm correct code entry. Alternately, successfully complete single player mode under any difficulty setting. Complete the game a second time under any difficulty setting to unlock two more stages.

Unlock All characters and levels in versus mode:
Successfully complete the game easy mode with at least a "D" rating.

Defeating Tyrant:
When you first meet this Boss, Jehuty is infected with a deadly virus that causes it to die if hit just once. Tyrant also has a Lock On attack to which you cannot escape. Instead of taking him on, leave the area and return later. Obtain the vaccine from Factory 2 to get rid of the virus. Be sure to avoid all battles when obtaining the vaccine. When Tyrant has gone past 50% damage he will start to rush you. When he reaches you, drop a decoy and fly over his head. He will release missiles which will target the decoy rather than you, and will therefore cause considerable damage to Tyrant himself.

Defeating Zombie Neith:
As soon as the battle starts, begin firing your gun without using your Dash Laser attack. She should use her shield. Continue firing, approaching her as you fire. When you get into close range, begin using your slash combo. She cannot use her homing energy balls if she is being shot.

Enemy's vital meter:
To check how much vitality your enemy has (not Bosses), check the colour of its level indicator. Vitality ranges from high (light blue) to low (red).

Defeating Tempest:
In his first form, hit him with your Burst Attack (be sure to keep your distance), until he changes. Put your shield up, get as close to his head as possible, and hit him several times with Burst Attack. When he goes high in the air, do not move until you see him release the small bombs. Dash to the place where none are coming down. When he returns to the ground, repeat until he is defeated.

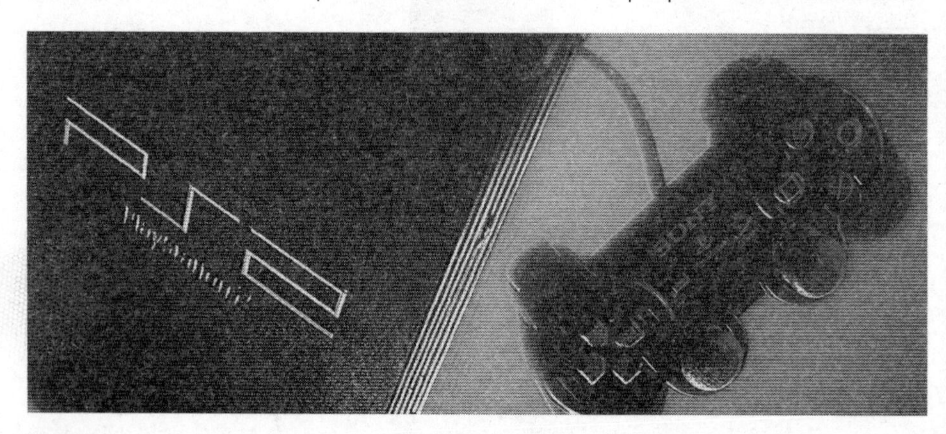